McGRAW-HILL SERIES IN
POLITICAL SCIENCE
Joseph P. Harris, CONSULTING EDITOR

BASIC DOCUMENTS
OF INTERNATIONAL RELATIONS

McGRAW-HILL SERIES IN POLITICAL SCIENCE

Joseph P. Harris, CONSULTING EDITOR

✓ ✓ ✓

BASIC DOCUMENTS OF INTERNATIONAL RELATIONS

Edited by Frederick H. Hartmann

ASSISTANT PROFESSOR OF POLITICAL SCIENCE
THE UNIVERSITY OF FLORIDA

FIRST EDITION

New York   Toronto   London
McGRAW-HILL BOOK COMPANY, INC.
1951

BASIC DOCUMENTS OF INTERNATIONAL RELATIONS

To
REGGIE

PREFACE

THERE IS today a growing belief that the undergraduate student can gain both profit and perspective through contact with source materials. Of no study is this more true than international relations. Even the most conscientious synthesis of some of the documents included in this book fails to provide an adequate substitute for a firsthand acquaintance with the materials themselves. A reading of the documents provides an otherwise lacking third dimension to be added to the written word of the general textbook and the spoken word of the lecture. Nowhere, for example, can the student find such a simple yet thoroughgoing presentation of the procedure for the peaceful settlement of international disputes as is contained in the Hague Convention of 1907. Nowhere is the complexity of an alliance system so well and succinctly illustrated as in the various documents concerning pre-World War I alliances and alignments.

This collection of documents is not intended as a substitute for the general textbooks in international relations but is designed as a companion volume to be used in conjunction with them. The undergraduate student would find it difficult to understand the complex subject of international relations without the guidance of the general analytical text. General texts, however, are necessarily limited in the number of basic documents, and any presented are usually printed either in appendixes or compressed into footnotes in print so small as to discourage reading.

It is hoped that the present collection will prove of use in bringing together in one convenient volume the most basic documents of the field. Such a collection has been necessarily selective, and many documents which might well have been included have been omitted. The criterion in every case has been whether the editor felt the document contributes enough to an understanding of the elements, forces, and problems of world politics and international organization to warrant its inclusion in a volume restricted to fifty documents.

The arrangement of materials is in chronological order, although occasionally exceptions have been made where it seemed useful. The addition of a descriptive note preceding each document, it is hoped, will increase the usefulness of the book. These contain data which are pertinent to the document in question, indicating the parties to the agreement and referring to other documents which subsequently altered the meaning or the effect of the original document. While these notes are designed to assist in an understanding of the document itself, they do not attempt to link the selections together in such a fashion that the book may be read connectedly.

In editing the documents it was found desirable to adopt a standard method for indicating omissions. Accordingly, a full line of periods has been used to indicate the omission in entirety of articles or paragraphs, while the omission of some part or portion within an article or paragraph has been indicated by ellipses. The omission of preambles or signatures has not been indicated.

The editor has kept in mind the necessity of having the book extremely flexible in order to permit maximum use of its contents. It is for this reason that the documents have been kept in chronological order and have not been arranged in chapters according to subject. The wide variation in methods of presentation of materials in general courses in international relations makes it desirable that the documents be arranged so that they may be assigned by number. For convenience, a table of documents classified by subject matter has also been included. Since documents are listed in this table under the appropriate heading or headings, some are listed more than once.

To Professor Manning J. Dauer, Chairman of the Department of Political Science, and Professors Franklin A. Doty and John H. Reynolds of the University College, University of Florida, for their encouragement and helpful comments, my deep appreciation is due.

FREDERICK H. HARTMANN

GAINESVILLE, FLA.
November, 1950

CONTENTS

TABLE OF DOCUMENTS BY SUBJECT

TREATY OF CHAUMONT [1]

THE HOLY Alliance system marked the first attempt since the emergence of the Western state system in the seventeenth century to bring the great powers into institutionalized consultation on a multilateral basis. The system was not created with formal covenant or charter, as were the League of Nations and the United Nations subsequently, but rested instead upon a military alliance (Document 1), periodic conferences (Document 2), and a supposedly common ideology (Document 3). The Treaty of Chaumont provided the military basis of the system. It was a twenty-year alliance against Napoleon and Bonapartist France, signed on March 1, 1814, by Austria, Prussia, Russia, and Britain.

Although the system which grew out of the wartime collaboration of these powers at first did not include all the great powers, France was admitted in 1818 upon a basis of full equality. Periodic congresses were summoned, beginning with that at Vienna in 1815 when the map of Europe was redrawn. France, slightly larger than in pre-Napoleonic days, was placed once more under the rule of the House of Bourbon. At Aix-la-Chapelle in 1818, rules of diplomatic precedence and procedure were evolved. In 1820, at the Congress of Troppau, Metternich proposed intervention to put down the revolutions then going on in both Naples and Spain. At the Laibach Congress in 1821, Austria was given the responsibility of restoring monarchial control in Italy, and at

[1] *British and Foreign State Papers,* Vol. I, pp. 121*ff.*

Verona in 1822, France was given a similar mandate in Spain.

Metternich's proposal in 1820 met with opposition from Castlereagh, British foreign minister. As a constitutional monarchy, Britain could not recognize the validity of the principle that people did not have the right to circumscribe the power of their rulers. The actions of Austria in Italy and of France in Spain subsequently drove a wedge between the British and the other powers, with the result that Great Britain did not attend any congress after Verona. When Louis Philippe in 1830 replaced the Bourbons in France and, contrary to the spirit of the alliance, ruled as a constitutional monarch, another serious weakening of the system occurred. The dissensions arising out of the Greek revolt against the Ottomans helped complete the process of disruption, Austria and Russia finding their interests in opposition in the Balkans. Russia, animated by a desire to weaken Turkey and obtain the Straits, even gave aid to the Greeks in their revolt against their rulers. By 1848 the Holy Alliance system had completely disappeared. The rudimentary international organization had, however, established a precedent for the creation by a wartime coalition of a postwar system designed to preserve the peace.

In the Name of the Most Holy and Undivided Trinity.

His Majesty the King of the United Kingdom of Great Britain and Ireland, His Imperial and Royal Apostolic Majesty the Emperor of Austria, King of Hungary and Bohemia, His Majesty the Emperor of All the Russias, and His Majesty the King of Prussia, have transmitted to the French Government proposals for concluding a General Peace, and being desirous, should France refuse the Conditions therein contained, to draw closer the ties which unite them for the vigorous prosecution of a War undertaken for the salutary purpose of putting an end to the miseries of Europe, of securing its future repose, by re-establishing a just balance of Power, and being at the same time desirous, should the Almighty bless their pacific intentions, to fix the means of maintaining against every attempt the order of things which shall have been the happy consequence of their efforts, have agreed to sanction by a solemn Treaty, signed separately by each of the four Powers with the three others, this twofold engagement.

. . . The said Plenipotentiaries, after having exchanged their Full Powers, found to be in due and proper form, have agreed upon the following Articles:

Article I

The High Contracting Parties above named solemnly engage by the present Treaty, and in the event of France refusing to accede to the Conditions of Peace now proposed, to apply all the means of their respective States to the vigorous prosecution of the War against that Power, and to employ them in perfect concert, in order to obtain for themselves and for Europe a General Peace, under the protection of which the rights and liberties of all Nations may be established and secured.

This engagement shall in no respect affect the Stipulations which the several Powers have already contracted relative to the number of Troops to be kept against the Enemy; and it is understood that the Courts of England, Austria, Russia, and Prussia, engage by the present Treaty to keep in the field, each of them, one hundred and fifty thousand effective men, exclusive of garrisons, to be employed in active service against the common Enemy.

. . . .

Article XVI

The present Treaty of Defensive Alliance having for its object to maintain the equilibrium of Europe, to secure the repose and independence of its States, and to prevent the invasions which during so many years have desolated the World, the High Contracting Parties have agreed to extend the duration of it to twenty years, to take date from the day of its Signature; and they reserve to themselves, to concert upon its ulterior prolongation, three years before its expiration, should circumstances require it.

Religion—precepts of Justice, Charity, and Peace—which, far from being solely applicable to private life, must on the contrary have a direct influence on the policies of Princes and guide all their acts, as being the only means of consolidating human institutions and remedying their imperfections. In consequence, their Majesties have agreed on the following Articles:

Article I

In conformance with the words of the Holy Scriptures, which command all men to consider each other as brothers, the Three Contracting Monarchs will remain united by the bonds of a true and indissoluble fraternity, and, considering each other as compatriots, they will, on all occasions and in all places, lend each other assistance, aid and help; regarding themselves toward their subjects and armies as fathers of families, they will direct them, in the same spirit of fraternity with which they are inspired, to protect Religion, Peace and Justice.

Article II

In consequence, the sole principle in effect, both between the said Governments and their Subjects, shall be that of rendering reciprocal service, and by an unalterable good will, to bear witness to the mutual affection with which they ought to be inspired, to consider themselves all but as members of one Christian Nation; the three Allied Princes looking upon themselves but as delegated by Providence to govern three branches of the same family, namely, Austria, Prussia, and Russia, thus confessing that the Christian Nation, of which they and their people are a part, has truly no other Sovereign than Him to Whom alone belongs the Power, because in Him alone are found all the treasures of love, science, and infinite wisdom, that is to say, God, our Divine Saviour, Jesus Christ, the Word of the Most High, the Word of Life. Their Majesties consequently recommend to their People, with the most tender solicitude, as the sole means of enjoying that Peace which is born out of a good conscience, and which alone is lasting, to strengthen themselves more each day in the principles and performance of the tasks which the Divine Saviour has taught to Mankind.

Article III

All the Powers who shall solemnly choose to avow the sacred principles which have dictated the present Act, and who shall acknowledge how important it is for the happiness of nations, too long disturbed, that these truths should exercise hereafter over the destinies of Mankind all the influence which to them belongs, will be received with equal earnestness and affection into this Holy Alliance.[2]

[2] The Treaty of the Holy Alliance was subsequently adhered to by all the governments of Europe except Turkey, the Papal States, and Great Britain (whose king could not formally adhere because of constitutional limitations).

TREATY OF PARIS [1]

BY THE middle of the nineteenth century the great powers of Europe were no longer cooperating in maintaining absolute monarchy. They were increasingly concerned with the alteration of the balance of power which resulted from the relinquishment by the Turks of their European possessions. Tension arose in the Near East, culminating in the Crimean War. On March 30, 1856, the Treaty of Paris was signed by Britain, France, Russia, Austria, Prussia, Sardinia, and Turkey. Russian ambitions for empire were decisively defeated, and she was forced to agree to the neutralization of the Black Sea.

During the Franco-Prussian War, Russia remained neutral. In return Bismarck supported the Russians when, on October 31, 1870, with France preoccupied by war, they denounced the treaty articles given below. Much diplomatic discussion followed, but it was evident that the will and the power to enforce the treaty no longer existed. Two conferences were therefore held. At the first of these, in London, a declaration was issued (January 17, 1871) to the effect ". . . that it is an essential principle of the Law of Nations that no Power can liberate itself from the engagements of a Treaty, nor modify the stipulations thereof, unless with the consent of the Contracting Powers by means of an amicable arrangement." [2] At the second conference (March 13, 1871) attended by the same powers (North Germany, Austria-Hungary, Great Brit-

---

[1] *British and Foreign State Papers,* Vol. XLVI, pp. 8ff.

[2] Hertslet, *The Map of Europe by Treaty* (1875), Vol. III, p. 1904.

ain, Russia, and Turkey), together with France, abroga-
tion of Articles XI, XIII, and XIV of the Treaty of Paris
was decreed. Thus Russia's *fait accompli* was legitimatized.

Article XI

The Black Sea is Neutralised; its Waters and its Ports, thrown
open to the Mercantile Marine of every Nation, are formally and
in perpetuity interdicted to the Flag of War, either of the
powers possessing its Coasts, or of any other Power, with the exceptions mentioned in Articles XIV and XIX of the present
Treaty.

.   .   .   .

Article XIII

The Black Sea being Neutralised according to the terms of
Article XI, the maintenance or establishment upon its Coast of
Military-Maritime Arsenals becomes alike unnecessary and pur-
poseless; in consequence, His Majesty the Emperor of All the
Russias, and His Imperial Majesty the Sultan, engage not to
establish or to maintain upon that Coast any Military-Maritime
Arsenal.

Article XIV

Their Majesties the Emperor of All the Russias and the Sultan
having concluded a Convention for the purpose of settling the
Force and the Number of Light Vessels, necessary for the service
of their Coasts, which they reserve to themselves to maintain in
the Black Sea, that Convention is annexed to the present Treaty,
and shall have the same force and validity as if it formed an integral part thereof. It cannot be either annulled or modified
without the assent of the Powers signing the present Treaty.

THE TRIPLE ALLIANCE [1]

THE ORIGINAL Treaty of the Triple Alliance, signed in 1882, was extended and amplified in 1887, 1891, 1902, and 1912. The text of the third treaty, signed on May 6, 1891, by Germany, Austria-Hungary, and Italy, is given below. Articles VI to XI were added at renewals of the original treaty.

Whereas the Triple Alliance bound Germany, Austria, and Italy together, Austria was unable to count upon German assistance (prior to 1890) if she were to force war upon Russia (see note and Document 6). Czarist Russia, through her "Reinsurance" Treaty with Germany (Document 6), felt sufficiently protected from Austria to refrain from alliance with republican France. Italy was assured of German aid if France forced war upon her, but she reciprocally agreed with France in 1902 that, should the other be the object of "a direct or indirect aggression" or, if one of them, acting under "direct provocation," declared war on a third power, the other would remain neutral. In 1882 Italy had made a Ministerial Declaration to the effect that the alliance could under no circumstances be regarded as directed against England. This declaration was still in effect in 1914. Thus Italy had a foot in both camps. There was no clear-cut division into rival and exclusive alliances such as evolved subsequently. These developments had the effect of making the system of European alliances extremely complex, and this very com-

---

[1] *Die Grosse Politik der Europäischen Kabinette, 1871–1914,* Vol. VII, pp. 99*ff*. (Editor's translation.)

plexity kept Europe and the world from becoming involved in war. No one nation dared to go too far in the absence of unconditional assurances of support in case of difficulty.

Article I

The High Contracting Parties promise to each other peace and friendship, and will not enter into any alliance or engagement directed against any one of their States.

They undertake to proceed to an exchange of ideas on any political and economic questions of a general nature which may arise, and they further promise each other their mutual support within the limits of their proper interests.

Article II

In the event that Italy, without direct provocation on her part, should be attacked by France for any reason whatsoever, the other two Contracting Parties shall be obligated to give the Party attacked aid and assistance with all their forces.

This same obligation shall be incumbent upon Italy in the event of an aggression without direct provocation by France against Germany.

Article III

If one, or two, of the High Contracting Parties, without direct provocation on their part, should happen to be attacked and find itself engaged in war with two or more Great Powers nonsignatory to the present Treaty, a *casus foederis* will occur simultaneously for all the High Contracting Parties.

Article IV

In the event that a Great Power nonsignatory to the present Treaty should threaten the security of the dominions of one of the High Contracting Parties, and the threatened Party should find itself compelled because of this to go to war, the two others obligate themselves to observe a benevolent neutrality towards their Ally. Each of them reserves the right in this event to take part in the war, if it should deem it necessary in order to make common cause with its Ally.

Article V

If the peace of one of the High Contracting Parties should happen to be threatened under the circumstances anticipated in the foregoing Articles, the High Contracting Parties shall consult together in good time on the military measures to be taken with a view to eventual cooperation.

They engage, henceforth, in every case of common participation in a war, not to conclude either an armistice, a peace, or a treaty, except by common agreement among themselves.

Article VI

Germany and Italy, having no other object in view but the maintenance, as far as possible, of the territorial status quo in the Orient, obligate themselves to use their influence to prevent any territorial change of the Ottoman coasts and islands in the Adriatic and Aegean Seas which might injure any of the Powers signatory to the present Treaty. They will communicate to one another for this purpose any information of a nature to inform one another as to their respective arrangements, as well as those of other Powers.

Article VII

Austria-Hungary and Italy, having no other object in view but the maintenance, as far as possible, of the territorial status quo in the Orient, obligate themselves to use their influence to prevent any territorial change which might injure any of the Powers signatory to the present Treaty. They will communicate to one another for this purpose any information of a nature to inform one another as to their respective arrangements, as well as those of other Powers. However, in a case where, through a sequence of events, the maintenance of the status quo of the Balkan regions or of the Ottoman coasts and islands in the Adriatic and Aegean Seas should become impossible, and if, whether because of the action of a third Power or otherwise, Austria-Hungary or Italy should feel themselves under the necessity of changing it by a temporary or permanent occupation on their part, this occupation shall not take place until after a preliminary agreement between the two Powers, based upon the principle of reciprocal compensation for every advantage, territorial or otherwise, which each of them might obtain over and above the present status quo, and giving satisfaction to the interests and justified claims of the two Parties.   .

. . . .

Article IX

Germany and Italy obligate themselves to work for the maintenance of the territorial status quo in the North African regions on the Mediterranean, namely, Cyrenaica, Tripolitania, and Tunisia. The Representatives of the two Powers in these regions shall be instructed to enter into the closest intimacy concerning mutual communication and assistance.

If unfortunately, following a mature examination of the situation, Germany and Italy should both recognize that the maintenance of the status quo has become impossible, Germany promises, after a preliminary and formal agreement, to support Italy in any action in the form of occupation or other taking of guaranty which the latter should undertake in these regions in view of an interest in equilibrium and legitimate compensation.

It is understood that in such an eventuality the two Powers would endeavour to place themselves equally in accord with England.

Article X

Should it happen that France in any manner should act to enlarge her occupation, or else her protectorate or her sovereignty, over the North African territories, and that in consequence of this, Italy believes herself obliged, in order to safeguard her position in the Mediterranean, also to undertake action in the said North African territories, or to have recourse to extreme measures in French territory in Europe, the state of war which would then follow between Italy and France would constitute *ipso facto,* upon the request of Italy, and as a common burden of Germany and Italy, the *casus foederis* foreseen by Articles II and V of the present Treaty, as if such an eventuality were expressly intended therein.

Article XI

If the fortunes of any war undertaken by the two Powers in common against France should cause Italy to desire territorial guaranties with regard to France for the security of the frontiers of the Kingdom and her maritime position, and at the same time with a view to stability and peace, Germany will place no obstacle thereto, and, in case of need and to the extent compatible with circumstances, will apply herself to facilitate the means of attaining such an objective.

"REINSURANCE" TREATY [1]

THE "REINSURANCE" Treaty was signed for a period of three years by Germany and Russia on June 18, 1887, and expired in 1890. Russia desired to renew the treaty, but Kaiser Wilhelm felt that the "Reinsurance" Treaty was incompatible with Germany's obligations under the Triple Alliance. A close study of the two documents (compare with Document 5) shows that the two treaties were compatible as regards the exact letter, if not the spirit, of the obligations. The issue which Germany faced was whether to continue what was in effect a guarantee against unprovoked Austrian attack, since Austria would not dare to attack Russia without German assistance, or to refuse to renew the treaty, and thus cause Russia to open negotiations with France for an alliance, which followed. In 1914, Germany was forced to fight on both East and West—a consequence which stemmed directly from the Kaiser's decision not to renew the treaty with Russia in 1890.

Article I

In the event that one of the High Contracting Parties should find itself at war with a third great Power, the other will maintain a benevolent neutrality towards it, and will dedicate its attention to the localization of the conflict. This arrangement will not apply to a war against Austria or France in a case where

[1] *Die Grosse Politik der Europäischen Kabinette, 1871–1914,* Vol. V, pp. 253*ff.* (Editor's translation.)

this war should result from an attack directed against one of these two latter Powers by one of the High Contracting Parties.

Article II

Germany recognizes the rights historically acquired by Russia in the Balkan Peninsula, and particularly the rightfulness of her preponderant and conclusive influence in Bulgaria and Eastern Rumelia. The two Courts undertake to allow no modification of the territorial status quo of the said peninsula without a preliminary agreement between them, and to resist whenever necessary any attempt to infringe upon this status quo or alter it without their consent.

Article III

The two Courts recognize the European and mutually obligatory character of the principle of the closing of the Straits of the Bosphorus and the Dardanelles, founded upon international law, sanctioned by treaties, and recapitulated in the declaration of the second Plenipotentiary of Russia at the session of July 12th of the Congress of Berlin (Protocol 19).

They will both take care that Turkey shall make no exception to this rule in favor of the interests of any Government whatsoever, by permitting the use of the part of her Empire formed by the Straits for the martial operations of a belligerent power. In the event of violation, or to prevent it if such violation is foreseen, the two Courts will warn Turkey that they would consider her, in that case, as putting herself in a state of war vis-à-vis the injured Party, and as putting herself from that time outside the security benefits assured to her territorial status quo by the Treaty of Berlin.

.   .   .   .

ADDITIONAL AND VERY SECRET PROTOCOL

.   .   .   .

2

In the event that His Majesty the Emperor of Russia should find himself under the necessity of assuming the task of defending the entrance of the Black Sea in order to safeguard the interests of Russia, Germany promises to grant her benevolent neutrality and her moral and diplomatic support to the measures which His Majesty might judge necessary to take to guard the key of His Empire.

DOCUMENT 7

DUAL ALLIANCE OF FRANCE AND RUSSIA [1]

THE MILITARY Convention of 1892 (below) was signed by France and Russia. It supplemented an exchange of notes in 1891 in which agreement to concert measures was reached. It will be noted that the negotiations which culuminated in the Convention were initiated the year after Kaiser Wilhelm refused to renew the "Reinsurance" Treaty (see note and Document 6). The Military Convention was the basis for the Dual Alliance of Russia and France in 1894. The consummation of the alliance seriously altered the balance of power in Europe because until then France had been isolated. When France concluded the Entente Cordiale with England in 1904, after coming to agreement over Egypt and Morocco, the path was clear for a combination against the Triple Alliance. In 1907, Britain and Russia settled their differences and divided Persia (Iran) into spheres of influence. Thereafter, these nations, together with France, formed the Triple Entente. From this time forward the flexibility which had characterized the pre-1890 system disappeared (see note preceding Document 5).

France and Russia, being animated by an equal desire to maintain peace, and having no other purpose than to anticipate the necessities of a defensive war provoked by an attack of the

[1] *Documents diplomatiques français (1871–1914)*, First Series (1871–1900), Vol. IX, pp. 643*ff.* (The text is taken from No. 444, with the minor corrections made as noted in No. 461, p. 682.) (Editor's translation.)

forces of the Triple Alliance against either of them, have agreed upon the following arrangements:

1

If France is attacked by Germany, or by Italy supported by Germany, Russia shall employ all her available forces in order to attack Germany.

If Russia is attacked by Germany, or by Austria supported by Germany, France shall employ all her available forces in order to fight Germany.

2

In the event that the forces of the Triple Alliance, or of one of the Powers composing it, should mobilize, France and Russia, at the first indication of the event and without the necessity of any previous concert, shall mobilize the whole of their forces immediately and simultaneously, and shall move them as near as possible to their frontiers.

3

The available forces to be employed against Germany shall be, on the part of France, 1,300,000 men, on the part of Russia, from 700,000 to 800,000 men.

These forces shall engage fully and with all speed, so that Germany may have to fight at the same time in the East and in the West.

4

The General Staffs of the Armies of the two countries shall consult together at all times in order to prepare and facilitate the fulfillment of the measures foreseen above.

They shall communicate to each other, even in time of peace, all information relative to the armies of the Triple Alliance which is or shall be within their knowledge.

Ways and means of corresponding in times of war shall be studied and provided for in advance.

5

France and Russia shall not conclude peace separately.

6

The present Convention shall have the same duration as the Triple Alliance.

7

All of the clauses enumerated above shall be kept rigorously secret.

HAGUE CONVENTION FOR THE PACIFIC SETTLEMENT OF INTERNATIONAL DISPUTES [1]

THE HAGUE Convention, signed on October 18, 1907, by forty-four nations, came into force on February 28, 1910. It reflected the concern of the powers that the procedures for settlement short of war be strengthened at a time when the balance of power was becoming increasingly inflexible and the number of international crises was multiplying.

The *methods* of peaceful settlement listed in the Convention are (1) good offices and mediation, (2) international commissions of inquiry, (3) arbitration. Under the first method a nation not party to the dispute offers to assist in arranging a compromise settlement, and, if the offer is accepted, it acts as a go-between. Under the second method, each party nominates two commissioners who then together elect a fifth commissioner as chairman. They investigate the facts of the dispute, and on the basis of the facts, make a recommendation. The recommendation may be accepted or rejected. Thus both methods leave the disputants free to accept or reject the proposed settlement. This is not so under the third method, arbitration. The arbitral panel is chosen in the same way as the commission of inquiry, but its award (or decision) is binding upon the parties. It constitutes a legal settlement of the dispute, and both parties are expected to comply. Therefore, if a party to a dispute wishes to be free to reject any proposed settlement, it utilizes mediation by

[1] *Treaties, Conventions, International Acts, Protocols and Agreements between the United States of America and Other Powers, 1776–1909,* Senate Document No. 357, 61st Congress, 2d Session, pp. 2220*ff.*

a third state or investigation by a commission of inquiry; only if it is prepared to accept in advance as binding a legal decison of the controversy, will it agree to arbitration. (Since World War I an alternative method of legal settlement has been available—adjudication. See note and Document 40.)

The Hague Convention established the Permanent Court of Arbitration. A panel of some one hundred and twenty members was set up through the nomination by each member nation of four arbitrators. It was from this panel that the five arbitrators were chosen for any particular case. Any nation wishing then to resort to arbitration could do so much more conveniently than it could before the creation of the Permanent Court of Arbitration (also called the Hague Court).

The following states are parties to the Convention of 1907: [2] Argentina, Belgium, Bolivia, Brazil, Bulgaria, Chile, China, Colombia, Cuba, Czechoslovakia, Denmark, Dominican Republic, Ecuador, Finland, France, Germany, Great Britain, Greece, Guatemala, Haiti, Hungary, Iran, Italy, Japan, Luxemburg, Mexico, Netherlands, Nicaragua, Norway, Panama, Paraguay, Peru, Poland, Portugal, Rumania, El Salvador, Siam, Spain, Sweden, Switzerland, Turkey, United States of America, Uruguay, Venezuela, Yugoslavia.

PART I

THE MAINTENANCE OF GENERAL PEACE

Article 1

With a view to obviating as far as possible recourse to force in the relations between States, the *contracting* [3] Powers agree to use

[2] As of April 29, 1949. *Rapport du conseil administratif de la cour permanente d'arbitrage (1948)*, pp. 5ff., International Bureau of the Permanent Court of Arbitration, 1949.

[3] Italicized parts indicate changes in the original Convention of 1899.

their best efforts to insure the pacific settlement of international differences.

PART II

GOOD OFFICES AND MEDIATION

Article 2

In case of serious disagreement or dispute, before an appeal to arms, the *contracting* Powers agree to have recourse, as far as circumstances allow, to the good offices or mediation of one or more friendly Powers.

Article 3

Independently of this recourse, the *contracting* Powers deem it expedient *and desirable* that one or more Powers, strangers to the dispute, should, on their own initiative and as far as circumstances may allow, offer their good offices or mediation to the States at variance.

Powers strangers to the dispute have the right to offer good offices or mediation even during the course of hostilities.

The exercise of this right can never be regarded by either of the parties in dispute as an unfriendly act.

Article 4

The part of the mediator consists in reconciling the opposing claims and appeasing the feelings of resentment which may have arisen between the States at variance.

Article 5

The functions of the mediator are at an end when once it is declared, either by one of the parties to the dispute or by the mediator himself, that the means of reconciliation proposed by him are not accepted.

Article 6

Good offices and mediation undertaken either at the request of the parties in dispute or on the initiative of Powers strangers to the dispute have exclusively the character of advice, and never have binding force.

Article 7

The acceptance of mediation can not, unless there be an agreement to the contrary, have the effect of interrupting, delaying, or hindering mobilization or other measures of preparation for war.

If it takes place after the commencement of hostilities, the military operations in progress are not interrupted in the absence of an agreement to the contrary.

Article 8

The *contracting* Powers are agreed in recommending the application, when circumstances allow, of special mediation in the following form:

In case of a serious difference endangering peace, the States at variance choose respectively a Power, to which they intrust the mission of entering into direct communication with the Power chosen on the other side, with the object of preventing the rupture of pacific relations.

For the period of this mandate, the term of which, unless otherwise stipulated, can not exceed thirty days, the States in dispute cease from all direct communication on the subject of the dispute, which is regarded as referred exclusively to the mediating Powers, which must use their best efforts to settle it.

In case of a definite rupture of pacific relations, these Powers are charged with the joint task of taking advantage of any opportunity to restore peace.

PART III

INTERNATIONAL COMMISSIONS OF INQUIRY

Article 9

In disputes of an international nature involving neither honor nor vital interests, and arising from a difference of opinion on points of fact, the *contracting* Powers deem it expedient *and* desirable that the parties who have not been able to come to an agreement by means of diplomacy, should, as far as circumstances allow, institute an international commission of inquiry, to facilitate a solution of these disputes by elucidating the facts by means of an impartial and conscientious investigation.

Article 10

International commissions of inquiry are constituted by special agreement between the parties in dispute.

The inquiry convention defines the facts to be examined; *it determines the mode and time in which the commission is to be formed* and the extent of the powers of the commissioners.

It also determines, if there is need, where the commission is to sit, and whether it may remove to another place, the language the commission shall use and the language the use of which shall be authorized before it, as well as the date on which each party must deposit its statement of facts, and generally speaking, all the conditions upon which the parties have agreed. . . .

. . . .

Article 17

In order to facilitate the constitution and working of commissions of inquiry, the contracting Powers recommend the following rules, which shall be applicable to the inquiry procedure in so far as the parties do not adopt other rules.

Article 18

The commission shall settle the details of the procedure not covered by the special inquiry convention or the present Convention, and shall arrange all the formalities required for dealing with the evidence.

Article 19

On the inquiry both sides must be heard.

At the dates fixed, each party communicates to the commission and to the other party the statements of facts, if any, and, in all cases, the instruments, papers, and documents which it considers useful for ascertaining the truth, as well as the list of witnesses and experts whose evidence it wishes to be heard.

Article 20

The commission is entitled, with the assent of the Powers, to move temporarily to any place where it considers it may be useful to have recourse to this means of inquiry or to send one or more of its members. Permission must be obtained from the State on whose territory it is proposed to hold the inquiry.

Article 21

Every investigation, and every examination of a locality, must be made in the presence of the agents and counsel of the parties or after they have been duly summoned.

Article 22

The commission is entitled to ask from either party for such explanations and information as it considers necessary.

Article 23

The *parties* undertake to supply the commission of inquiry, as fully as they may think possible, with all means and facilities necessary to enable it to become completely acquainted with, and to accurately understand, the facts in question.

They undertake to make use of the means at their disposal, under their municipal law, to insure the appearance of the witnesses or experts who are in their territory and have been summoned before the commission.

If the witnesses or experts are unable to appear before the commission, the parties will arrange for their evidence to be taken before the qualified officials of their own country.

Article 24

For all notices to be served by the commission in the territory of a third contracting Power, the commission shall apply direct to the Government of the said Power. The same rule applies in the case of steps being taken on the spot to procure evidence.

The requests for this purpose are to be executed so far as the means at the disposal of the Power applied to under its mu-

nicipal law allow. They can not be rejected unless the Power in question considers they are calculated to impair its sovereign rights or its safety.

The commission will equally be always entitled to act through the Power on whose territory it sits.

Article 25

The witnesses and experts are summoned on the request of the parties or by the commission of its own motion, and, in every case, through the Government of the State in whose territory they are.

The witnesses are heard in succession and separately, in the presence of the agents and counsel, and in the order fixed by the commission.

Article 26

The examination of witnesses is conducted by the president.

The members of the commission may however put to each witness questions which they consider likely to throw light on and complete his evidence, or get information on any point concerning the witness within the limits of what is necessary in order to get at the truth.

The agents and counsel of the parties may not interrupt the witness when he is making his statements, nor put any direct question to him, but they may ask the president to put such additional questions to the witness as they think expedient.

Article 27

The witness must give his evidence without being allowed to read any written draft. He may, however, be permitted by the president to consult notes or documents if the nature of the facts referred to necessitate their employment.

Article 28

A minute of the evidence of the witness is drawn up forthwith and read to the witness. The latter may make such alterations and additions as he thinks necessary, which will be recorded at the end of his statement.

When the whole of his statement has been read to the witness, he is asked to sign it.

Article 29

The agents are authorized, in the course of or at the close of the inquiry, to present in writing to the commission and to the other party such statements, requisitions, or summaries of the facts as they consider useful for ascertaining the truth.

Article 30

The commission considers its decisions in private and the proceedings are secret.

All questions are decided by a majority of the members of the commission.

If a member declines to vote, the fact must be recorded in the minutes.

Article 31

The sittings of the commission are not public, nor the minutes and documents connected with the inquiry published except in virtue of a decision of the commission taken with the consent of the parties.

Article 32

After the parties have presented all the explanations and evidence, and the witnesses have all been heard, the president declares the inquiry terminated, and the commission adjourns to deliberate and to draw up its report.

Article 33

The report is signed by all the members of the commission.

If one of the members refuses to sign, the fact is mentioned; but the validity of the report is not affected.

Article 34

The report of the commission is read at a public sitting, the agents and counsel of the parties being present or duly summoned.

A copy of the report is given to each party.

Article 35

The report of the commission is limited to a statement of facts, and has in no way the character of an award. It leaves to the parties entire freedom as to the effect to be given to the statement.

Article 36

Each party pays its own expenses and an equal share of the expenses incurred by the commission.

PART IV

INTERNATIONAL ARBITRATION

CHAPTER I. THE SYSTEM OF ARBITRATION

Article 37

International arbitration has for its object the settlement of disputes between States by judges of their own choice and on the basis of respect for law.

Recourse to arbitration implies an engagement to submit in good faith to the award.

Article 38

In questions of a legal nature, and especially in the interpretation or application of international conventions, arbitration is recognized by the *contracting* Powers as the most effective, and, at the same time, the most equitable means of settling disputes which diplomacy has failed to settle.

Consequently, it would be desirable that, in disputes about the above-mentioned questions, the contracting Powers should, if the case arose, have recourse to arbitration, in so far as circumstances permit.

Article 39

The arbitration convention is concluded for questions already existing or for questions which may arise eventually.

It may embrace any dispute or only disputes of a certain category.

Article 40

Independently of general or private treaties expressly stipulating recourse to arbitration as obligatory on the *contracting* Powers, the said Powers reserve to themselves the right of concluding new agreements, general or particular, with a view to extending compulsory arbitration to all cases which they may consider it possible to submit to it.

CHAPTER II. THE PERMANENT COURT OF ARBITRATION

Article 41

With the object of facilitating an immediate recourse to arbitration for international differences, which it has not been possible to settle by diplomacy, the *contracting* Powers undertake to *maintain the* Permanent Court of Arbitration, *as established by the First Peace Conference,* accessible at all times, and operating, unless otherwise stipulated by the parties, in accordance with the rules of procedure inserted in the present Convention.

Article 42

The Permanent Court *is* competent for all arbitration cases, unless the parties agree to institute a special tribunal.

Article 43

The Permanent Court sits at The Hague.

An International Bureau serves as registry for the Court. It is the channel for communications relative to the meetings of the Court; it has charge of the archives and conducts all the administrative business.

The *contracting* Powers undertake to communicate to the Bureau, *as soon as possible,* a certified copy of any conditions of arbitration arrived at between them and of any award concerning them delivered by a special tribunal.

They likewise undertake to communicate to the Bureau the laws, regulations, and documents eventually showing the execution of the awards given by the Court.

Article 44

Each *contracting* Power *selects* four persons at the most, of known competency in questions of international law, of the highest moral reputation, and disposed to accept the duties of arbitrator.

The persons thus selected *are* inscribed, as members of the Court, in a list which shall be notified to all the *contracting* Powers by the Bureau.

Any alteration in the list of arbitrators is brought by the Bureau to the knowledge of the *contracting* Powers.

Two or more Powers may agree on the selection in common of one or more members.

The same person can be selected by different Powers. The members of the Court are appointed for a term of six years. These appointments are renewable.

Should a member of the Court die or resign, the same procedure is followed for filling the vacancy as was followed for appointing him. *In this case the appointment is made for a fresh period of six years.*

Article 45

When the *contracting* Powers wish to have recourse to the Permanent Court for the settlement of a difference which has arisen between them, the arbitrators called upon to form the tribunal with jurisdiction to decide this difference must be chosen from the general list of members of the Court.

Failing the direct agreement of the parties on the composition of the arbitration tribunal, the following course shall be pursued:

Each party appoints two arbitrators, *of whom one only can be its national or chosen from among the persons selected by it as members of the Permanent Court.* These arbitrators together choose an umpire.

If the votes are equally divided, the choice of the umpire is intrusted to a third Power, selected by the parties by common accord.

If an agreement is not arrived at on this subject each party selects a different Power, and the choice of the umpire is made in concert by the Powers thus selected.

If, within two months' time, these two Powers cannot come to an agreement, each of them presents two candidates taken from the list of members of the Permanent Court, exclusive of the members selected by the parties and not being nationals of either of them. Drawing lots determines which of the candidates thus presented shall be umpire.

Article 46

The tribunal being thus composed, the parties notify to the Bureau their determination to have recourse to the Court, *the text of their compromis,*[4] and the names of the arbitrators.

The Bureau communicates without delay to each arbitrator the compromis, and the names of the other members of the tribunal.

The tribunal assembles at the date fixed by the parties. *The Bureau makes the necessary arrangements for the meeting.*

The members of the *tribunal,* in the exercise of their duties and out of their own country, enjoy diplomatic privileges and immunities.

Article 47

The Bureau is authorized to place its offices and staff at the disposal of the *contracting* Powers for the use of any special board of arbitration.

The jurisdiction of the Permanent Court may, within the conditions laid down in the regulations, be extended to disputes between *non-contracting* Powers or between *contracting* Powers and *non-contracting* Powers, if the parties are agreed on recourse to this tribunal.

Article 48

The *contracting* Powers consider it their duty, if a serious dispute threatens to break out between two or more of them, to remind these latter that the Permanent Court is open to them.

---

[4] The preliminary agreement in an international arbitration defining the point at issue and arranging the procedure to be followed.

Consequently, they declare that the fact of reminding the parties at variance of the provisions of the present Convention, and the advice given to them, in the highest interests of peace, to have recourse to the Permanent Court, can only be regarded as friendly actions.

In case of dispute between two Powers, one of them can always address to the International Bureau a note containing a declaration that it would be ready to submit the dispute to arbitration.

The Bureau must at once inform the other Power of the declaration.

Article 49

The Permanent Administrative Council, composed of the diplomatic representatives of the *contracting* Powers accredited to The Hague and of the Netherland Minister for Foreign Affairs, who will act as president, is charged with the direction and control of the International Bureau. . . .

. . . .

CHAPTER III. ARBITRATION PROCEDURE

Article 51

With a view to encouraging the development of arbitration, the *contracting* Powers have agreed on the following rules, which are applicable to arbitration procedure, unless other rules have been agreed on by the parties.

Article 52

The Powers which have recourse to arbitration sign a compromis, in which the subject of the dispute is clearly defined, *the time allowed for appointing arbitrators, the form, order, and time in which the communication referred to in Article 63 must be made, and the amount of the sum which each party must deposit in advance to defray the expenses.*

The compromis likewise defines, if there is occasion, the manner of appointing arbitrators, any special powers which may eventually belong to the tribunal, where it shall meet, the lan-

*guage it shall use, and the languages the employment of which
shall be authorized before it, and, generally speaking, all the
conditions on which the parties are agreed.*

Article 53

*The Permanent Court is competent to settle the compromis,
if the parties are agreed to have recourse to it for the purpose.*

*It is similarly competent, even if the request is only made by
one of the parties, when all attempts to reach an understanding
through the diplomatic channel have failed, in the case of—*

*1. A dispute covered by a general treaty of arbitration con-
cluded or renewed after the present Convention has come into
force, and providing for a compromis in all disputes and not
either explicitly or implicitly excluding the settlement of the
compromis from the competence of the Court. Recourse can not,
however, be had to the Court if the other party declares that in
its opinion the dispute does not belong to the category of disputes which can be submitted to compulsory arbitration, unless
the treaty of arbitration confers upon the arbitration tribunal
the power of deciding this preliminary question.*

*2. A dispute arising from contract debts claimed from one
Power by another Power as due to its nationals, and for the settlement of which the offer of arbitration has been accepted. This
arrangement is not applicable if acceptance is subject to the condition that the compromis should be settled in some other way.*

Article 54

*In the cases contemplated in the preceding article, the com-
promis shall be settled by a commission consisting of five members selected in the manner arranged for in Article 45, paragraphs 3 to 6.*

The fifth member is president of the commission ex officio.

Article 55

The duties of arbitrator may be conferred on one arbitrator
alone or on several arbitrators selected by the parties as they

please, or chosen by them from the members of the Permanent Court of Arbitration established by the present Convention.

Failing the constitution of the tribunal by direct agreement between the parties, the course *referred to in Article 45, paragraphs 3 to 6, is followed.*

Article 56

When a sovereign or the chief of a State is chosen as arbitrator, the arbitration procedure is settled by him.

Article 57

The umpire is president of the tribunal ex officio.

When the tribunal does not include an umpire, it appoints its own president.

Article 58

When the compromis is settled by a commission, as contemplated in Article 54, and in the absence of an agreement to the contrary, the commission itself shall form the arbitration tribunal.

.   .   .   .

Article 60

The tribunal sits at The Hague, unless some other place is selected by the parties.

The tribunal can only sit in the territory of a third Power with the latter's consent. . . .

.   .   .   .

Article 63

As a general rule, arbitration procedure comprises two distinct phases: pleadings and oral discussions.

The pleadings consist in the communication by the respective agents to the members of the tribunal and the opposite party of *cases, counter-cases, and, if necessary, of replies; the parties annex thereto all papers* and documents called for in the case. This communication shall be made *either directly or through the intermediary of the International Bureau,* in the *order* and within the time fixed by the *compromis.*

The time fixed by the compromis may be extended by mutual agreement by the parties, or by the tribunal when the latter considers it necessary for the purpose of reaching a just decision.

The discussions consist in the oral development before the tribunal of the arguments of the parties.

Article 64

A *certified copy* of every document produced by one party must be communicated to the other party.

Article 65

Unless special circumstances arise, the tribunal does not meet until the pleadings are closed.

Article 66

The discussions are under the control of the president.

They are only public if it be so decided by the tribunal, with the assent of the parties.

They are recorded in minutes drawn up by the secretaries appointed by the president. These minutes *are signed by the president and by one of the secretaries and* alone have an authentic character.

Article 67

After the close of the pleadings, the tribunal is entitled to refuse discussion of all new papers or documents which one of the parties may wish to submit to it without the consent of the other party.

Article 68

The tribunal is free to take into consideration new papers or documents to which its attention may be drawn by the agents or counsel of the parties.

In this case, the tribunal has the right to require the production of these papers or documents, but is obliged to make them known to the opposite party.

Article 69

The tribunal can, besides, require from the agents of the parties the production of all papers, and can demand all necessary explanations. In case of refusal the tribunal takes note of it.

Article 70

The agents and the counsel of the parties are authorized to present orally to the tribunal all the arguments they may consider expedient in defense of their case.

Article 71

They are entitled to raise objections and points. The decisions of the tribunal on these points are final and can not form the subject of any subsequent discussion.

Article 72

The members of the tribunal are entitled to put questions to the agents and counsel of the parties, and to ask them for explanations on doubtful points.

Neither the questions put, nor the remarks made by members of the tribunal in the course of the discussions, can be regarded as an expression of opinion by the tribunal in general or by its members in particular.

Article 73

The tribunal is authorized to declare its competence in interpreting the compromis, as well as the other *treaties* which may be invoked, and in applying the principles of law.

Article 74

The tribunal is entitled to issue rules of procedure for the conduct of the case, to decide the forms, *order,* and time in which each party must conclude its arguments, and to arrange all the formalities required for dealing with the evidence.

Article 75

The parties undertake to supply the tribunal, as fully as they consider possible, with all the information required for deciding the case.

Article 76

For all notices which the tribunal has to serve in the territory of a third contracting Power, the tribunal shall apply direct to the Government of that Power. The same rule applies in the case of steps being taken to procure evidence on the spot.

The requests for this purpose are to be executed as far as the means at the disposal of the Power applied to under its municipal law allow. They can not be rejected unless the Power in question considers them calculated to impair its own sovereign rights or its safety.

The Court will equally be always entitled to act through the Power on whose territory it sits.

Article 77

When the agents and counsel of the parties have submitted all the explanations and evidence in support of their case the president shall declare the discussion closed.

Article 78

The tribunal considers its decisions in private and *the proceedings remain secret.*

All questions are decided by a majority of the members of the tribunal.

Article 79

The award must give the reasons on which it is based. *It contains the names of the arbitrators; it is signed by the president and registrar or by the secretary acting as registrar.*

Article 80

The award is read out in public sitting, the agents and counsel of the parties being present or duly summoned to attend.

Article 81

The award, duly pronounced and notified to the agents of the parties, settles the dispute definitively and without appeal.

Article 82

Any dispute arising between the parties as to the interpretation and execution of the award shall, in the absence of an agreement to the contrary, be submitted to the tribunal which pronounced it.

Article 83

The parties can reserve in the compromis the right to demand the revision of the award.

In this case and unless there be an agreement to the contrary, the demand must be addressed to the tribunal which pronounced the award. It can only be made on the ground of the discovery of some new fact calculated to exercise a decisive influence upon the award and which was unknown to the tribunal and to the party which demanded the revision at the time the discussion was closed.

Proceedings for revision can only be instituted by a decision of the tribunal expressly recording the existence of the new fact, recognizing in it the character described in the preceding paragraph, and declaring the demand admissible on this ground.

The compromis fixes the period within which the demand for revision must be made.

Article 84

The award is not binding except on the parties *in dispute*.

When it concerns the interpretation of a Convention to which Powers other than those in dispute are parties, they shall inform all the signatory Powers *in good time*. Each of these Powers is entitled to intervene in the case. If one or more avail themselves of this right, the interpretation contained in the award is equally binding on them.

Article 85

Each party pays its own expenses and an equal share of the expenses of the tribunal.

CHAPTER IV. ARBITRATION BY SUMMARY PROCEDURE

Article 86

With a view to facilitating the working of the system of arbitration in disputes admitting of a summary procedure, the contracting Powers adopt the following rules, which shall be observed in the absence of other arrangements and subject to the reservation that the provisions of Chapter III apply so far as may be.

Article 87

Each of the parties in dispute appoints an arbitrator. The two arbitrators thus selected choose an umpire. If they do not agree on this point, each of them proposes two candidates taken from the general list of the members of the Permanent Court exclusive of the members appointed by either of the parties and not being nationals of either of them; which of the candidates thus proposed shall be the umpire is determined by lot.

The umpire presides over the tribunal, which gives its decisions by a majority of votes.

Article 88

In the absence of any previous agreement the tribunal, as soon as it is formed, settles the time within which the two parties must submit their respective cases to it.

Article 89

Each party is represented before the tribunal by an agent, who serves as intermediary between the tribunal and the Government who appointed him.

Article 90

The proceedings are conducted exclusively in writing. Each party, however, is entitled to ask that witnesses and experts should be called. The tribunal has, for its part, the right to demand oral explanations from the agents of the two parties, as well as from the experts and witnesses whose appearance in Court it may consider useful.

PART V

FINAL PROVISIONS

·   ·   ·   ·   ·   ·   ·   ·   ·   ·   ·   ·   ·   ·

Article 96

In the event of one of the contracting *Powers wishing to* denounce the present Convention, *the* denunciation shall be notified in writing to the Netherland Government, *which shall* immediately communicate *a duly certified copy* of the notification to all the other Powers *informing them of the date on which it was received.*

The denunciation shall only have effect in regard to the notifying Power, *and one year after the notification has reached the Netherland Government.*

DOCUMENT 9

WILSON'S FOURTEEN POINTS [1]

THE FOURTEEN Points were presented to a joint session of Congress in an address by President Wilson on January 8, 1918. They were accepted as a basis of negotiation for ending the war by both the Allies and the German government, and an armistice was proclaimed on November 11, 1918. Actually the Germans did not "negotiate" the Treaty of Versailles which followed. They were forced to sign the treaty without any substantial changes, once it was completed by the Allied and Associated Powers. Although they had no real choice, since their military power was exhausted and the Kaiser had been driven from his throne by revolution, the Versailles *Diktat* subsequently proved fertile propaganda for Hitler, especially when contrasted with the Fourteen Points. The fourteenth point, calling for "a general association of nations" was realized with the creation of the League of Nations.

I

Open covenants of peace, openly arrived at, after which there shall be no private international understandings of any kind but diplomacy shall proceed always frankly and in the public view.

II

Absolute freedom of navigation upon the seas, outside territorial waters, alike in peace and in war, except as the seas

[1] *Congressional Record,* Vol. 56, 65th Congress, 2d Session, pp. 680*ff.*

may be closed in whole or in part by international action for the enforcement of international covenants.

III

The removal, so far as possible, of all economic barriers and the establishment of an equality of trade conditions among all the nations consenting to the peace and associating themselves for its maintenance.

IV

Adequate guarantees given and taken that national armaments will be reduced to the lowest point consistent with domestic safety.

V

A free, open-minded, and absolutely impartial adjustment of all colonial claims, based upon a strict observance of the principle that in determining all such questions of sovereignty the interests of the populations concerned must have equal weight with the equitable claims of the government whose title is to be determined.

VI

The evacuation of all Russian territory and such a settlement of all questions affecting Russia as will secure the best and freest co-operation of the other nations of the world in obtaining for her an unhampered and unembarrassed opportunity for the independent determination of her own political development and national policy and assure her of a sincere welcome into the society of free nations under institutions of her own choosing; and, more than a welcome, assistance also of every kind that she may need and may herself desire. The treatment accorded Russia by her sister nations in the months to come will be the acid test of their good will, of their comprehension of her needs as distinguished from their own interests, and of their intelligent and unselfish sympathy.

VII

Belgium, the whole world will agree, must be evacuated and restored, without any attempt to limit the sovereignty which she enjoys in common with all other free nations. No other single act will serve as this will serve to restore confidence among the nations in the laws which they have themselves set and determined for the government of their relations with one another. Without this healing act the whole structure and validity of international law is forever impaired.

VIII

All French territory should be freed and the invaded portions restored, and the wrong done to France by Prussia in 1871 in the matter of Alsace-Lorraine, which has unsettled the peace of the world for nearly fifty years, should be righted, in order that peace may once more be made secure in the interest of all.

IX

A readjustment of the frontiers of Italy should be effected along clearly recognizable lines of nationality.

X

The peoples of Austria-Hungary, whose place among the nations we wish to see safeguarded and assured, should be accorded the freest opportunity of autonomous development.

XI

Rumania, Serbia, and Montenegro should be evacuated; occupied territories restored; Serbia accorded free and secure access to the sea; and the relations of the several Balkan states to one another determined by friendly counsel along historically established lines of allegiance and nationality; and international guarantees of the political and economic independence and territorial integrity of the several Balkan states should be entered into.

XII

The Turkish portions of the present Ottoman Empire should be assured a secure sovereignty, but the other nationalities which are now under Turkish rule should be assured an undoubted security of life and an absolutely unmolested opportunity of autonomous development, and the Dardanelles should be per-

manently opened as a free passage to the ships and commerce
of all nations under international guarantees.

XIII

An independent Polish state should be erected which should
include the territories inhabited by indisputably Polish populations, which should be assured a free and secure access to the
sea, and whose political and economic independence and territorial integrity should be guaranteed by international covenant.

XIV

A general association of nations must be formed under specific
covenants for the purpose of affording mutual guarantees of
political independence and territorial integrity to great and
small states alike.

DOCUMENT 10

COVENANT OF THE LEAGUE OF NATIONS [1]

THE COVENANT, signed on June 28, 1919, constituted Part I of the Treaty of Versailles. It entered into force on January 10, 1920. The subsequent amendments (as indicated in italics) were Article 6, as of August 13, 1924; Articles 12, 13, and 15, as of September 26, 1924; and Article 4, as of July 29, 1926. Proposed amendments to Article 16, paragraph 1, and Article 26 were never ratified.

Of the proposed "Original Members" named in the Annex, the United States and Hedjaz never accepted membership by ratification of the Treaty of Peace. Ecuador, although it did not ratify the treaty, became a member in 1934. All the other states listed in the Annex became members in 1920. In addition to the "Original Members" and the "States Invited to Accede," the following states became members:

Afghanistan	Sept. 27, 1934	Germany	Sept. 8, 1926
Albania	Dec. 17, 1920	Hungary	Sept. 18, 1922
Austria	Dec. 15, 1920	Iraq	Oct. 3, 1932
Bulgaria	Dec. 16, 1920	Irish Free State	
Costa Rica	Dec. 16, 1920	(Eire)	Sept. 10, 1923
Dominican Republic	Sept. 29, 1924	Latvia	Sept. 22, 1921
Ecuador	Sept. 28, 1934	Lithuania	Sept. 22, 1921
Egypt	May 26, 1937	Luxemburg	Dec. 16, 1920
Estonia	Sept. 22, 1921	Mexico	Sept. 12, 1931
Ethiopia	Sept. 28, 1923	Turkey	July 18, 1932
Finland	Dec. 16, 1920	U.S.S.R.	Sept. 18, 1934

[1] Text taken from League of Nations Secretariat, Information Section publication, 1938. The paragraphs are as officially numbered by an Assembly resolution of Sept. 21, 1926. *League of Nations Official Journal,* Special Supplement No. 43, p. 10.

On December 14, 1939, the Soviet Union was expelled from the League, the only instance of expulsion of a state. In addition, the following states withdrew:

Country	Notice of withdrawal	Membership expired
Brazil..........	June 14, 1926	June 13, 1928
Chile...........	June 2, 1938	June 1, 1920
Costa Rica......	Dec. 24, 1924	Jan. 1, 1927
Germany.......	Oct. 21, 1933	Oct. 20, 1935
Guatemala......	May 26, 1936	May 25, 1938
Honduras.......	July 10, 1936	July 9, 1938
Hungary........	Apr. 11, 1939	Apr. 10, 1941
Italy...........	Dec. 11, 1937	Dec. 10, 1939
Japan..........	Mar. 27, 1933	Mar. 26, 1935
Nicaragua......	June 27, 1936	June 26, 1938
Paraguay.......	Feb. 24, 1937	Feb. 23, 1939
Peru...........	Apr. 9, 1939	Apr. 8, 1941
Rumania.......	July 11, 1940	July 10, 1942
Salvador........	Aug. 10, 1937	Aug. 9, 1939
Spain...........	May 9, 1939	May 8, 1941
Venezuela.......	July 11, 1938	July 10, 1940

The High Contracting Parties,

In order to promote international cooperation and to achieve international peace and security

by the acceptance of obligations not to resort to war,

by the prescription of open, just and honorable relations between nations,

by the firm establishment of the understandings of international law as the actual rule of conduct among Governments, and

by the maintenance of justice and a scrupulous respect for all treaty obligations in the dealings of organized peoples with one another,

Agree to this Covenant of the League of Nations.

Article 1

1. The original Members of the League of Nations shall be those of the Signatories which are named in the Annex to this Covenant and also such of those other States named in the Annex as shall accede without reservation to this Covenant. Such accessions shall be effected by a declaration deposited with the Secretariat within two months of the coming into force of the Covenant. Notice thereof shall be sent to all other Members of the League.

2. Any fully self-governing State, Dominion or Colony not named in the Annex may become a Member of the League if its admission is agreed to by two-thirds of the Assembly, provided that it shall give effective guarantees of its sincere intention to observe its international obligations, and shall accept such regulations as may be prescribed by the League in regard to its military, naval and air forces and armaments.

3. Any Member of the League may, after two years' notice of its intention so to do, withdraw from the League, provided that all its international obligations and all its obligations under this Covenant shall have been fulfilled at the time of its withdrawal.

Article 2

The action of the League under this Covenant shall be effected through the instrumentality of an Assembly and of a Council, with a permanent Secretariat.

Article 3

1. The Assembly shall consist of Representatives of the Members of the League.

2. The Assembly shall meet at stated intervals and from time to time, as occasion may require, at the Seat of the League or at such other place as may be decided upon.

3. The Assembly may deal at its meetings with any matter within the sphere of action of the League or affecting the peace of the world.

4. At meetings of the Assembly each Member of the League

shall have one vote and may have not more than three Representatives.

Article 4

1. The Council shall consist of representatives of the Principal Allied and Associated Powers [United States, Great Britain, France, Italy, and Japan], together with Representatives of four other Members of the League.[2] These four Members of the League shall be selected by the Assembly from time to time in its discretion. Until the appointment of the Representatives of the four Members of the League first selected by the Assembly, Representatives of Belgium, Brazil, Spain and Greece shall be Members of the Council.

2. With the approval of the majority of the Assembly, the Council may name additional Members of the League, whose Representatives shall always be Members of the Council; the Council with like approval may increase the number of Members of the League to be selected by the Assembly for representation on the Council.

2. *bis. The Assembly shall fix by a two-thirds majority the rules dealing with the election of the non-permanent Members of the Council, and particularly such regulations as relate to their term of office and the conditions of reeligibility.*[3]

3. The Council shall meet from time to time as occasion may require, and at least once a year, at the Seat of the League, or at such other place as may be decided upon.

4. The Council may deal at its meetings with any matter within the sphere of action of the League or affecting the peace of the world.

---

[2] Germany in 1926 was admitted and given a permanent seat but later resigned. When Japan resigned, Russia was given a permanent seat. Eventually, Italy withdrew. The number of permanent seats thus fluctuated. The same was true of the nonpermanent seats, the number being six in 1922, nine in 1926, ten in 1933, and eleven in 1936. The Covenant was sufficiently flexible to permit this (Article 4, paragraph 2).

[3] Italicized parts indicate changes in the original Covenant.

5. Any Member of the League not represented on the Council shall be invited to send a Representative to sit as a member at any meeting of the Council during the consideration of matters specially affecting the interests of that Member of the League.

6. At meetings of the Council, each Member of the League represented on the Council shall have one vote, and may have not more than one Representative.

Article 5

1. Except where otherwise expressly provided in this Covenant or by the terms of the present Treaty, decisions at any meeting of the Assembly or of the Council shall require the agreement of all the Members of the League represented at the meeting.

2. All matters of procedure at meetings of the Assembly or of the Council, including the appointment of Committees to investigate particular matters, shall be regulated by the Assembly or by the Council and may be decided by a majority of the Members of the League represented at the meeting.

3. The first meeting of the Assembly and the first meeting of the Council shall be summoned by the President of the United States of America.

Article 6

1. The permanent Secretariat shall be established at the Seat of the League. The Secretariat shall comprise a Secretary-General and such secretaries and staffs as may be required.

2. The first Secretary-General shall be the person named in the Annex; thereafter the Secretary-General shall be appointed by the Council with the approval of the majority of the Assembly.

3. The secretaries and the staff of the Secretariat shall be appointed by the Secretary-General with the approval of the Council.

4. The Secretary-General shall act in that capacity at all meetings of the Assembly and of the Council.

5. *The expenses of the League shall be borne by the Members of the League in the proportion decided by the Assembly.*

Article 7

1. The Seat of the League is established at Geneva.

2. The Council may at any time decide that the Seat of the League shall be established elsewhere.

3. All positions under or in connection with the League, including the Secretariat, shall be open equally to men and women.

4. Representatives of the Members of the League and officials of the League when engaged on the business of the League shall enjoy diplomatic privileges and immunities.

5. The buildings and other property occupied by the League or its officials or by Representatives attending its meetings shall be inviolable.

Article 8

1. The Members of the League recognize that the maintenance of peace requires the reduction of national armaments to the lowest point consistent with national safety and the enforcement by common action of international obligations.

2. The Council, taking account of the geographical situation and circumstances of each State, shall formulate plans for such reduction for the consideration and action of the several Governments.

3. Such plans shall be subject to reconsideration and revision at least every ten years.

4. After these plans shall have been adopted by the several Governments, the limits of armaments therein fixed shall not be exceeded without the concurrence of the Council.

5. The Members of the League agree that the manufacture by private enterprise of munitions and implements of war is open to grave objections. The Council shall advise how the evil effects attendant upon such manufacture can be prevented, due regard being had to the necessities of those Members of the League which are not able to manufacture the munitions and implements of war necessary for their safety.

6. The Members of the League undertake to interchange full and frank information as to the scale of their armaments, their military, naval and air programs and the condition of such of their industries as are adaptable to warlike purposes.

Article 9

A permanent Commission shall be constituted to advise the Council on the execution of the provisions of Articles 1 and 8 and on military, naval and air questions generally.

Article 10

The Members of the League undertake to respect and preserve as against external aggression the territorial integrity and existing political independence of all Members of the League. In case of any such aggression or in case of any threat or danger of such aggression the Council shall advise upon the means by which this obligation shall be fulfilled.

Article 11

1. Any war or threat of war, whether immediately affecting any of the Members of the League or not, is hereby declared a matter of concern to the whole League, and the League shall take any action that may be deemed wise and effectual to safeguard the peace of nations. In case any such emergency should arise the Secretary-General shall on the request of any Member of the League forthwith summon a meeting of the Council.

2. It is also declared to be the friendly right of each Member of the League to bring to the attention of the Assembly or of the Council any circumstance whatever affecting international relations which threatens to disturb international peace or the good understanding between nations upon which peace depends.

Article 12

1. The Members of the League agree that, if there should arise between them any dispute likely to lead to a rupture, they will submit the matter either to arbitration *or judicial settlement* or to inquiry by the Council, and they agree in no case to resort to war until three months after the award by the arbitrators *or the judicial decision,* or the report by the Council.

2. In any case under this Article the award of the arbitrators *or the judicial decision* shall be made within a reasonable time,

and the report of the Council shall be made within six months after the submission of the dispute.

Article 13

1. The Members of the League agree that, whenever any dispute shall arise between them which they recognize to be suitable for submission to arbitration *or judicial settlement,* and which can not be satisfactorily settled by diplomacy, they will submit the whole subject-matter to arbitration *or judicial settlement.*

2. Disputes as to the interpretation of a treaty, as to any question of international law, as to the existence of any fact which, if established, would constitute a breach of any international obligation, or as to the extent and nature of the reparation to be made for any such breach, are declared to be among those which are generally suitable for submission to arbitration *or judicial settlement.*

3. *For the consideration of any such dispute, the court to which the case is referred shall be the Permanent Court of International Justice, established in accordance with Article 14, or any tribunal agreed on by the parties to the dispute or stipulated in any convention existing between them.*

4. The Members of the League agree that they will carry out in full good faith any award *or decision* that may be rendered, and that they will not resort to war against a Member of the League which complies therewith. In the event of any failure to carry out such an award *or decision,* the Council shall propose what steps should be taken to give effect thereto.

Article 14

The Council shall formulate and submit to the Members of the League for adoption plans for the establishment of a Permanent Court of International Justice. The Court shall be competent to hear and determine any dispute of an international character which the parties thereto submit to it. The Court may also give an advisory opinion upon any dispute or question referred to it by the Council or by the Assembly.

Article 15

1. If there should arise between Members of the League any dispute likely to lead to a rupture, which is not submitted to arbitration *or judicial settlement* in accordance with Article 13, the Members of the League agree that they will submit the matter to the Council. Any party to the dispute may effect such submission by giving notice of the existence of the dispute to the Secretary-General, who will make all necessary arrangements for a full investigation and consideration thereof.

2. For this purpose the parties to the dispute will communicate to the Secretary-General, as promptly as possible, statements of their case with all the relevant facts and papers, and the Council may forthwith direct the publication thereof.

3. The Council shall endeavor to effect a settlement of the dispute, and, if such efforts are successful, a statement shall be made public giving such facts and explanations regarding the dispute and the terms of settlement thereof as the Council may deem appropriate.

4. If the dispute is not thus settled, the Council either unanimously or by a majority vote shall make and publish a report containing a statement of the facts of the dispute and the recommendations which are deemed just and proper in regard thereto.

5. Any member of the League represented on the Council may make a public statement of the facts of the dispute and of its conclusions regarding the same.

6. If a report by the Council is unanimously agreed to by the Members thereof other than the Representatives of one or more of the parties to the dispute, the Members of the League agree that they will not go to war with any party to the dispute which complies with the recommendation of the report.

7. If the Council fails to reach a report which is unanimously agreed to by the members thereof, other than the Representatives of one or more of the parties to the dispute, the Members of the League reserve to themselves the right to take such action as they shall consider necessary for the maintenance of right and justice.

8. If the dispute between the parties is claimed by one of them,

and is found by the Council, to arise out of a matter which by international law is solely within the domestic jurisdiction of that party, the Council shall so report, and shall make no recommendation as to its settlement.

9. The Council may in any case under this Article refer the dispute to the Assembly. The dispute shall be so referred at the request of either party to the dispute, provided that such request be made within fourteen days after the submission of the dispute to the Council.

10. In any case referred to the Assembly, all the provisions of this Article and of Article 12 relating to the action and powers of the Council shall apply to the action and powers of the Assembly, provided that a report made by the Assembly, if concurred in by the Representatives of those Members of the League represented on the Council and of a majority of the other Members of the League, exclusive in each case of the Representatives of the parties to the dispute, shall have the same force as a report by the Council concurred in by all the members thereof other than the Representatives of one or more of the parties to the dispute.

Article 16

1. Should any Member of the League resort to war in disregard of its covenants under Articles 12, 13 or 15, it shall *ipso facto* be deemed to have committed an act of war against all other Members of the League, which hereby undertake immediately to subject it to the severance of all trade or financial relations, the prohibition of all intercourse between their nationals and the nationals of the covenant-breaking State, and the prevention of all financial, commercial or personal intercourse between the nationals of the covenant-breaking State and the nationals of any other State, whether a Member of the League or not.

2. It shall be the duty of the Council in such case to recommend to the several Governments concerned what effective military, naval or air force the Members of the League shall severally contribute to the armed forces to be used to protect the covenants of the League.

3. The Members of the League agree, further, that they will mutually support one another in the financial and economic measures which are taken under this Article, in order to minimize the loss and inconvenience resulting from the above measures, and that they will mutually support one another in resisting any special measures aimed at one of their number by the covenant-breaking State, and that they will take the necessary steps to afford passage through their territory to the forces of any of the Members of the League which are cooperating to protect the covenants of the League.

4. Any Member of the League which has violated any covenant of the League may be declared to be no longer a Member of the League by a vote of the Council concurred in by the Representatives of all the other Members of the League represented thereon.

Article 17

1. In the event of a dispute between a Member of the League and a State which is not a Member of the League, or between States not Members of the League, the State or States not Members of the League shall be invited to accept the obligations of membership in the League for the purposes of such dispute, upon such conditions as the Council may deem just. If such invitation is accepted, the provisions of Articles 12 to 16, inclusive, shall be applied with such modifications as may be deemed necessary by the Council.

2. Upon such invitation being given, the Council shall immediately institute an inquiry into the circumstances of the dispute and recommend such action as may seem best and most effectual in the circumstances.

3. If a State so invited shall refuse to accept the obligations of membership in the League for the purposes of such dispute, and shall resort to war against a Member of the League, the provisions of Article 16 shall be applicable as against the State taking such action.

4. If both parties to the dispute when so invited refuse to accept the obligations of Membership in the League for the pur-

poses of such dispute, the Council may take such measures and make such recommendations as will prevent hostilities and will result in the settlement of the dispute.

Article 18

Every treaty or international engagement entered into hereafter by any Member of the League shall be forthwith registered with the Secretariat and shall as soon as possible be published by it. No such treaty or international engagement shall be binding until so registered.

Article 19

The Assembly may from time to time advise the reconsideration by Members of the League of treaties which have become inapplicable, and the consideration of international conditions whose continuance might endanger the peace of the world.

Article 20

1. The Members of the League severally agree that this Covenant is accepted as abrogating all obligations or understandings *inter se* which are inconsistent with the terms thereof, and solemnly undertake that they will not hereafter enter into any engagements inconsistent with the terms thereof.

2. In case any Member of the League shall, before becoming a Member of the League, have undertaken any obligations inconsistent with the terms of this Covenant, it shall be the duty of such Member to take immediate steps to procure its release from such obligations.

Article 21

Nothing in this Covenant shall be deemed to affect the validity of international engagements, such as treaties of arbitration or regional understandings like the Monroe doctrine, for securing the maintenance of peace.

Article 22

1. To those colonies and territories which as a consequence of the late war have ceased to be under the sovereignty of the States

which formerly governed them and which are inhabited by peoples not yet able to stand by themselves under the strenuous conditions of the modern world, there should be applied the principle that the well-being and development of such peoples form a sacred trust of civilization and that securities for the performance of this trust should be embodied in this Covenant.

2. The best method of giving practical effect to this principle is that the tutelage of such peoples should be intrusted to advanced nations who by reason of their resources, their experience or their geographical position can best undertake this responsibility, and who are willing to accept it, and that this tutelage should be exercised by them as Mandatories on behalf of the League.

3. The character of the mandate must differ according to the stage of the development of the people, the geographical situation of the territory, its economic conditions and other similar circumstances.

4. Certain communities formerly belonging to the Turkish Empire have reached a stage of development where their existence as independent nations can be provisionally recognized subject to the rendering of administrative advice and assistance by a Mandatory until such time as they are able to stand alone. The wishes of these communities must be a principal consideration in the selection of the Mandatory.

5. Other peoples, especially those of Central Africa, are at such a stage that the Mandatory must be responsible for the administration of the territory under conditions which will guarantee freedom of conscience and religion, subject only to the maintenance of public order and morals, the prohibition of abuses such as the slave trade, the arms traffic and the liquor traffic, and the prevention of the establishment of fortifications of military and naval bases and of military training of the natives for other than police purposes and the defense of territory, and will also secure equal opportunities for the trade and commerce of other Members of the League.

6. There are territories, such as Southwest Africa and certain of the South Pacific islands, which, owing to the sparseness of

their population, or their small size, or their remoteness from the centers of civilization, or their geographical contiguity to the territory of the Mandatory, and other circumstances, can be best administered under the laws of the Mandatory as integral portions of its territory, subject to the safeguards above mentioned in the interests of the indigenous population.

7. In every case of mandate, the Mandatory shall render to the Council an annual report in reference to the territory committed to its charge.

8. The degree of authority, control or administration to be exercised by the Mandatory shall, if not previously agreed upon by the Members of the League, be explicitly defined in each case by the Council.

9. A permanent Commission shall be constituted to receive and examine the annual reports of the Mandatories and to advise the Council on all matters relating to the observance of the mandates.

Article 23

Subject to and in accordance with the provisions of international conventions existing or hereafter to be agreed upon, the Members of the League:

(a) will endeavor to secure and maintain fair and humane conditions of labor for men, women and children, both in their own countries and in all countries to which their commercial and industrial relations extend, and for that purpose will establish and maintain the necessary international organizations;

(b) undertake to secure just treatment of the native inhabitants of territories under their control;

(c) will intrust the League with the general supervision over the execution of agreements with regard to traffic in women and children, and the traffic in opium and other dangerous drugs;

(d) will intrust the League with the general supervision of the trade in arms and ammunition with the countries in which the control of this traffic is necessary in the common interest;

(e) will make provision to secure and maintain freedom of communications and of transit and equitable treatment for the commerce of all Members of the League. In this connection, the special necessities of the regions devastated during the war of 1914–1918 shall be borne in mind;

(f) will endeavor to take steps in matters of international concern for the prevention and control of disease.

Article 24

1. There shall be placed under the direction of the League all international bureaus already established by general treaties if the parties to such treaties consent. All such international bureaus and all commissions for the regulation of matters of international interest hereafter constituted shall be placed under the direction of the League.

2. In all matters of international interest which are regulated by general conventions but which are not placed under the control of international bureaus or commissions, the Secretariat of the League shall, subject to the consent of the Council and if desired by the parties, collect and distribute all relevant information and shall render any other assistance which may be necessary or desirable.

3. The Council may include as part of the expenses of the Secretariat the expenses of any bureau or commission which is placed under the direction of the League.

Article 25

The Members of the League agree to encourage and promote the establishment and cooperation of duly authorized voluntary national Red Cross organizations having as purposes the improvement of health, the prevention of disease and the mitigation of suffering throughout the world.

Article 26

1. Amendments to this Covenant will take effect when ratified by the Members of the League whose Representatives compose the Council and by a majority of the Members of the League whose Representatives compose the Assembly.

2. No such amendment shall bind any Member of the League

which signifies its dissent therefrom, but in that case it shall cease to be a Member of the League.

Annex

I. *Original Members of the League of Nations Signatories of the Treaty of Peace.*

United States of America
Belgium
Bolivia
Brazil
British Empire
  Canada
  Australia
  South Africa
  New Zealand
  India
China
Cuba
Ecuador
France
Greece
Guatemala
Haiti

Hedjaz
Honduras
Italy
Japan
Liberia
Nicaragua
Panama
Peru
Poland
Portugal
Rumania
Serb-Croat-Slovene State [Yugo-
  slavia]
Siam
Czechoslovakia
Uruguay

States Invited to Accede to the Covenant.

Argentine Republic
Chile
Colombia
Denmark
Netherlands
Norway
Paraguay

Persia [Iran]
Salvador
Spain
Sweden
Switzerland
Venezuela

II. *First Secretary-General of the League of Nations. The Honorable Sir James Eric Drummond, K.C.M.G., C.B.*

THE TREATY OF VERSAILLES—LODGE RESERVATIONS TO UNITED STATES' RATIFICATION [1]

MOST OF the Lodge Reservations, which were presented to Congress on November 19, 1919, related to Articles 1 to 26 (Part I of the treaty) which was the Covenant of the League. Ratification of the treaty with these reservations would have been equivalent to rewriting the Covenant. Note that ratification by the United States was also contingent upon acceptance of these terms by three of the four Allied powers. Reservation 13 concerned membership in the International Labor Organization.

On March 19, 1920, the treaty, with these reservations attached, was defeated in the Senate by a vote of 49 for and 35 against ratification. Seven votes were lacking for the needed two-thirds majority. Of the 35 against, 20 were pro-League who regarded the reservations as unacceptable.

Since the United States was technically still at war with Germany, it negotiated (and ratified) a separate treaty of peace, signed at Berlin, August 25, 1921, which stipulated:

Article I. Germany undertakes to accord to the United States, and the United States shall have and enjoy, all the rights, privileges, indemnities, reparation or advantages specified in the aforesaid Joint Resolution of the Congress of the United States of July 2, 1921, including all the rights and advantages stipulated for the benefit of the United States in the Treaty of Versailles

[1] *Congressional Record*, Vol. 58, 66th Congress, 1st Session, pp. 8777*ff.*

which the United States shall fully enjoy notwithstanding the fact that such Treaty has not been ratified by the United States.

In Article II, paragraph 2, it was provided "That the United States shall not be bound by the provisions of Part I of that Treaty [of Versailles], nor by any provisions of that Treaty. . . ." [2]

Resolved (two-thirds of the Senators present concurring therein), That the Senate advise and consent to the ratification of the treaty of peace with Germany concluded at Versailles on the 28th day of June, 1919, subject to the following reservations and understandings, which are hereby made a part and condition of this resolution of ratification, which ratification is not to take effect or bind the United States until the said reservations and understandings adopted by the Senate have been accepted by an exchange of notes as a part and a condition of this resolution of ratification by at least three of the four principal allied and associated powers, to wit, Great Britain, France, Italy and Japan:

1. The United States so understands and construes article 1 that in case of notice of withdrawal from the league of nations, as provided in said article, the United States shall be the sole judge as to whether all its international obligations and all its obligations under the said covenant have been fulfilled, and notice of withdrawal by the United States may be given by a concurrent resolution of the Congress of the United States.

2. The United States assumes no obligation to preserve the territorial integrity or political independence of any other country or to interfere in controversies between nations—whether members of the league or not—under the provisions of article 10, or to employ the military or naval forces of the United States under any article of the treaty for any purpose, unless in any particular case the Congress, which, under the Constitution, has

[2] *The Statutes at Large of the United States,* Vol. 42, Part 2, pp. 1939*ff.*

the sole power to declare war or authorize the employment of the military or naval forces of the United States, shall by act or joint resolution so provide.

3. No mandate shall be accepted by the United States under article 22, part 1, or any other provision of the treaty of peace with Germany, except by action of the Congress of the United States.

4. The United States reserves to itself exclusively the right to decide what questions are within its domestic jurisdiction and declares that all domestic and political questions relating wholly or in part to its internal affairs, including immigration, labor, coastwise traffic, the tariff, commerce, the suppression of traffic in women and children, and in opium and other dangerous drugs, and all other domestic questions, are solely within the jurisdiction of the United States and are not under this treaty to be submitted in any way either to arbitration or to the consideration of the council or of the assembly of the league of nations, or any agency thereof, or to the decision or recommendation of any other power.

5. The United States will not submit to arbitration or to inquiry by the assembly or by the council of the league of nations, provided for in said treaty of peace, any questions which in the judgment of the United States depend upon or relate to its long-established policy, commonly known as the Monroe doctrine; said doctrine is to be interpreted by the United States alone and is hereby declared to be wholly outside the jurisdiction of said league of nations and entirely unaffected by any provision contained in the said treaty of peace with Germany.

6. The United States withholds its assent to articles 156, 157, and 158,[3] and reserves full liberty of action with respect to any controversy which may arise under said articles between the Republic of China and the Empire of Japan.

7. The Congress of the United States will provide by law for the appointment of the representatives of the United States in the assembly and the council of the league of nations, and may

[3] Dealing with the disposition of the Shantung Peninsula.

in its discretion provide for the participation of the United States in any commission, committee, tribunal, court, council, or conference, or in the selection of any members thereof and for the appointment of members of said commissions, committees, tribunals, courts, councils, or conferences, or any other representatives under the treaty of peace, or in carrying out its provisions, and until such participation and appointment have been so provided for and the powers and duties of such representatives have been defined by law, no person shall represent the United States under either said league of nations or the treaty of peace with Germany or be authorized to perform any act for or on behalf of the United States thereunder, and no citizen of the United States shall be selected or appointed as a member of said commissions, committees, tribunals, courts, councils, or conferences except with the approval of the Senate of the United States.

8. The United States understands that the reparation commission will regulate or interfere with exports from the United States to Germany, or from Germany to the United States, only when the United States by act or joint resolution of Congress approves such regulation or interference.

9. The United States shall not be obligated to contribute to any expenses of the league of nations, or of the secretariat, or of any commission, or committee, or conference, or other agency, organized under the league of nations or under the treaty or for the purpose of carrying out the treaty provisions, unless and until an appropriation of funds available for such expenses shall have been made by the Congress of the United States.

10. If the United States shall at any time adopt any plan for the limitation of armaments proposed by the council of the league of nations under the provisions of article 8, it reserves the right to increase such armaments without the consent of the council whenever the United States is threatened with invasion or engaged in war.

11. The United States reserves the right to permit, in its discretion, the nationals of a covenant-breaking State, as defined in article 16 of the covenant of the league of nations, residing

within the United States or in countries other than that violating said article 16, to continue their commercial, financial, and personal relations with the nationals of the United States.

12. Nothing in articles 296, 297,[4] or in any of the annexes thereto or in any other article, section, or annex of the treaty of peace with Germany, shall, as against citizens of the United States, be taken to mean any confirmation, ratification, or approval of any act otherwise illegal or in contravention of the rights of citizens of the United States.

13. The United States withholds its assent to Part XIII (articles 387 to 427, inclusive) unless Congress by act or joint resolution shall hereafter make provision for representation in the organization established by said Part XIII,[5] and in such event the participation of the United States will be governed and conditioned by the provisions of such act or joint resolution.

14. The United States assumes no obligation to be bound by any election, decision, report, or finding of the council or assembly in which any member of the league and its self-governing dominions, colonies, or parts of empire, in the aggregate have cast more than one vote, and assumes no obligation to be bound by any decision, report, or finding of the council or assembly arising out of any dispute between the United States and any member of the league if such member, or any self-governing dominion, colony, empire, or part of empire united with it politically has voted.

[4] Dealing with debts, property, rights, and interests.
[5] The International Labor Organization.

DOCUMENT 12

CONSTITUTION OF THE INTERNATIONAL LABOR ORGANIZATION [1]

THE CONSTITUTION of the International Labor Organization was Part XIII (Articles 387 to 427) of the Treaty of Versailles and came into force with that treaty, although actually its first meeting was held in October, 1919, and it began to function before ratification of the treaty. Its creation was the result of widespread feeling that social and humanitarian activities were properly a part of international organization and that cooperation on a world-wide scale could best give practical effect to these aspirations.

Representation was based upon the highly unusual principle that accorded delegates to labor and employer groups of each member state, as well as to states. Delegates from each state were not required to vote in the name of their state and as a unit but could and did vote independently. The only change in the Constitution made between the wars was to broaden the basis of this representation upon the Governing Body, the new text of Article 7 going into effect in 1934. Since World War II other amendments to the Constitution have been made, and the amended Constitution entered into force on April 20, 1948. The changes redefine the aims and purposes of the ILO (International Labor Organization) and make the necessary revisions in the text to permit affiliation with the United Nations.

[1] *United States Treaty Series,* No. 874, Washington, 1934, contains the Constitution as it was before the amendments which entered into force in 1948. For the revised text given here, see *The Constitution of the International Labor Organization (Revised—1946),* a publication of the Washington Branch of the International Labor Office.

It was possible for a state to be a member of the ILO without being a member of the League. Similarly, it is possible today for a state to be a member of the ILO without being a member of the United Nations. The United States became a member of the ILO on August 20, 1934, although it never joined the League of Nations. As many as sixty-two states have belonged at one time. Owing to the incorporation of the Baltic states into the Soviet Union and the conquest for a time of others, the membership fell during the war. However, since affiliation with the United Nations the membership has steadily increased and is now sixty.[2]

The following states are at present members: Afghanistan, Albania, Argentina, Australia, Austria, Belgium, Bolivia, Brazil, Bulgaria, Burma, Canada, Ceylon, Chile, China, Colombia, Costa Rica, Cuba, Czechoslovakia, Denmark, Dominican Republic, Ecuador, Egypt, El Salvador, Ethiopia, Finland, France, Greece, Guatemala, Haiti, Hungary, Iceland, India, Iran, Iraq, Ireland, Israel, Italy, Lebanon, Liberia, Luxemburg, Mexico, Netherlands, New Zealand, Norway, Pakistan, Panama, Peru, Philippines, Poland, Portugal, Sweden, Switzerland, Syria, Thailand, Turkey, Union of South Africa, United Kingdom, United States, Uruguay, Venezuela.

Preamble

Whereas universal and lasting peace can be established only if it is based upon social justice;

And whereas conditions of labour exist involving such injustice, hardship and privation to large numbers of people as to produce unrest so great that the peace and harmony of the world are imperilled; and an improvement of those conditions is

[2] As of Feb. 1, 1950. The listing is taken from *United Nations Department of Public Information Press Release* SA/49 of Oct. 20, 1949.

urgently required: as, for example, by the regulation of the hours of work, including the establishment of a maximum working day and week, the regulation of the labour supply, the prevention of unemployment, the provision of an adequate living wage, the protection of the worker against sickness, disease and injury arising out of his employment, the protection of children, young persons and women, provision for old age and injury, protection of the interests of workers when employed in countries other than their own, recognition of the principle of equal remuneration for work of equal value, recognition of the principle of freedom of association, the organisation of vocational and technical education and other measures;

Whereas also the failure of any nation to adopt humane conditions of labour is an obstacle in the way of other nations which desire to improve the conditions in their own countries;

The High Contracting Parties, moved by sentiments of justice and humanity as well as by the desire to secure the permanent peace of the world, and with a view to attaining the objectives set forth in this Preamble, agree to the following Constitution of the International Labour Organisation:

CHAPTER I. ORGANISATION

Article 1

1. A permanent organisation is hereby established for the promotion of the objects set forth in the Preamble. . . .

2. The Members of the International Labour Organisation shall be the States which were Members of the Organisation on 1 November 1945, and such other States as may become Members. . . .

3. Any original Member of the United Nations and any State admitted to membership of the United Nations . . . may become a Member of the International Labour Organisation by communicating to the Director-General of the International Labour Office its formal acceptance of the obligations of the Constitution of the International Labour Organisation.

4. The General Conference of the International Labour Organisation may also admit Members to the Organisation by a vote concurred in by two-thirds of the delegates attending the session, including two-thirds of the Government delegates present and voting. . . .

5. No Member of the International Labour Organisation may withdraw from the Organisation without giving notice of its intention so to do to the Director-General of the International Labour Office. Such notice shall take effect two years after the date of its reception by the Director-General, subject to the Member having at that time fulfilled all financial obligations arising out of its membership. . . .

Article 2

The permanent organisation shall consist of:

(a) a General Conference of representatives of the Members;

(b) a Governing Body composed as described in Article 7; and

(c) an International Labour Office controlled by the Governing Body.

Article 3

1. The meetings of the General Conference of representatives of the Members shall be held from time to time as occasion may require, and at least once in every year. It shall be composed of four representatives of each of the Members, of whom two shall be Government delegates and the two others shall be delegates representing respectively the employers and the workpeople of each of the Members.

2. Each delegate may be accompanied by advisers. . . .

5. The Members undertake to nominate non-Government delegates and advisers chosen in agreement with the industrial organisations, if such organisations exist, which are most representative of employers or workpeople, as the case may be, in their respective countries.

6. Advisers shall not speak except on a request made by the delegate whom they accompany and by the special authorisation of the President of the Conference. and may not vote. . . .

Article 4

1. Every delegate shall be entitled to vote individually on all matters which are taken into consideration by the Conference.

2. If one of the Members fails to nominate one of the non-Government delegates whom it is entitled to nominate, the other non-Government delegate shall be allowed to sit and speak at the Conference, but not to vote. . . .

Article 5

The meetings of the Conference shall, subject to any decisions which may have been taken by the Conference itself at a previous meeting, be held at such place as may be decided by the Governing Body.

Article 6

Any change in the seat of the International Labour Office shall be decided by the Conference by a two-thirds majority of the votes cast by the delegates present.

Article 7 [3]

1. The Governing Body shall consist of thirty-two persons:
   Sixteen representing Governments,
   Eight representing the employers, and
   Eight representing the workers.

2. Of the sixteen persons representing Governments, eight shall be appointed by the Members of chief industrial importance, and eight shall be appointed by the Members selected for that purpose by the Government delegates to the Conference, excluding the delegates of the eight Members mentioned above. Of the sixteen Members represented, six shall be non-European States.

3. The Governing Body shall as occasion requires determine

[3] Article 7 was the subject of the only revision of the Constitution made between the two World Wars. The version given here is again slightly revised. The original text provided for twelve governmental representatives, six employers' representatives, and six workers' representatives.

which are the Members of the Organisation of chief industrial importance and shall make rules to ensure that all questions relating to the selection of the Members of chief industrial importance are considered by an impartial committee before being decided by the Governing Body. Any appeal made by a Member from the declaration of the Governing Body as to which are the Members of chief industrial importance shall be decided by the Conference, but an appeal to the Conference shall not suspend the application of the declaration until such time as the Conference decides the appeal.

4. The persons representing the employers and the persons representing the workers shall be elected respectively by the employers' delegates and the workers' delegates to the Conference. Two employers' representatives and two workers' representatives shall belong to non-European States.

5. The period of office of the Governing Body shall be three years. . . .

8. The Governing Body shall regulate its own procedure and shall fix its own times of meeting. A special meeting shall be held if a written request to that effect is made by at least twelve of the representatives on the Governing Body.

Article 8

1. There shall be a Director-General of the International Labour Office, who shall be appointed by the Governing Body, and, subject to the instructions of the Governing Body, shall be responsible for the efficient conduct of the International Labour Office and for such other duties as may be assigned to him.

2. The Director-General or his deputy shall attend all meetings of the Governing Body.

Article 9

1. The staff of the International Labour Office shall be appointed by the Director-General under regulations approved by the Governing Body.

2. So far as is possible with due regard to the efficiency of the

work of the Office, the Director-General shall select persons of different nationalities.

3. A certain number of these persons shall be women.

4. The responsibilities of the Director-General and the staff shall be exclusively international in character. In the performance of their duties, the Director-General and the staff shall not seek or receive instructions from any Government or from any other authority external to the Organisation. They shall refrain from any action which might reflect on their position as international officials responsible only to the Organisation.

5. Each Member of the Organisation undertakes to respect the exclusively international character of the responsibilities of the Director-General and the staff and not to seek to influence them in the discharge of their responsibilities.

Article 10

1. The functions of the International Labour Office shall include the collection and distribution of information on all subjects relating to the international adjustment of conditions of industrial life and labour, and particularly the examination of subjects which it is proposed to bring before the Conference with a view to the conclusion of international Conventions, and the conduct of such special investigations as may be ordered by the Conference or by the Governing Body.

2. Subject to such directions as the Governing Body may give, the Office will—

(a) prepare the documents on the various items of the agenda. . . .

(b) accord to Governments at their request all appropriate assistance. . . .

(c) carry out the duties required of it by the provisions of this Constitution in connection with the effective observance of Conventions;

(d) edit and issue, in such languages as the Governing Body may think desirable, publications dealing with problems of industry and employment of international interest.

3. Generally, it shall have such other powers and duties as may be assigned to it by the Conference or by the Governing Body.

Article 11

The Government departments of any of the Members which deal with questions of industry and employment may communicate directly with the Director-General through the representative of their Government on the Governing Body of the International Labour Office or, failing any such representative, through such other qualified official as the Government may nominate for the purpose.

Article 12

1. The International Labour Organisation shall co-operate within the terms of this Constitution with any general international organisation entrusted with the co-ordination of the activities of public international organisations having specialised responsibilities and with public international organisations having specialised responsibilities in related fields. . . .

Article 13

1. The International Labour Organisation may make such financial and budgetary arrangements with the United Nations as may appear appropriate. . . .

.   .   .   .

CHAPTER II. PROCEDURE

Article 14

1. The agenda for all meetings of the Conference will be settled by the Governing Body, which shall consider any suggestion as to the agenda that may be made by the Government of any of the Members or by any representative organisation recognised for the purpose of Article 3, or by any public international organisation. . . .

Article 15

1. The Director-General shall act as the Secretary-General of the Conference, and shall transmit the agenda so as to reach the

Members four months before the meeting of the Conference, and, through them, the non-Government delegates when appointed. . . .

Article 16

1. Any of the Governments of the Members may formally object to the inclusion of any item or items in the agenda. . . .

2. Items to which such objection has been made shall not, however, be excluded from the agenda, if at the Conference a majority of two-thirds of the votes cast by the delegates present is in favour of considering them. . . .

Article 17

1. . . . The Conference shall regulate its own procedure and may appoint committees to consider and report on any matter.

2. Except as otherwise expressly provided in this Constitution . . . all matters shall be decided by a simple majority of the votes cast by the delegates present.

3. The voting is void unless the total number of votes cast is equal to half the number of the delegates attending the Conference.

.   .   .   .

Article 19

1. When the Conference has decided on the adoption of proposals with regard to an item in the agenda, it will rest with the Conference to determine whether these proposals should take the form: (a) of an international Convention, or (b) of a Recommendation to meet circumstances where the subject, or aspect of it, dealt with is not considered suitable or appropriate at that time for a Convention.

2. In either case a majority of two-thirds of the votes cast by the delegates present shall be necessary on the final vote for the adoption of the Convention or Recommendation, as the case may be, by the Conference.

3. In framing any Convention or Recommendation of general application the Conference shall have due regard to those countries in which climatic conditions, the imperfect development of

industrial organisation, or other special circumstances make the industrial conditions substantially different and shall suggest the modifications, if any, which it considers may be required to meet the case of such countries. . . .

5. In the case of a Convention—

(a) the Convention will be communicated to all Members for ratification;

(b) each of the Members undertakes that it will, within the period of one year at most from the closing of the session of the Conference, or if it is impossible owing to exceptional circumstances to do so within the period of one year, then at the earliest practicable moment and in no case later than eighteen months from the closing of the session of the Conference, bring the Convention before the authority or authorities within whose competence the matter lies, for the enactment of legislation or other action. . . .

(d) if the Member obtains the consent of the authority or authorities within whose competence the matter lies, it will communicate the formal ratification of the Convention to the Director-General and will take such action as may be necessary to make effective the provisions of such Convention;

(e) if the Member does not obtain the consent of the authority or authorities within whose competence the matter lies, no further obligation shall rest upon the Member except that it shall report . . . at appropriate intervals . . . the position of its law and practice in regard to the matters dealt with in the Convention. . . .

6. In the case of a Recommendation—

(a) the Recommendation will be communicated to all Members for their consideration with a view to effect being given to it by national legislation or otherwise;

(b) each of the Members undertakes that it will, within a period of one year at most from the closing of the session of the Conference, or if it is impossible owing to exceptional circumstances to do so within the period of one year, then at the earliest practicable moment and in no case later than eighteen months after the closing of the Conference, bring the Recommendation before the authority or authorities within whose competence the matter lies for the enactment of legislation or other action. . . .

(d) apart from bringing the Recommendation before the said competent authority or authorities, no further obligation shall rest upon the Members, except that they shall report . . . at appropriate intervals . . . the position of the law and practice in their country in regard to the matters dealt with in the Recommendation. . . .

7. In the case of a federal State, the following provisions shall apply: . . .

(b) in respect of Conventions and Recommendations which the federal government regards as appropriate under its constitutional system, in whole or in part, for action by the constituent States, provinces, or cantons rather than for federal action, the federal Government shall—

(i) make, in accordance with its Constitution and the Constitutions of the States, provinces or cantons concerned, effective arrangements for the reference of such Conventions and Recommendations not later than eighteen months from the closing of the session of the Conference to the appropriate federal, State, provincial or cantonal authorities for the enactment of legislation or other action; . . .

(iv) in respect of each such Convention which it has not ratified, report to the Director-General . . . at appropriate intervals . . . the position of the law and practice of the federation and its constituent States, provinces or cantons in regard to the Convention. . . .

(v) in respect of each such Recommendation, report . . . at appropriate intervals . . . the position of the law and practice of the federation and its constituent States, provinces or cantons in regard to the Recommendation. . . .

8. In no case shall the adoption of any Convention or Recommendation by the Conference, or the ratification of any Convention by any Member, be deemed to affect any law, award, custom or agreement which ensures more favourable conditions to the

workers concerned than those provided for in the Convention or Recommendation.

Article 20

Any Convention so ratified shall be communicated by the Director-General of the International Labour Office to the Secretary-General of the United Nations for registration in accordance with the provisions of Article 102 of the Charter of the United Nations but shall only be binding upon the Members which ratify it.

Article 21

1. If any Convention coming before the Conference for final consideration fails to secure the support of two-thirds of the votes cast by the delegates present, it shall nevertheless be within the right of any of the Members of the Organisation to agree to such Convention among themselves. . . .

Article 22

Each of the Members agrees to make an annual report to the International Labour Office on the measures which it has taken to give effect to the provisions of Conventions to which it is a party. These reports shall be made in such form and shall contain such particulars as the Governing Body may request.

. . . .

Article 24

In the event of any representation being made to the International Labour Office by an industrial association of employers or of workers that any of the Members has failed to secure in any respect the effective observance within its jurisdiction of any Convention to which it is a party, the Governing Body may communicate this representation to the Government against which it is made, and may invite that Government to make such statement on the subject as it may think fit.

Article 25

If no statement is received within a reasonable time from the Government in question, or if the statement when received is not deemed to be satisfactory by the Governing Body, the latter shall have the right to publish the representation and the statement, if any, made in reply to it.

Article 26

1. Any of the Members shall have the right to file a complaint with the International Labour Office if it is not satisfied that any other Member is securing the effective observance of any Convention which both have ratified in accordance with the foregoing Articles.

2. The Governing Body may, if it thinks fit, before referring such a complaint to a Commission of Enquiry, as hereinafter provided for, communicate with the Government in question in the manner described in Article 24.

3. If the Governing Body does not think it necessary to communicate the complaint to the Government in question, or if, when it has made such communication, no statement in reply has been received within a reasonable time which the Governing Body considers to be satisfactory, the Governing Body may appoint a Commission of Enquiry to consider the complaint and to report thereon.

4. The Governing Body may adopt the same procedure either of its own motion or on receipt of a complaint from a delegate to the Conference.

5. When any matter arising out of Articles 25 or 26 is being considered by the Governing Body, the Government in question shall, if not already represented thereon, be entitled to send a representative to take part in the proceedings of the Governing Body while the matter is under consideration. Adequate notice of the date on which the matter will be considered shall be given to the Government in question.

．　．　．　．　．　．　．　．　．　．　．　．　．

Article 28

When the Commission of Enquiry has fully considered the complaint, it shall prepare a report embodying its findings on all questions of fact relevant to determining the issue between the parties and containing such recommendations as it may think proper as to the steps which should be taken to meet the complaint and the time within which they should be taken.

Article 29

1. The Director-General of the International Labour Office shall communicate the report of the Commission of Enquiry to the Governing Body and to each of the Governments concerned in the complaint, and shall cause it to be published.

2. Each of these Governments shall within three months inform the Director-General of the International Labour Office whether or not it accepts the recommendations contained in the report of the Commission; and if not, whether it proposes to refer the complaint to the International Court of Justice.

Article 30

In the event of any Member failing to take the action required by paragraphs 5 (b), 6 (b) or 7 (b) (i) of Article 19 with regard to a Convention or Recommendation, any other Member shall be entitled to refer the matter to the Governing Body. In the event of the Governing Body finding that there has been such a failure, it shall report the matter to the Conference.

Article 31

The decision of the International Court of Justice in regard to a complaint or matter which has been referred to it in pursuance of Article 29 shall be final.

Article 32

The International Court of Justice may affirm, vary or reverse any of the findings or recommendations of the Commission of Enquiry, if any.

Article 33

In the event of any Member failing to carry out within the time specified the recommendations, if any, contained in the report of the Commission of Enquiry, or in the decision of the International Court of Justice, as the case may be, the Governing

Body may recommend to the Conference such action as it may deem wise and expedient to secure compliance therewith.

. . . .

CHAPTER III. GENERAL

Article 35

1. The Members undertake that Conventions which they have ratified in accordance with the provisions of this Constitution shall be applied to the non-metropolitan territories for whose international relations they are responsible, including any trust territories for which they are the administering authority, except where the subject matter of the Convention is within the self-governing powers of the territory or the Convention is inapplicable owing to the local conditions or subject to such modifications as may be necessary to adapt the Convention to local conditions. . . .

Article 36

Amendments to this Constitution which are adopted by the Conference by a majority of two-thirds of the votes cast by the delegates present shall take effect when ratified or accepted by two-thirds of the Members of the Organisation including five of the eight Members which are represented on the Governing Body as Members of chief industrial importance in accordance with the provisions of paragraph 3 of Article 7 of this Constitution.

Article 37

1. Any question or dispute relating to the interpretation of this Constitution or of any subsequent Convention concluded by the Members in pursuance of the provisions of this Constitution shall be referred for decision to the International Court of Justice. . . .[4]

[4] Articles 39 and 40, which are omitted, provide for full juridical personality and diplomatic privileges and immunities for the ILO and its staff.

INTERPRETATIVE RESOLUTIONS OF THE SECOND LEAGUE ASSEMBLY [1]

THE THREE Scandinavian nations of Denmark, Norway, and Sweden were disturbed in 1921 by the prospect of being called upon to bear a burden of economic sanctions out of proportion to their strength should Article 16 of the Covenant be invoked against Germany, and they sponsored the interpretations given in final form below. The intent of the resolutions is made perfectly clear in resolution 4: "It is the duty of each Member of the League to *decide for itself* [2] whether a breach of the Covenant has been committed." No nation could be compelled by the League, under such an interpretation, to apply sanctions unless it wished to. The freedom of decision surrendered when each nation ratified the Covenant was thus in large measure regained. The basic provisions of the interpretations were incorporated as well in an amendment to Article 16, paragraph 1, of the Covenant, but it was never ratified by a sufficient number of nations to be put into effect. While the Covenant therefore was not changed textually, the interpretative resolutions stood approved by the League Assembly. For this reason, the interpretations themselves were considered the authoritative statement of what was intended under Article 16. Although the automatic character of sanctions was thereby weakened, these interpretations did not prevent the imposition of sanctions

[1] *League of Nations Official Journal,* Special Supplement No. 6 (October, 1921), pp. 24*ff.*

[2] Italics added.

against Italy in 1935, where the violation of the Covenant was too clear to be ignored (see also note and Document 14).

The resolutions were adopted by the League Assembly on October 4, 1921.

The Assembly adopts the following resolutions:

1. The resolutions and the proposals for amendments to Article 16 which have been adopted by the Assembly shall, so long as the amendments have not been put in force in the form required by the Covenant, constitute rules for guidance which the Assembly recommends, as a provisional measure, to the Council and to the Members of the League in connection with the application of Article 16.

2. Subject to the special provisions of Article 17, the economic measures referred to in Article 16 shall be applicable only in the specific case referred to in this article.

3. The unilateral action of the defaulting State cannot create a state of war: it merely entitles the other Members of the League to resort to acts of war or to declare themselves in a state of war with the Covenant-breaking State; but it is in accordance with the spirit of the Covenant that the League of Nations should attempt, at least at the outset, to avoid war, and to restore peace by economic pressure.

4. It is the duty of each Member of the League to decide for itself whether a breach of the Covenant has been committed. The fulfillment of their duties under Article 16 is required from Members of the League by the express terms of the Covenant, and they cannot neglect them without breach of their Treaty obligations.

5. All cases of breach of Covenant under Article 16 shall be referred to the Council as a matter of urgency at the request of any Member of the League. Further, if a breach of Covenant be committed, or if there arise a danger of such breach being committed, the Secretary-General shall at once give notice thereof to all the Members of the Council. Upon receipt of such a re-

quest by a Member of the League, or of such a notice by the Secretary-General, the Council will meet as soon as possible. The Council shall summon representatives of the parties to the conflict and of all States which are neighbors of the defaulting State, or which normally maintain close economic relations with it, or whose cooperation would be especially valuable for the application of Article 16.

6. If the Council is of opinion that a State has been guilty of a breach of Covenant, the Minutes of the meeting at which that opinion is arrived at shall be immediately sent to all Members of the League, accompanied by a statement of reasons and by an invitation to take action accordingly. The fullest publicity shall be given to this decision.

7. For the purpose of assisting it to enforce Article 16, the Council may, if it thinks fit, be assisted by a *technical* Committee. This Committee, which will remain in permanent session as soon as the action decided on is taken, may include, if desirable, representatives of the States specially affected.

8. The Council shall recommend the date on which the enforcement of economic pressure, under Article 16, is to be begun, and shall give notice of that date to all the Members of the League.

9. All States must be treated alike as regards the application of the measures of economic pressure, with the following reservations:

(a) It may be necessary to recommend the execution of special measures by certain States.

(b) If it is thought desirable to postpone, wholly or partially, in the case of certain States, the effective application of the economic sanctions laid down in Article 16, such postponement shall not be permitted except in so far as it is desirable for the success of the common plan of action, or reduces to a minimum the losses and embarrassments which may be entailed in the case of certain Members of the League by the application of the sanctions.

10. It is not possible to decide beforehand, and in detail, the various measures of an economic, commercial and financial na-

ture to be taken in each case where economic pressure is to be applied.

When the case arises, the Council shall recommend to the Members of the League a plan for joint action.

11. The interruption of diplomatic relations may, in the first place, be limited to the withdrawal of the heads of Missions.

12. Consular relations may possibly be maintained.

13. For the purposes of the severance of relations between persons belonging to the Covenant-breaking State and persons belonging to other States Members of the League, the test shall be residence and not nationality.

14. In cases of prolonged application of economic pressure, measures of increasing stringency may be taken. The cutting-off of the food supplies of the civil population of the defaulting State shall be regarded as an extremely drastic measure which shall only be applied if the other measures available are clearly inadequate.

15. Correspondence and all other methods of communication shall be subjected to special regulations.

16. Humanitarian relations shall be continued.

17. Efforts should be made to arrive at arrangements which would ensure the cooperation of States non-Members of the League in the measures to be taken.

18. In special circumstances and in support of economic measures to be taken, it may become advisable: (a) to establish an effective blockade of the seaboard of the Covenant-breaking State; (b) to entrust to some Members of the League the execution of the blockade operations.

19. The Council shall urge upon all the States Members of the League, that their Governments should take the necessary preparatory measures, above all of a legislative character, to enable them to enforce at short notice the necessary measures of economic pressure.

PROPOSED INTERPRETATIVE RESOLUTION OF THE FOURTH LEAGUE ASSEMBLY [1]

ARTICLE 10 OF the League Covenant, which provided that the members of the League undertook to "respect and preserve as against external aggression the territorial integrity and existing political independence" of all League members, was the subject of an interpretation sponsored by Canada in 1923. Canada feared particularly the complications inherent in fulfilling this pledge when the United States was not a member of the League. (Article 10 was considered by President Wilson to be the heart of the Covenant and was adopted in the expectation that America would be in the League. The vote in the Assembly was 29 in favor, 22 abstaining, and 1 (Persia) against. Since unanimity was required, and there was one negative vote, the interpretation failed of adoption. It was, however, a clear indication of prevailing League sentiment at the time and was another step toward the progressive weakening of the Covenant. (See note and Document 13.)

The Assembly, desirous of defining the scope of the obligations contained in Article 10 of the Covenant so far as regards the points raised by the Canadian Delegation, adopts the following resolution:

1. It is in conformity with the spirit of Article 10 that, in the event of the Council considering it to be its duty to recommend the application of military measures in consequence of an aggres-

[1] *League of Nations Official Journal,* Special Supplement No. 14 (September, 1923), p. 27.

sion, or danger or threat of aggression, the Council shall be bound to take account, more particularly, of the geographical situation and of the special conditions of each state.

2. It is for the constitutional authorities of each Member to decide, in reference to the obligation of preserving the independence and the integrity of the territory of Members, in what degree the Member is bound to assure the execution of this obligation by employment of its military forces.

3. The recommendation made by the Council shall be regarded as being of the highest importance and shall be taken into consideration by all the Members of the League with the desire to execute their engagements in good faith.

WASHINGTON TREATY ON THE LIMITATION OF NAVAL ARMAMENT [1]

THE TREATY was signed by the United States, the British Empire, France, Italy, and Japan on February 6, 1922, and took effect on August 21, 1923. It was to remain in effect until December 31, 1936. The extent of the agreement which was reached on naval disarmament in the treaty was never approached in subsequent disarmament conferences. It should be recognized, however, that the disarmament provisions were an integral part of the security arrangements reached in the Nine-Power and Four-Power Treaties (Documents 16 and 17). The restrictions of the treaty had the effect of granting naval control of the Western Pacific to Japan and control of the Eastern Pacific to the United States. Guam remained unfortified. From the viewpoint of the United States the potential weak point in the arrangement was the Philippines. On the other hand, Japan was not willing to suspend the armaments race upon terms which would have given us naval hegemony in that region. The result was a compromise which for a time brought a degree of stabilization to the Pacific area. It furthermore ended the naval race between the United States and Britain which had threatened to endanger the relations of the two nations.

Article III

Subject to the provisions of Article II, the Contracting Powers shall abandon their respective capital ship building programs, and no new capital ships shall be constructed or acquired by any

[1] *United States Treaty Series*, No. 671, Washington, 1923.

of the Contracting Powers except replacement tonnage which may be constructed or acquired as specified. . . .

Article IV

The total capital ship replacement tonnage of each of the Contracting Powers shall not exceed in standard displacement, for the United States, 525,000 tons (533,400 metric tons); for the British Empire 525,000 tons (533,400 metric tons); for France 175,000 tons (177,800 metric tons); for Italy 175,000 tons (177,800 metric tons); for Japan 315,000 tons (320,040 metric tons).

Article V

No capital ship exceeding 35,000 tons (35,560 metric tons) standard displacement shall be acquired by, or constructed by, for, or within the jurisdiction of, any of the Contracting Powers.

Article VI

No capital ship of any of the Contracting Powers shall carry a gun with a calibre in excess of 16 inches (406 millimetres).

Article VII

The total tonnage for aircraft carriers of each of the Contracting Powers shall not exceed in standard displacement, for the United States 135,000 tons (137,160 metric tons); for the British Empire 135,000 tons (137,160 metric tons); for France 60,000 tons (60,960 metric tons); for Italy 60,000 tons (60,960 metric tons); for Japan 81,000 tons (82,296 metric tons).

.   .   .   .

Article XI

No vessel of war exceeding 10,000 tons (10,160 metric tons) standard displacement, other than a capital ship or aircraft carrier,[2] shall be acquired by, or constructed by, for, or within the jurisdiction of, any of the Contracting Powers. . . .

.   .   .   .

[2] Aircraft carriers were restricted to 27,000 tons by Article IX; they were not to carry guns larger than 8-inch caliber (Article X).

Article XIX

The United States, the British Empire and Japan agree that the status quo at the time of the signing of the present Treaty, with regard to fortifications and naval bases, shall be maintained in their respective territories and possessions specified hereunder:

(1) The insular possessions which the United States now holds or may hereafter acquire in the Pacific Ocean, except (a) those adjacent to the coast of the United States, Alaska and the Panama Canal Zone, not including the Aleutian Islands, and (b) the Hawaiian Islands;

(2) Hongkong and the insular possessions which the British Empire now holds or may hereafter acquire in the Pacific Ocean, east of the meridian of 110 east longitude, except (a) those adjacent to the coast of Canada, (b) the Commonwealth of Australia and its Territories, and (c) New Zealand;

(3) The following insular territories and possessions of Japan in the Pacific Ocean, to wit: the Kurile Islands, the Bonin Islands, Anami-Oshima, the Loochoo Islands, Formosa and the Pescadores, and any insular territories or possessions in the Pacific Ocean which Japan may hereafter acquire.

The maintenance of the status quo under the foregoing provisions implies that no new fortifications or naval bases shall be established in the territories and possessions specified, that no measures shall be taken to increase the existing naval facilities for the repair and maintenance of naval forces, and that no increase shall be made in the coast defenses of the territories and possessions above specified. This restriction, however, does not preclude such repair and replacement of worn-out weapons and equipment as is customary in naval and military establishments in time of peace. . . .

THE NINE-POWER TREATY [1]

THE NINE-POWER Treaty was signed by the United States, Belgium, the British Empire, China, France, Italy, Japan, the Netherlands, and Portugal on February 6, 1922, and was subsequently adhered to by Bolivia, Denmark, Mexico, Norway, and Sweden. It was ratified and came into force on August 5, 1925. It was designed, as the preamble states, ". . . to stabilize conditions in the Far East, to safeguard the rights and interests of China, and to promote intercourse between China and other Powers upon the basis of equality of opportunity."

The Nine-Power Treaty attempted to solve one of the key questions of international relations in the Far East—the future of China. Ever since China had first been opened to Western penetration and imperialism, its independent existence had remained precarious. The most important reason that China existed more or less intact was the failure of the great powers to agree on an equitable division. Since the United States preferred to keep China intact and had no desire for Chinese territory, the American delegation to the Conference suggested that the wisest course of action under the circumstances was to maintain the *status quo* and adopt as a general rule the principle of the Open Door, or equal commercial opportunity, in China for all. It is essentially this viewpoint which was incorporated into the treaty. It was accepted primarily because of lack of agreement among the

---

[1] *United States Treaty Series*, No. 723, Washington, 1937.

other powers as to any alternative course of conduct (see also notes and Documents 15 and 17).

Article I

The Contracting Powers, other than China, agree:

(1) To respect the sovereignty, the independence, and the territorial and administrative integrity of China;

(2) To provide the fullest and most unembarrassed opportunity to China to develop and maintain for herself an effective and stable government;

(3) To use their influence for the purpose of effectually establishing and maintaining the principle of equal opportunity for the commerce and industry of all nations throughout the territory of China;

(4) To refrain from taking advantage of conditions in China in order to seek special rights or privileges which would abridge the rights of subjects or citizens of friendly States, and from countenancing action inimical to the security of such States.

Article II

The Contracting Powers agree not to enter into any treaty, agreement, arrangement, or understanding, either with one another, or, individually or collectively, with any Power or Powers, which would infringe or impair the principles stated in Article I.

Article III

With a view to applying more effectually the principles of the Open Door or equality of opportunity in China for the trade and industry of all nations, the Contracting Powers, other than China, agree that they will not seek, nor support their respective nationals in seeking—

(a) any arrangement which might purport to establish in favor of their interests any general superiority of rights with respect to commercial or economic development in any designated region of China;

(b) any such monopoly or preference as would deprive the nationals of any other Power of the right of undertaking any legitimate trade or industry in China, or of participating with the Chinese Government, or with any local authority, in any category of public enterprise, or which by reason of its scope, duration or geographical extent is calculated to frustrate the practical application of the principle of equal opportunity.

It is understood that the foregoing stipulations of this Article are not to be so construed as to prohibit the acquisition of such properties or rights as may be necessary to the conduct of a particular commercial, industrial, or financial undertaking or to the encouragement of invention and research.

China undertakes to be guided by the principles stated in the foregoing stipulations of this Article in dealing with applications for economic rights and privileges from Governments and nationals of all foreign countries, whether parties to the present Treaty or not.

Article IV

The Contracting Powers agree not to support any agreements by their respective nationals with each other designed to create Spheres of Influence or to provide for the enjoyment of mutually exclusive opportunities in designated parts of Chinese territory.

Article V

China agrees that, throughout the whole of the railways in China, she will not exercise or permit unfair discrimination of any kind. In particular there shall be no discrimination whatever, direct or indirect, in respect of charges or of facilities on the ground of the nationality of passengers or the countries from which or to which they are proceeding, or the origin or ownership of goods or the country from which or to which they are consigned, or the nationality or ownership of the ship or other means of conveying such passengers or goods before or after their transport on the Chinese Railways.

The Contracting Powers, other than China, assume a corresponding obligation in respect of any of the aforesaid railways over which they or their nationals are in a position to exercise any control in virtue of any concession, special agreement or otherwise.

Article VI

The Contracting Powers, other than China, agree fully to respect China's rights as a neutral in time of war to which China is not a party; and China declares that when she is a neutral she will observe the obligations of neutrality.

Article VII

The Contracting Powers agree that, whenever a situation arises which in the opinion of any one of them involves the application of the stipulations of the present Treaty, and renders desirable discussion of such application, there shall be full and frank communication between the Contracting Powers concerned.

DOCUMENT 17

THE FOUR-POWER TREATY [1]

THE FOUR-POWER Treaty, signed by the United States, the British Empire, France, and Japan, was proclaimed in effect on August 17, 1923. It was part of the attempt to maintain the Pacific Ocean *status quo* and was an integral part of the naval disarmament arrangements concluded in Washington in 1921. Japan reluctantly agreed in Article IV to the termination of the Anglo-Japanese Alliance agreement of July 13, 1911, in return for the more general guarantees contained in this treaty. Britain was thus released from an arrangement which conceivably could have brought her into war on the side of Japan against the United States. The Four-Power Treaty therefore represented a distinct diplomatic triumph for the United States.

Since the treaty provided no enforcement measures but stipulated merely that in the event of an emergency the four powers would confer, it was destined to last only until it was seriously challenged. This was implicit in the reservation included in the ratification by the United States Senate that ". . . The United States understands that under the statement in the preamble and under the terms of this treaty there is no commitment to armed force, no alliance, no obligation to join in any defense." When Japan challenged the *status quo* in 1931, the United States and Great Britain failed to coordinate their efforts to restrain her. No conference was called, and the treaty was not implemented.

---

[1] *United States Treaty Series,* No. 669, Washington, 1923.

Article I

The High Contracting Parties agree as between themselves to respect their rights in relation to their insular possessions and insular dominions in the region of the Pacific Ocean.

If there should develop between any of the High Contracting Parties a controversy arising out of any Pacific question and involving their said rights which is not satisfactorily settled by diplomacy and is likely to affect the harmonious accord now happily subsisting between them, they shall invite the other High Contracting Parties to a joint conference to which the whole subject will be referred for consideration and adjustment.

Article II

If the said rights are threatened by the aggressive action of any other Power, the High Contracting Parties shall communicate with one another fully and frankly in order to arrive at an understanding as to the most efficient measures to be taken, jointly or separately, to meet the exigencies of the particular situation.

Article III

This Treaty shall remain in force for 10 years from the time it shall take effect, and after the expiration of said period it shall continue to be in force subject to the right of any of the High Contracting Parties to terminate it upon twelve months' notice.

THE GENEVA PROTOCOL [1]

THE GENEVA Protocol (known formally as the Protocol for the Pacific Settlement of International Disputes) was signed on October 2, 1924, by Albania, Brazil, Bulgaria, Chile, Estonia, France, Greece, Latvia, Poland, Portugal, Yugoslavia, and Czechoslovakia and subsequently by seven other states. It represented the most important attempt made to strengthen the League of Nations. (For efforts to weaken the League, see Documents 13 and 14.) It was prepared and adopted unanimously by the Fifth Assembly of the League but never was ratified and never went into effect since Article XXI provided that the Protocol would be null and void unless the forthcoming Disarmament Conference (see Article XVII) adopted a plan for the reduction of armaments. This the Conference failed to do. Great Britain's opposition to compulsory arbitration and compulsory sanctions, supplemented by Dominion opposition, dealt the death blow to the Protocol in 1925.

The Geneva Protocol was the most ambitious plan ever to approach actual adoption which sought (1) to define an aggressor and (2) to provide for the settlement of *all* disputes by peaceful means. The aggressor was to be any party to the dispute who failed to compromise or mediate the dispute and who rejected compulsory arbitration or adjudication and resorted to force. It would have closed the "gaps" in the League Covenant and provided a logically complete system

[1] *Protocol for the Pacific Settlement of International Disputes,* League of Nations Publication C.606. M.211. 1924. IX.

of collective security. It failed of adoption ultimately because of the unwillingness of all the League members to see the gaps in the Covenant closed and a system of automatic sanctions introduced.

Article I

The signatory States undertake to make every effort in their power to secure the introduction into the Covenant of amendments on the lines of the provisions contained in the following articles.

They agree that, as between themselves, these provisions shall be binding as from the coming into force of the present Protocol and that, so far as they are concerned, the Assembly and the Council of the League of Nations shall thenceforth have power to exercise all the rights and perform all the duties conferred upon them by the Protocol.

Article II

The signatory States agree in no case to resort to war either with one another or against a State which, if the occasion arises, accepts all the obligations hereinafter set out, except in case of resistance to acts of aggression or when acting in agreement with the Council or the Assembly of the League of Nations in accordance with the provisions of the Covenant and of the present Protocol.

Article III

The signatory States undertake to recognise as compulsory, *ipso facto* and without special agreement, the jurisdiction of the Permanent Court of International Justice in the cases covered by paragraph 2 of Article 36 of the Statute of the Court, but without prejudice to the right of any State, when acceding to the special protocol provided for in the said article and opened for signature on December 16th, 1920, to make reservations compatible with the said clause.

Accession to this special protocol, opened for signature on December 16th, 1920, must be given within the month following the coming into force of the present Protocol.

States which accede to the present Protocol after its coming into force must carry out the above obligation within the month following their accession.

Article IV

With a view to render more complete the provisions of paragraphs 4, 5, 6 and 7 of Article 15 of the Covenant, the signatory States agree to comply with the following procedure:

1. If the dispute submitted to the Council is not settled by it as provided in paragraph 3 of the said Article 15, the Council shall endeavour to persuade the parties to submit the dispute to judicial settlement or arbitration.

2. (a) If the parties cannot agree to do so, there shall, at the request of at least one of the parties, be constituted a Committee of Arbitrators. The Committee shall so far as possible be constituted by agreement between the parties.

(b) If within the period fixed by the Council the parties have failed to agree, in whole or in part, upon the number, the names and the powers of the arbitrators and upon the procedure, the Council shall settle the points remaining in suspense. It shall with the utmost possible despatch select in consultation with the parties the arbitrators and their President from among persons who by their nationality, their personal character and their experience appear to it to furnish the highest guarantees of competence and impartiality.

(c) After the claims of the parties have been formulated, the Committee of Arbitrators, on the request of any party, shall through the medium of the Council request an advisory opinion upon any points of law in dispute from the Permanent Court of International Justice, which in such case shall meet with the utmost possible despatch.

3. If none of the parties asks for arbitration, the Council shall again take the dispute under consideration. If the Council reaches a report which is unanimously agreed to by the members thereof other than the representatives of any of the parties to the

dispute, the signatory States agree to comply with the recommendations therein.

4. If the Council fails to reach a report which is concurred in by all its members, other than the representatives of any of the parties to the dispute, it shall submit the dispute to arbitration. It shall itself determine the composition, the powers and the procedure of the Committee of Arbitrators and, in the choice of the arbitrators, shall bear in mind the guarantees of competence and impartiality referred to in paragraph 2 (b) above.

5. In no case may a solution upon which there has already been a unanimous recommendation of the Council accepted by one of the parties concerned be again called in question.

6. The signatory States undertake that they will carry out in full good faith any judicial sentence or arbitral award that may be rendered and that they will comply, as provided in paragraph 3 above, with the solutions recommended by the Council. In the event of a State failing to carry out the above undertakings, the Council shall exert all its influence to secure compliance therewith. If it fails therein, it shall propose what steps should be taken to give effect thereto, in accordance with the provision contained at the end of Article 13 of the Covenant. Should a State in disregard of the above undertakings resort to war, the sanctions provided for by Article 16 of the Covenant, interpreted in the manner indicated in the present Protocol, shall immediately become applicable to it.

7. The provisions of the present article do not apply to the settlement of disputes which arise as the result of measures of war taken by one or more signatory States in agreement with the Council or Assembly.

Article V

The provisions of paragraph 8 of Article 15 of the Covenant shall continue to apply in proceedings before the Council.

If in the course of an arbitration, such as is contemplated in Article IV above, one of the parties claims that the dispute, or part thereof, arises out of a matter which by international law is solely within the domestic jurisdiction of that party, the arbitrators shall on this point take the advice of the Permanent

Court of International Justice through the medium of the Council. The opinion of the Court shall be binding upon the arbitrators, who, if the opinion is affirmative, shall confine themselves to so declaring in their award.

If the question is held by the Court or by the Council to be a matter solely within the domestic jurisdiction of the State, this decision shall not prevent consideration of the situation by the Council or by the Assembly under Article 11 of the Covenant.

Article VI

If in accordance with paragraph 9 of Article 15 of the Covenant a dispute is referred to the Assembly, that body shall have for the settlement of the dispute all the powers conferred upon the Council as to endeavouring to reconcile the parties in the manner laid down in paragraphs 1, 2 and 3 of Article 15 of the Covenant and in paragraph 1 of Article IV above.

Should the Assembly fail to achieve an amicable settlement:

If one of the parties asks for arbitration, the Council shall proceed to constitute the Committee of Arbitrators in the manner provided in sub-paragraphs (a), (b) and (c) of paragraph 2 of Article IV above.

If no party asks for arbitration, the Assembly shall again take the dispute under consideration and shall have in this connection the same powers as the Council. Recommendations embodied in a report of the Assembly, provided that it secures the measure of support stipulated at the end of paragraph 10 of Article 15 of the Covenant, shall have the same value and effect, as regards all matters dealt with in the present Protocol, as recommendations embodied in a report of the Council adopted as provided in paragraph 3 of Article IV above.

If the necessary majority cannot be obtained, the dispute shall be submitted to arbitration and the Council shall determine the composition, the powers and the procedure of the Committee of Arbitrators as laid down in paragraph 4 of Article IV above.

Article VII

In the event of a dispute arising between two or more signatory States, these States agree that they will not, either before the dispute is submitted to proceedings for pacific settlement or during such proceedings, make any increase of their armaments or effectives which might modify the position established by the Conference for the Reduction of Armaments provided for by Article XVII of the present Protocol, nor will they take any measure of military, naval, air, industrial or economic mobilisation, nor, in general, any action of a nature likely to extend the dispute or render it more acute.

It shall be the duty of the Council, in accordance with the provisions of Article 11 of the Covenant, to take under consideration any complaint as to infraction of the above undertakings which is made to it by one or more of the States parties to the dispute. Should the Council be of opinion that the complaint requires investigation, it shall, if it deems it expedient, arrange for enquiries and investigations in one or more of the countries concerned. Such enquiries and investigations shall be carried out with the utmost possible despatch and the signatory States undertake to afford every facility for carrying them out.

The sole object of measures taken by the Council as above provided is to facilitate the pacific settlement of disputes and they shall in no way prejudge the actual settlement.

If the result of such enquiries and investigations is to establish an infraction of the provisions of the first paragraph of the present article, it shall be the duty of the Council to summon the State or States guilty of the infraction to put an end thereto. Should the State or States in question fail to comply with such summons, the Council shall declare them to be guilty of a violation of the Covenant or of the present Protocol, and shall decide upon the measures to be taken with a view to end as soon as possible a situation of a nature to threaten the peace of the world.

For the purposes of the present article decisions of the Council may be taken by a two-thirds majority.

Article VIII

The signatory States undertake to abstain from any act which might constitute a threat of aggression against another State.

If one of the signatory States is of opinion that another State is making preparations for war, it shall have the right to bring the matter to the notice of the Council.

The Council, if it ascertains that the facts are as alleged, shall proceed as provided in paragraphs 2, 4 and 5 of Article VII.

Article IX

The existence of demilitarised zones being calculated to prevent aggression and to facilitate a definite finding of the nature provided for in Article X below, the establishment of such zones between States mutually consenting thereto is recommended as a means of avoiding violations of the present Protocol.

The demilitarised zones already existing under the terms of certain treaties or conventions, or which may be established in future between States mutually consenting thereto, may, at the request and at the expense of one or more of the conterminous States, be placed under a temporary or permanent system of supervision to be organized by the Council.

Article X

Every State which resorts to war in violation of the undertakings contained in the Covenant or in the present Protocol is an aggressor. Violation of the rules laid down for a demilitarised zone shall be held equivalent to resort to war.

In the event of hostilities having broken out, any State shall be presumed to be an aggressor, unless a decision of the Council, which must be taken unanimously, shall otherwise declare:

(1) If it has refused to submit the dispute to the procedure of pacific settlement provided by Articles 13 and 15 of the Covenant as amplified by the present Protocol, or to comply with a judicial sentence or arbitral award or with a unanimous recommendation of the Council, or has disregarded a unanimous report of the Council, a judicial sentence or an arbitral award recognising

that the dispute between it and the other belligerent State arises out of a matter which by international law is solely within the domestic jurisdiction of the latter State; nevertheless, in the last case the State shall only be presumed to be an aggressor if it has not previously submitted the question to the Council or the Assembly, in accordance with Article 11 of the Covenant;

(2) If it has violated provisional measures enjoined by the Council for the period while the proceedings are in progress as contemplated by Article VII of the present Protocol.

Apart from the cases dealt with in paragraphs 1 and 2 of the present Article, if the Council does not at once succeed in determining the aggressor, it shall be bound to enjoin upon the belligerents an armistice, and shall fix the terms, acting, if need be, by a two-thirds majority, and shall supervise its execution.

Any belligerent which has refused to accept the armistice or has violated its terms shall be deemed an aggressor.

The Council shall call upon the signatory States to apply forthwith against the aggressor the sanctions provided by Article XI of the present Protocol, and any signatory State thus called upon shall thereupon be entitled to exercise the rights of a belligerent.

Article XI

As soon as the Council has called upon the signatory States to apply sanctions, as provided in the last paragraph of Article X of the present Protocol, the obligations of the said States, in regard to the sanctions of all kinds mentioned in paragraphs 1 and 2 of Article 16 of the Covenant will immediately become operative in order that such sanctions may forthwith be employed against the aggressor.

These obligations shall be interpreted as obliging each of the signatory States to co-operate loyally and effectively in support of the Covenant of the League of Nations, and in resistance to any act of aggression, in the degree which its geographical position and its particular situation as regards armaments allow.

In accordance with paragraph 3 of Article 16 of the Covenant the signatory States give a joint and several undertaking to come to the assistance of the State attacked or threatened, and to give each other mutual support by means of facilities and reciprocal exchanges as regards the provision of raw materials and supplies of every kind, openings of credits, transport and transit, and for this purpose to take all measures in their power to preserve the safety of communications by land and by sea of the attacked or threatened State.

If both parties to the dispute are aggressors within the meaning of Article X, the economic and financial sanctions shall be applied to both of them.

Article XII

In view of the complexity of the conditions in which the Council may be called upon to exercise the functions mentioned in Article XI of the present Protocol concerning economic and financial sanctions, and in order to determine more exactly the guarantees afforded by the present Protocol to the signatory States, the Council shall forthwith invite the economic and financial organisations of the League of Nations to consider and report as to the nature of the steps to be taken to give effect to the financial and economic sanctions and measures of co-operation contemplated in Article 16 of the Covenant and in Article XI of this Protocol.

When in possession of this information, the Council shall draw up through its competent organs:

1. Plans of action for the application of the economic and financial sanctions against an aggressor State;
2. Plans of economic and financial co-operation between a State attacked and the different States assisting it;

and shall communicate these plans to the Members of the League and to the other signatory States.

Article XIII

In view of the contingent military, naval and air sanctions provided for by Article 16 of the Covenant and by Article XI of the present Protocol, the Council shall be entitled to receive undertakings from States determining in advance the military, naval and air forces which they would be able to bring into action immediately to ensure the fulfilment of the obligations in regard to sanctions which result from the Covenant and the present Protocol.

Furthermore, as soon as the Council has called upon the signatory States to apply sanctions, as provided in the last paragraph of Article X above, the said States may, in accordance with any agreements which they may previously have concluded, bring to the assistance of a particular State, which is the victim of aggression, their military, naval and air forces.

The agreements mentioned in the preceding paragraph shall be registered and published by the Secretariat of the League of Nations. They shall remain open to all States Members of the League which may desire to accede thereto.

Article XIV

The Council shall alone be competent to declare that the application of sanctions shall cease and normal conditions be re-established.

Article XV

In conformity with the spirit of the present Protocol, the signatory States agree that the whole cost of any military, naval or air operations undertaken for the repression of an aggression under the terms of the Protocol, and reparation for all losses suffered by individuals, whether civilians or combatants, and for all material damage caused by the operations of both sides, shall be borne by the aggressor State up to the extreme limit of its capacity.

Nevertheless, in view of Article 10 of the Covenant, neither the territorial integrity nor the political independence of the aggressor State shall in any case be affected as the result of the application of the sanctions mentioned in the present Protocol.

Article XVI

The signatory States agree that in the event of a dispute between one or more of them and one or more States which have not signed the present Protocol and are not Members of the League of Nations, such non-Member States shall be invited, on the conditions contemplated in Article 17 of the Covenant, to submit, for the purpose of a pacific settlement, to the obligations accepted by the States signatories of the present Protocol.

If the State so invited, having refused to accept the said conditions and obligations, resorts to war against a signatory State, the provisions of Article 16 of the Covenant as defined by the present Protocol, shall be applicable against it.

Article XVII

The signatory States undertake to participate in an International Conference for the Reduction of Armaments which shall meet at Geneva on Monday, June 15th, 1925. All other States, whether Members of the League or not, shall be invited to this Conference.

In preparation for the convening of the Conference, the Council shall draw up with due regard to the undertakings contained in Articles XI and XIII of the present Protocol, a general programme for the reduction and limitation of armaments, which shall be laid before the Conference and which shall be communicated to the Governments at the earliest possible date, and at the latest three months before the Conference meets.

If by May 1st, 1925, ratifications have not been deposited by at least a majority of the permanent Members of the Council and ten other Members of the League, the Secretary-General of the League shall immediately consult the Council as to whether he shall cancel the invitations or merely adjourn the Conference to a subsequent date to be fixed by the Council so as to permit the necessary number of ratifications to be obtained.

Article XVIII

Wherever mention is made in Article X or in any other provision of the present Protocol, of a decision of the Council, this shall be understood in the sense of Article 15 of the Covenant, namely, that the votes of the representatives of the parties to the dispute shall not be counted when reckoning unanimity or the necessary majority.

Article XIX

Except as expressly provided by its terms, the present Protocol shall not affect in any way the rights and obligations of Members of the League as determined by the Covenant.

Article XX

Any dispute as to the interpretation of the present Protocol shall be submitted to the Permanent Court of International Justice.

Article XXI

The present Protocol, of which the French and English texts are both authentic, shall be ratified.

The deposit of ratifications shall be made at the Secretariat of the League of Nations as soon as possible.

States of which the seat of government is outside Europe will be entitled merely to inform the Secretariat of the League of Nations that their ratification has been given; in that case, they must transmit the instrument of ratification as soon as possible.

So soon as the majority of the permanent Members of the Council and ten other Members of the League have deposited or have effected their ratifications, a *proces-verbal* to that effect shall be drawn up by the Secretariat.

After the said *proces-verbal* has been drawn up, the Protocol shall come into force as soon as the plan for the reduction of armaments has been adopted by the Conference provided for in Article XVII.

If within such period after the adoption of the plan for the reduction of armaments as shall be fixed by the said Conference, the plan has not been carried out, the Council shall make a declaration to that effect; this declaration shall render the present Protocol null and void.

THE LOCARNO PACT [1]

THE LOCARNO Pact was signed by Germany, Belgium, France, Great Britain, and Italy on October 16, 1925,[2] and came into effect on September 14, 1926. It was adopted after the failure of the Geneva Protocol (see Document 18) as a substitute *regional* security measure. The Franco-Belgian-German frontier was declared inviolate, with Italy and Great Britain guaranteeing their assistance to any of the other parties attacked across that frontier. Like the Geneva Protocol, the Locarno Pact sought to supplement the provisions of the League Covenant guaranteeing the territory and security of every member of the League by pledging automatic sanctions against any designated aggressor.

The effect of the Interpretative Resolutions adopted October 4, 1921, by the Assembly (see Document 13) had been to make the application of League sanctions highly uncertain in any given case; both the Geneva Protocol and the Locarno Pact sought to reverse this trend. Whereas the Protocol was to apply everywhere in the world, the pact was strictly limited to Germany's western frontier. This difference accounted for Britain's altered attitude. The British, although unwilling to accept the obligation of enforcing automatic sanctions everywhere in the world, were quite willing to guarantee the Lowlands region, since that was in accord with permanent British policy. To prevent opposition from the Dominions

[1] *League of Nations Treaty Series*, Vol. 54 (No. 1292), pp. 289*ff.*

[2] Actually the treaty was signed at London on Dec. 1, 1925, but it was agreed that it would bear the date of initialling at Locarno (Oct. 16, 1925). Manley O. Hudson, *International Legislation*, Vol. III, p. 1689.

and India, such as had contributed toward the defeat of the Geneva Protocol, they were excused from any obligations under the pact (Article IX).

The unique feature of the pact was that the guaranteeing powers promised to aid *either* France *or* Germany, depending upon which was attacked.

Article I

The high contracting parties collectively and severally guarantee, in the manner provided in the following articles, the maintenance of the territorial *status quo* resulting from the frontiers between Germany and Belgium and between Germany and France, and the inviolability of the said frontiers as fixed by or in pursuance of the Treaty of Peace signed at Versailles on June 28, 1919, and also the observance of the stipulations of Articles 42 and 43 of the said treaty concerning the demilitarised zone.

Article II

Germany and Belgium, and also Germany and France, mutually undertake that they will in no case attack or invade each other or resort to war against each other.

This stipulation shall not, however, apply in the case of:

(1) The exercise of the right of legitimate defence, that is to say, resistance to a violation of the undertaking contained in the previous paragraph or to a flagrant breach of Articles 42 or 43 of the said Treaty of Versailles, if such breach constitutes an unprovoked act of aggression and by reason of the assembly of armed forces in the demilitarised zone immediate action is necessary;

(2) Action in pursuance of Article 16 of the Covenant of the League of Nations;

(3) Action as the result of a decision taken by the Assembly or by the Council of the League of Nations or in pursuance of Article 15, paragraph 7, of the Covenant of the League of Nations, provided that in this last event the action is directed against a State which was the first to attack.

Article III

In view of the undertakings entered into in Article II of the present treaty, Germany and Belgium, and Germany and France, undertake to settle by peaceful means and in the manner laid down herein all questions of every kind which may arise between them and which it may not be possible to settle by the normal methods of diplomacy:

Any question with regard to which the parties are in conflict as to their respective rights shall be submitted to judicial decision, and the parties undertake to comply with such decision.

All other questions shall be submitted to a conciliation commission. If the proposals of this commission are not accepted by the two parties, the question shall be brought before the Council of the League of Nations, which will deal with it in accordance with Article 15 of the Covenant of the League.

The detailed arrangements for effecting such peaceful settlement are the subject of special agreements signed this day.

Article IV

(1) If one of the high contracting parties alleges that a violation of Article II of the present treaty or a breach of Articles 42 or 43 of the Treaty of Versailles has been or is being committed, it shall bring the question at once before the Council of the League of Nations.

(2) As soon as the Council of the League of Nations is satisfied that such violation or breach has been committed, it will notify its finding without delay to the Powers signatory of the present treaty, who severally agree that in such case they will each of them come immediately to the assistance of the Power against whom the act complained of is directed.

(3) In case of a flagrant violation of Article II of the present treaty or of a flagrant breach of Articles 42 or 43 of the Treaty of Versailles by one of the high contracting parties, each of the other contracting parties hereby undertakes immediately to come to the help of the party against whom such a violation or breach has been directed as soon as the said Power has been able to

satisfy itself that this violation constitutes an unprovoked act of aggression and that by reason either of the crossing of the frontier or of the outbreak of hostilities or of the assembly of armed forces in the demilitarised zone immediate action is necessary. Nevertheless, the Council of the League of Nations, which will be seized of the question in accordance with the first paragraph of this article, will issue its findings, and the high contracting parties undertake to act in accordance with the recommendations of the Council provided that they are concurred in by all the members other than the representatives of the parties which have engaged in hostilities.

Article V

The provisions of Article III of the present treaty are placed under the guarantee of the high contracting parties as provided by the following stipulations:

If one of the Powers referred to in Article III refuses to submit a dispute to peaceful settlement or to comply with an arbitral or judicial decision and commits a violation of Article II of the present treaty or a breach of Articles 42 or 43 of the Treaty of Versailles, the provisions of Article IV of the present treaty shall apply.

Where one of the Powers referred to in Article III without committing a violation of Article II of the present treaty or a breach of Articles 42 or 43 of the Treaty of Versailles, refuses to submit a dispute to peaceful settlement or to comply with an arbitral or judicial decision, the other party shall bring the matter before the Council of the League of Nations, and the Council shall propose what steps shall be taken; the high contracting parties shall comply with these proposals.

Article VI

The provisions of the present treaty do not affect the rights and obligations of the high contracting parties under the Treaty of Versailles or under arrangements supplementary thereto, including the agreements signed in London on August 30, 1924.

Article VII

The present treaty, which is designed to ensure the maintenance of peace, and is in conformity with the Covenant of the League of Nations, shall not be interpreted as restricting the duty of the League to take whatever action may be deemed wise and effectual to safeguard the peace of the world.

Article VIII

The present treaty shall be registered at the League of Nations in accordance with the Covenant of the League. It shall remain in force until the Council, acting on a request of one or other of the high contracting parties notified to the other signatory Powers three months in advance, and voting at least by a two-thirds majority, decides that the League of Nations ensures sufficient protection to the high contracting parties; the treaty shall cease to have effect on the expiration of a period of one year from such decision.

Article IX

The present treaty shall impose no obligation upon any of the British dominions, or upon India, unless the Government of such dominion, or of India, signifies its acceptance thereof.

Article X

The present treaty shall be ratified and the ratifications shall be deposited at Geneva in the archives of the League of Nations as soon as possible.

It shall enter into force as soon as all the ratifications have been deposited and Germany has become a member of the League of Nations.

The present treaty, done in a single copy, will be deposited in the archives of the League of Nations, and the Secretary-General will be requested to transmit certified copies to each of the high contracting parties.

In faith whereof the above-mentioned plenipotentiaries have signed the present treaty.

BRIAND-KELLOGG PACT [1]

THE BRIAND-KELLOGG Pact (also known as the Pact of Paris, and more formally as the General Treaty for the Renunciation of War) was signed on August 27, 1928, and was ratified by the largest number of states ever to accept a multilateral political instrument. It came into effect on July 24, 1929.

The Briand-Kellogg Pact did not make all wars illegal— the inherent right of self-defense was explicitly reaffirmed by Secretary of State Kellogg during the negotiations. This interpretation was accepted by the other signatory nations who remained individually competent to decide when circumstances required recourse to war in self-defense. Much controversy was aroused by this pact. Some international law experts claimed that since self-defense remained legal, and each state had the right to interpret the pact for itself, the result was that each state could designate any war in which it became involved as a war of self-defense. Consequently the pact could and would have no practical effect. This view was opposed by others who claimed that no state could unilaterally interpret a treaty in such a way as to free itself from contractual obligations. (On this point see note and Document 4.) Without a generally accepted definition of what constitutes aggression, it is difficult to resolve this conflict of views.

The more serious objection to the pact was that it provided no machinery for action in the event of a violation of its provisions. At the time of its consideration in the Senate, it

[1] *United States Treaty Series,* No. 796, Washington, 1929.

was made clear that many Senators believed that the most potent enforcement of the pact would stem from aroused world public opinion. During the Manchurian crisis in 1931 to 1932, Secretary Stimson refused to recognize the Japanese puppet state of Manchukuo on the ground that it was created contrary to the principles of the Pact of Paris. The League Assembly endorsed this method of enforcing the pact in its resolution of March 11, 1932, declaring that it was incumbent upon the members of the League not to recognize any situation, agreement, or treaty which might be brought about by means contrary to the Briand-Kellogg Pact.

The signatory states and those which have adhered to the pact are Afghanistan, Albania, Australia, Austria, Belgium, Brazil, Bulgaria, Canada, Chile, China, Colombia, Costa Rica, Cuba, Czechoslovakia, Denmark, Dominican Republic, Ecuador, Egypt, Estonia, Ethiopia, Finland, France, Free City of Danzig, Germany, Great Britain, Greece, Guatemala, Haiti, Honduras, Hungary, Iceland, India, Iran, Iraq, Ireland, Italy, Japan, Latvia, Liberia, Lithuania, Luxemburg, Mexico, Netherlands, New Zealand, Nicaragua, Norway, Panama, Paraguay, Peru, Poland, Portugal, Rumania, Saudi Arabia, Spain, Sweden, Switzerland, Thailand, Turkey, Union of South Africa, Union of Soviet Socialist Republics, United States of America, Venezuela, and Yugoslavia.

Article I

The high contracting parties solemnly declare in the names of their respective peoples that they condemn recourse to war for the solution of international controversies, and renounce it as an instrument of national policy in their relations with one another.

Article II

The high contracting parties agree that the settlement or solution of all disputes or conflicts, of whatever nature or of whatever origin they may be, which may arise among them, shall never be sought except by pacific means.

Article III

The present treaty shall be ratified by the high contracting parties named in the preamble in accordance with their respective constitutional requirements, and shall take effect as between them as soon as all their several instruments of ratification shall have been deposited at Washington.

This treaty shall, when it has come into effect as prescribed in the preceding paragraph, remain open as long as may be necessary for adherence by all the other Powers of the world. Every instrument evidencing the adherence of a Power shall be deposited at Washington and the treaty shall immediately upon such deposit become effective as between the Power thus adhering and the other Powers parties hereto.

FRANCO-SOVIET TREATY OF MUTUAL ASSISTANCE [1]

THE FRANCO-SOVIET Treaty of Mutual Assistance, signed on May 2, 1935, reflected the alarm of these two nations over the rise of Hitlerite Germany. Even so, France vacillated, not ratifying the pact until after the remilitarization of the Rhineland. The treaty was proclaimed in effect on March 27, 1936.

It is interesting to compare this pact with the Franco-Russian Alliance of 1892 (see Document 7). Far from stipulating for immediate use of a specified number of troops, the pact of 1935 merely provided (Article 1) for "immediate consultation." When such consultations were actually held in the summer of 1939, following the dismemberment of Czechoslovakia, no concrete agreement was reached. Instead, the Soviet Union concluded a treaty of nonaggression with Germany.

The language in which the Treaty of Mutual Assistance was framed was designed to make it compatible with the provisions of the League Covenant. It was provided that should either France or Russia become the victim of unprovoked aggression because of their actions under Article 15, section 7, or Article 16 of the Covenant, the other would give all "aid and assistance" possible. Since the League never considered the crisis which brought war in 1939, these provisions were never called into effect and only the obligation to consult remained—with the consequences noted above.

The creation of this treaty was a significant measure of the

[1] *League of Nations Treaty Series*, Vol. 167 (No. 3881), pp. 404ff.

actual failure of the general system of security under the League of Nations. It will be noted that this pact and the Locarno Treaty (see Document 19) were both arrangements for the security of *particular* nations. (In contrast, the Geneva Protocol [see note and Document 18] was to provide security for *all* nations.) It was another step toward a balance-of-power arrangement and away from collective security.

Article I

In the event of France or the Union of Soviet Socialist Republics being threatened with or in danger of aggression on the part of any European State, the Union of Soviet Socialist Republics and reciprocally France undertake mutually to proceed to an immediate consultation as regards the measures to be taken for the observance of the provisions of Article 10 of the Covenant of the League of Nations.

Article II

Should, in the circumstances specified in Article 15, paragraph 7, of the Covenant of the League of Nations, France or the Union of Soviet Socialist Republics be the object, notwithstanding the sincerely peaceful intentions of both countries, of an unprovoked aggression on the part of a European State, the Union of Soviet Socialist Republics and reciprocally France shall immediately come to each other's aid and assistance.

Article III

In consideration of the fact that under Article 16 of the Covenant of the League of Nations any Member of the League which resorts to war in disregard of its covenants under Articles 12, 13 or 15 of the Covenant is *ipso facto* deemed to have committed an act of war against all other Members of the League, France, and reciprocally the Union of Soviet Socialist Republics undertake, in the event of one of them being the object, in these conditions and notwithstanding the sincerely peaceful intentions of both countries, of an unprovoked aggression on the part of a European State, immediately to come to each other's aid and assistance in application of Article 16 of the Covenant.

The same obligation is assumed in the event of France or the Union of Soviet Socialist Republics being the object of an aggression on the part of a European State in the circumstances specified in Article 17, paragraphs 1 and 3, of the Covenant of the League of Nations.

Article IV

The undertakings stipulated above being consonant with the obligations of the High Contracting Parties as Members of the League of Nations, nothing in the present Treaty shall be interpreted as restricting the duty of the latter to take any action that may be deemed wise and effectual to safeguard the peace of the world or as restricting the obligations resulting for the High Contracting Parties from the Covenant of the League of Nations.

Article V

The present Treaty, both the French and the Russian texts whereof shall be equally authentic, shall be ratified and the instruments of ratification shall be exchanged at Moscow as soon as possible. It shall be registered with the Secretariat of the League of Nations.

It shall take effect as soon as the ratifications have been exchanged and shall remain in force for five years. If it is not denounced by either of the High Contracting Parties giving notice thereof at least one year before the expiry of that period, it shall remain in force indefinitely, each of the High Contracting Parties being at liberty to terminate it at a year's notice by a declaration to that effect.

THE ANTI-COMINTERN PACT [1]

THE ANTI-COMINTERN Pact was signed by Germany and Japan on November 25, 1936. It was later adhered to by Italy on November 6, 1937, and by Hungary and Manchukuo on February 24, 1939. Spain adhered on March 27, 1939.

Since its very name denoted opposition to Communism, the Anti-Comintern Pact was accepted as a contribution to stability by many elements in the nations of the Western world. It was the first step toward the Axis alliance which was to overthrow the balance of power and ultimately range Western Europe, in cooperation with Soviet Russia, against the Axis states.

The Imperial Government of Japan and the Government of Germany,

In cognizance of the fact that the object of the Communistic International (the so-called Komintern) is the disintegration of, and the commission of violence against, existing States by the exercise of all means at its command,

Believing that the toleration of interference by the Communistic International in the internal affairs of nations not only endangers their internal peace and social welfare, but threatens the general peace of the world,

Desiring to co-operate for defence against communistic disintegration, have agreed as follows:

[1] Department of State, *Foreign Relations of the United States: Japan, 1931–1941,* Vol. II, pp. 153*ff.*

Article I

The High Contracting States agree that they will mutually keep each other informed concerning the activities of the Communistic International, will confer upon the necessary measures of defence, and will carry out such measures in close co-operation.

Article II

The High Contracting States will jointly invite third States whose internal peace is menaced by the disintegrating work of the Communistic International, to adopt defensive measures in the spirit of the present Agreement or to participate in the present Agreement.

Article III

The Japanese and German texts are each valid as the original text of this Agreement. The Agreement shall come into force on the day of its signature and shall remain in force for the term of five years. The High Contracting States will, in a reasonable time before the expiration of the said term, come to an understanding upon the further manner of their cooperation.

THE MUNICH AGREEMENT [1]

THE MUNICH Agreement is one of the most remarkable documents of recent times. Despite the fact that France and Czechoslovakia were bound together by a defensive alliance, France, in concert with Great Britain, put pressure upon the Czechs to grant the German demands. The Czechs were warned that any other course of action would produce a situation for which France and Britain could take no responsibility. On September 21, 1938, therefore, the Czechs agreed to the cession of all areas containing over 50 per cent Germans. On September 29, 1938, Germany, the United Kingdom, France, and Italy signed the Munich Agreement to specify the method of transfer of territory.

Actually the Czechs were not even invited to the Munich Conference which partitioned their state. Moreover, the agreement was never lived up to; no plebiscites were ever held in the frontier areas, and the boundary which was finally drawn transferred to Germany territory beyond that surrendered at Munich. The international guarantee of the new frontiers never materialized, the offer to guarantee was never implemented, and on March 17, 1939, a German protectorate over Bohemia and Moravia was proclaimed. The remaining portion of Czechoslovakia, Slovakia, became an "autonomous" state under full German control. In this way the Czech army of twenty-one regular divisions, fifteen to sixteen reserve but mobilized divisions, and the Czech "Maginot

[1] *British Command Paper* No. 5848.

Line" were surrendered to the Germans, thus freeing some thirty German divisions for use elsewhere.

The political consequences were even more disastrous. Russia was not invited to the conference and took no part in its decisions. The Soviets felt that they had been given ample grounds for distrusting the motives of the Western powers. They construed the agreement as an attempt to turn German aggression toward the East. With this the seeds were sown for the mutual distrust whose harvest was reaped with the signing of the Nazi-Soviet Non-Aggression Pact (see Document 25).

Germany, the United Kingdom, France and Italy, taking into consideration the agreement, which has been already reached in principle for the cession to Germany of the Sudeten German territory, have agreed on the following terms and conditions governing the said cession and the measures consequent thereon, and by this agreement they each hold themselves responsible for the steps necessary to secure its fulfilment:

(1) The evacuation will begin on 1st October.

(2) The United Kingdom, France and Italy agree that the evacuation of the territory shall be completed by the 10th October, without any existing installations having been destroyed and that the Czechoslovak Government will be held responsible for carrying out the evacuation without damage to the said installations.

(3) The conditions governing the evacuation will be laid down in detail by an international commission composed of representatives of Germany, the United Kingdom, France, Italy and Czechoslovakia.

(4) The occupation by stages of the predominantly German territory by German troops will begin on the 1st October. The four territories marked on the attached map will be occupied by German troops in the following order: the territory marked No. I on the 1st and 2nd of October, the territory marked No.

II on the 2nd and 3rd of October, the territory marked No. III on the 3rd, 4th and 5th of October, the territory marked No. IV on the 6th and 7th of October. The remaining territory of predominantly German character will be ascertained by the aforesaid international commission forthwith and be occupied by German troops by the 10th of October.

(5) The international commission referred to in paragraph 3 will determine the territories in which a plebiscite is to be held. These territories will be occupied by international bodies until the plebiscite has been completed. The same commission will fix the conditions in which the plebiscite is to be held, taking as a basis the conditions of the Saar plebiscite. The commission will also fix a date, not later than the end of November, on which the plebiscite will be held.

(6) The final determination of the frontiers will be carried out by the international commission. This commission will also be entitled to recommend to the four Powers, Germany, the United Kingdom, France and Italy, in certain exceptional cases minor modifications in the strictly ethnographical determination of the zones which are to be transferred without plebiscite.

(7) There will be a right of option into and out of the transferred territories, the option to be exercised within six months from the date of this agreement. A German-Czechoslovak commission shall determine the details of the option, consider ways of facilitating the transfer of population and settle questions of principle arising out of the said transfer.

(8) The Czechoslovak Government will within a period of four weeks from the date of this agreement release from their military and police forces any Sudeten Germans who may wish to be released, and the Czechoslovak Government will within the same period release Sudeten German prisoners who are serving terms of imprisonment for political offences.

.   .   .   .

Annex to the Agreement

His Majesty's Government in the United Kingdom and the French Government have entered into the above agreement on the basis that they stand by the offer, contained in paragraph 6 of the Anglo-French proposals of the 19th September, [Cmd. 5847] relating to an international guarantee of the new boundaries of the Czechoslovak State against unprovoked aggression.

When the question of the Polish and Hungarian minorities in Czechoslovakia has been settled, Germany and Italy for their part will give a guarantee to Czechoslovakia.

THE BRITISH GUARANTEE TO POLAND [1]

CHAMBERLAIN REALIZED, after the Munich Agreement had been torn up by Hitler, that "peace in our time" was an illusion. The proclamation by Germany of a protectorate over Bohemia-Moravia, in the face of Hitler's solemn promise to guarantee what remained of Czechoslovakia after the Sudeten areas had been incorporated into the Third Reich, convinced Chamberlain that it was time to seek peace through other methods. Accordingly, in concert with the French, guarantees were given to Poland, Greece, and Rumania respectively on March 31, April 6, and April 13, 1939. The guarantee given to Poland was later transformed into a reciprocal treaty of mutual assistance between the United Kingdom and Poland, which was signed and came into force on August 25, 1939. The text is given below. It was hoped that the certainty of Anglo-French opposition to a further overthrow of the balance of power would make Hitler hesitate to use force. As Chamberlain wrote to Hitler on August 22, 1939: ". . . It has been alleged that, if His Majesty's Government had made their position more clear in 1914, the great catastrophe would have been avoided. Whether or not there is any force in that allegation, His Majesty's Government are resolved that on this occasion there shall be no such tragic misunderstanding. . . ." [2] Hitler's reply on August 23, 1939, rejected the warning: ". . . Germany, if attacked by England, will be found prepared and

[1] *British Command Paper* No. 6106, pp. 37*ff*.
[2] *Ibid.,* No. 6102.

determined. I have already more than once declared . . . that there can be no doubt concerning the determination of the new German Reich rather to accept, for however long it might be, every sort of misery and tribulation than to sacrifice its national interests, let alone its honour." [3]

The practical task of implementing the guarantee was complicated by the surrender of the Czech bastion at Munich (see note and Document 23). Furthermore, the Nazis, following their illegal remilitarization of the Rhineland, had steadily built the West Wall on the Franco-German frontier, making military action by the Allies to enforce the guarantees extremely difficult. There remained only the tenuous connections by air and sea by which aid could be given to Poland if she were attacked by Germany. What was needed was a firm alliance with Soviet Russia, and by the time of the above exchange of notes this had become impossible (see Document 25).

Article 1

Should one of the Contracting Parties become engaged in hostilities with a European Power in consequence of aggression by the latter against that Contracting Party, the other Contracting Party will at once give the Contracting Party engaged in hostilities all the support and assistance in its power.

Article 2

(1) The provisions of Article 1 will also apply in the event of any action by a European Power which clearly threatened, directly or indirectly, the independence of one of the Contracting Parties, and was of such a nature that the Party in question considered it vital to resist it with its armed forces.

(2) Should one of the Contracting Parties become engaged in hostilities with a European Power in consequence of action by

[3] *Ibid.*

that Power which threatened the independence or neutrality of another European State in such a way as to constitute a clear menace to the security of that Contracting Party, the provisions of Article 1 will apply, without prejudice, however, to the rights of the other European State concerned.[4]

Article 3

Should a European Power attempt to undermine the independence of one of the Contracting Parties by processes of economic penetration or in any other way, the Contracting Parties will support each other in resistance to such attempts. Should the European Power concerned thereupon embark on hostilities against one of the Contracting Parties, the provisions of Article 1 will apply.

.   .   .   .

Article 6

(1) The Contracting Parties will communicate to each other the terms of any undertakings of assistance against aggression which they have already given or may in future give to other States. . . .

Article 7

Should the Contracting Parties be engaged in hostilities in consequence of the application of the present Agreement, they will not conclude an armistice or treaty of peace except by mutual agreement.

[4] This provision might equally well apply to a threat by Germany against Belgium or the Danzig Free City.

NAZI-SOVIET NON-AGGRESSION TREATY [1]

DURING THE summer of 1939, two separate sets of negotiations were being conducted in Moscow; one was between the Soviets and Britain and France, the other between the Soviets and Nazi Germany. The attempts of Britain and France to come to terms with the Soviets were complicated by the stubborn fact that Russia would not undertake to defend Poland unless the Poles permitted Soviet troops to advance into Polish territory. From the Soviet point of view, the value of defending Poland was that it offered a possibility of preventing the Germans from invading Soviet soil. But the Poles adamantly refused these terms, fearing the Russians at least as much as the Germans. Negotiations thereupon reached a deadlock, the Soviets quickly came to terms with the Nazis, and the nonaggression pact, signed on August 23, 1939, was announced to a stunned world.

In the secret protocol to the pact the Machiavellian character of the agreement becomes very clear. In essence, Germany and Russia were dividing Eastern Europe into their respective spoils.

The Government of the German Reich and the Government of the Union of Soviet Socialist Republics, desirous of strengthening the cause of peace between Germany and the U.S.S.R., and proceeding from the fundamental provisions of the Neutrality

[1] Department of State Publication 3023, *Nazi-Soviet Relations, 1939–1941*, pp. 76*ff.*

Agreement concluded in April, 1926, between Germany and the U.S.S.R., have reached the following agreement:

Article I

Both High Contracting Parties obligate themselves to desist from any act of violence, any aggressive action, and any attack on each other, either individually or jointly with other powers.

Article II

Should one of the High Contracting Parties become the object of belligerent action by a third power, the other High Contracting Party shall in no manner lend its support to this third power.

Article III

The Governments of the two High Contracting Parties shall in the future maintain continual contact with one another for the purpose of consultation in order to exchange information on problems affecting their common interests.

Article IV

Neither of the two High Contracting Parties shall participate in any grouping of powers whatsoever that is directly or indirectly aimed at the other party.

Article V

Should disputes or conflicts arise between the High Contracting Parties over problems of one kind or another, both parties shall settle these disputes or conflicts exclusively through friendly exchange of opinion or, if necessary, through the establishment of arbitration commissions.

Article VI

The present treaty is concluded for a period of ten years, with the proviso that, in so far as one of the High Contracting Parties does not denounce it one year prior to the expiration of this period, the validity of this treaty shall automatically be extended for another five years.

Article VII

The present treaty shall be ratified within the shortest possible time. The ratifications shall be exchanged in Berlin. The agreement shall enter into force as soon as it is signed.

.   .   .   .

SECRET ADDITIONAL PROTOCOL

On the occasion of the signature of the Nonaggression Pact between the German Reich and the Union of Soviet Socialist Republics the undersigned plenipotentiaries of each of the two parties discussed in strictly confidential conversations the question of the boundary of their respective spheres of influence in Eastern Europe. These conversations led to the following conclusions:

1. In the event of a territorial and political rearrangement in the areas belonging to the Baltic States (Finland, Estonia, Latvia, Lithuania), the northern boundary of Lithuania shall represent the boundary of the spheres of influence of Germany and the U.S.S.R. In this connection the interest of Lithuania in the Vilna area is recognized by each party.

2. In the event of a territorial and political rearrangement of the areas belonging to the Polish state the spheres of influence of Germany and the U.S.S.R. shall be bounded approximately by the line of the rivers Narew, Vistula, and San.

The question of whether the interest of both parties make desirable the maintenance of an independent Polish state and how such a state should be bounded can only be definitely determined in the course of further political developments.

In any event both Governments will resolve this question by means of a friendly agreement.

3. With regard to Southeastern Europe attention is called by the Soviet side to its interest in Bessarabia. The German side declares its complete disinterestedness in these areas.

4. This protocol shall be treated by both parties as strictly secret.

DOCUMENT 26

THE NEUTRALITY ACT OF 1939 [1]

THE NEUTRALITY ACT of November 4, 1939, was the fourth
and last in a series of acts designed to preserve American
neutrality. By the time of the Nye munitions investigation
of 1934 to 1936, many Americans were disillusioned with the
postwar world and were willing to believe that the United
States had been "pushed into war" by profit-seeking bankers
and munitions makers. In short, prevailing opinion was that
America had participated in the "Great Crusade" for no
compelling reasons of vital national interest. For this reason
it was important that, in the event of a new war, the United
States did not repeat the same mistake by allowing America
to become involved economically, which would in turn bring
political involvement.

Under the spur of the isolationist bloc in Congress, the
First Neutrality Act of 1935 was passed. It instructed the
President to impose an arms embargo on American shipments
to *all* belligerents. In 1936, the Second Neutrality Act still
further narrowed the President's discretionary powers by
requiring him to order the arms embargo whenever he found
a state of war to exist. Although these provisions regarding
arms shipments were retained, the Third Neutrality Act
of 1937 permitted *war materials* such as oil and steel to be
exported on a "cash-and-carry" basis, provided these were
transported in non-American ships. Only a few months after
the passage of this act, the outbreak of the undeclared war

[1] Department of State, *Peace and War: United States Foreign Policy,
1931–1941,* pp. 494*ff.*

between China and Japan focused popular attention on the disastrous results which such legislation could produce. Had not President Roosevelt taken advantage of the technical fact that war had not been declared and refused to invoke the act in this connection, the United States would have been forced to aid Japan against China because Japan was not only effectively blockading the Chinese coast but she had the funds to buy from us and the ships in which to transport the materials.

Although there was considerable discussion in the next two years, no further amendment was made until after the actual outbreak of war in Europe. The President, as soon as hostilities had begun, imposed an arms embargo on all the belligerents which was seriously detrimental to the Allied war effort. Whereas Germany, being already rearmed, suffered relatively little, Britain and France were in the process of remedying belatedly the gaps in their equipment. In these circumstances, President Roosevelt called the Congress into special session in September, 1939. He declared to them: "I regret that the Congress passed that act [of 1937]. I regret equally that I signed that act."

The new measure, the Fourth Neutrality Act (1939), was then passed, providing that both arms and war materials might be exported to all belligerents on the "cash-and-carry" basis but that these had to be carried in non-American vessels. While, technically, Germany was permitted to trade with the United States on this basis, British superiority on the seas made this provision one which actually aided the Allies. Later, as the British progressively exhausted their resources in the United States, America was confronted with the stark fact that the "cash-and-carry" policy could not be continued indefinitely. After much heated debate, the Congress passed on March 11, 1941, the "Lend-Lease" Act (see note preceding

Document 30). This act marked the adoption of an entirely different policy; the Neutrality Act was thereby discarded.

Resolved, by the Senate and House of Representatives of the United States of America in Congress assembled,

Proclamation of a State of War between Foreign States

Section 1. (a) That whenever the President, or the Congress by concurrent resolution, shall find that there exists a state of war between foreign States, and that it is necessary to promote the security or preserve the peace of the United States or to protect the lives of citizens of the United States, the President shall issue a proclamation naming the States involved; and he shall, from time to time, by proclamation, name other States as and when they may become involved in the war.

.   .   .   .

Commerce with States Engaged in Armed Conflict

Section 2. (a) Whenever the President shall have issued a proclamation under the authority of Section 1 (a) it shall thereafter be unlawful for any American vessel to carry any passengers or any articles or materials to any State named in such proclamation.

.   .   .   .

(c) Whenever the President shall have issued a proclamation under the authority of Section 1 (a) it shall thereafter be unlawful to export or transport or attempt to export or transport, or cause to be exported or transported, from the United States to any State named in such proclamation, any articles or materials (except copyrighted articles or materials) until all right, title and interest therein shall have been transferred to some foreign government, agency, institution, association, partnership, corporation, or national. . . .

Combat Areas

Section 3. (a) Whenever the President shall have issued a proclamation under the authority of 1 (a), and he shall thereafter find that the protection of citizens of the United States so requires, he shall, by proclamation, define combat areas, and thereafter it shall be unlawful, except under such rules and regulations as may be prescribed, for any citizen of the United States or any American vessel to proceed into or through any such combat area. The combat areas so defined may be made to apply to surface vessels or aircraft, or both.

. . . .

(c) The President may from time to time modify or extend any proclamation issued under the authority of this section, and when the conditions which shall have caused him to issue any such proclamation shall have ceased to exist he shall revoke such proclamation and the provisions of this section shall thereupon cease to apply, except as to offenses committed prior to such revocation.

. . . .

Travel on Vessels of Belligerent States

Section 5. (a) Whenever the President shall have issued a proclamation under the authority of Section 1 (a) it shall thereafter be unlawful for any citizen of the United States to travel on any vessel of any State named in such proclamation, except in accordance with such rules and regulations as may be prescribed.

. . . .

Arming of American Merchant Vessels Prohibited

Section 6. Whenever the President shall have issued a proclamation under the authority of Section 1 (a), it shall thereafter be unlawful, until such proclamation is revoked, for any American vessel engaged in commerce with any foreign State to be armed, except with small arms and ammunition therefor, which the President may deem necessary and shall publicly designate for the preservation of discipline aboard any such vessel.

Financial Transactions

Section 7. (a) Whenever the President shall have issued a proclamation under the authority of Section 1 (a), it shall thereafter be unlawful for any person within the United States to purchase, sell, or exchange bonds, securities, or other obligations of the government of any State named in such proclamation, or of any political subdivision of any such State, or of any person acting for or on behalf of the government of any such State or political subdivision thereof, issued after the date of such proclamation, or to make any loan or extend any credit (other than necessary credits accruing in connection with the transmission of telegraph, cable, wireless, and telephone services) to any such government, political subdivision, or person. . . .

Solicitation and Collection of Funds and Contributions

Section 8. (a) Whenever the President shall have issued a proclamation under the authority of Section 1 (a), it shall thereafter be unlawful for any person within the United States to solicit or receive any contribution for or on behalf of the government of any State named in such proclamation or for or on behalf of any agent or instrumentality of any such State. . . .

American Republics

Section 9. This joint resolution, except Section 12, shall not apply to any American republic engaged in war against a non-American State or States, provided the American republic is not cooperating with a non-American State or States in such war.

.   .   .   .

National Munitions Control Board

Section 12 . . . (b) Every person who engages in the business of manufacturing, exporting, or importing any arms, ammunition, or implements of war listed in a proclamation issued under authority of subsection (i) of this section, whether as an exporter, importer, manufacturer or dealer, shall register with the Secretary of State his name, or business name, principal place of business, and places of business in the United States, and a list of the arms, ammunition, and implements of war which he manufactures, imports, or exports. . . .

(d) It shall be unlawful for any person to export, or attempt to export, from the United States to any other State, any arms, ammunition, or implements of war listed in a proclamation issued under the authority of subsection (i) of this section, or to import, or attempt to import, to the United States from any other State, any of the arms, ammunition, or implements of war listed in any such proclamation, without first having submitted to the Secretary of State the name of the purchaser and the terms of sale and having obtained a license therefor. . . .

THE ATLANTIC CHARTER [1]

THE ATLANTIC Charter contained the first authoritative statement of British war aims, suitable for propaganda use, which went beyond a determination to restore the *status quo* of the prewar era. It provided the ideological basis upon which the United States and Great Britain fought World War II. It should be noted that the Charter was signed *before* America entered the war and was another evidence of growing coordination of the foreign policies of the two English-speaking nations. It was another step in the long process by which America moved toward an active participation in the war.

The Atlantic Charter took the form of a statement signed by President Roosevelt and Prime Minister Churchill on August 14, 1940, and was, technically, an executive agreement. As such it did not bind subsequent administrations.

Joint Declaration of the President of the United States of America and the Prime Minister, Mr. Churchill, representing His Majesty's Government in the United Kingdom, being met together, deem it right to make known certain common principles in the national policies of their respective countries on which they base their hopes for a better future for the world.

First, their countries seek no aggrandizement, territorial or other;

Second, they desire to see no territorial changes that do not accord with the freely expressed wishes of the peoples concerned;

[1] Department of State Publication 1732, *United States Executive Agreement Series,* No. 236, Washington, 1942.

Third, they respect the right of all peoples to choose the form of government under which they will live; and they wish to see sovereign rights and self-government restored to those who have been forcibly deprived of them;

Fourth, they will endeavor, with due respect for their existing obligations, to further the enjoyment by all States, great or small, victor or vanquished, of access, on equal terms, to the trade and to the raw materials of the world which are needed for their economic prosperity;

Fifth, they desire to bring about the fullest collaboration between all nations in the economic field with the object of securing, for all, improved labor standards, economic advancement and social security;

Sixth, after the final destruction of the Nazi tyranny, they hope to see established a peace which will afford to all nations the means of dwelling in safety within their own boundaries, and which will afford assurance that all the men in all the lands may live out their lives in freedom from fear and want;

Seventh, such a peace should enable all men to traverse the high seas and oceans without hindrance;

Eighth, they believe that all of the nations of the world, for realistic as well as spiritual reasons must come to the abandonment of the use of force. Since no future peace can be maintained if land, sea or air armaments continue to be employed by nations which threaten, or may threaten, aggression outside of their frontiers, they believe, pending the establishment of a wider and permanent system of general security, that the disarmament of such nations is essential. They will likewise aid and encourage all other practicable measures which will lighten for peace-loving peoples the crushing burden of armaments.

FRANKLIN D. ROOSEVELT
WINSTON S. CHURCHILL

THE TRIPARTITE PACT [1]

AMERICAN PEACETIME conscription, extensive rearmament, and a determination to extend to Great Britain "all aid short of war" following the fall of France, confronted the Axis powers with the likelihood of American belligerency in the near future. In order, if possible, to discourage the United States from entrance into the war on the side of Britain by threatening America with a two-front war, the Tripartite Pact was concluded by Germany, Italy, and Japan on September 27, 1940. It was obviously directed against the United States (see Article 3), since Article 5 specifically exempted the provisions of the pact from applying to the Soviet Union, and all the other Great Powers were already involved.

If the pact succeeded in keeping the United States neutral, alternate and successive crises in Europe and in Asia might keep America in a state of ineffective indecision. If, on the other hand, the United States refused to heed the Axis warning, the pact would ensure that America's energies would be divided and prevent the United States' war effort from being concentrated against any one of them. When the pact failed to deter America from the policy of opposition to the Axis, Japan seized the opportunity to strike the first blow. The later decision of the United States to concentrate first on the defeat of Germany, and Germany's subsequent collapse, brought about the very danger the Axis had hoped to avoid.

---

[1] Department of State, *Foreign Relations of the United States: Japan, 1931–1941,* Vol. II, pp. 165*ff.*

. . . The Governments of Germany, Italy and Japan have agreed as follows:

Article I

Japan recognizes and respects the leadership of Germany and Italy in the establishment of a new order in Europe.

Article II

Germany and Italy recognize and respect the leadership of Japan in the establishment of a new order in Greater East Asia.

Article III

Germany, Italy and Japan agree to cooperate in their efforts on aforesaid lines. They further undertake to assist one another with all political, economic and military means when one of the three Contracting Powers is attacked by a Power at present not involved in the European war or in the Chinese-Japanese conflict.

Article IV

With the view to implementing the present Pact, Joint Technical Commissions, members of which are to be appointed by the respective Governments of Germany, Italy and Japan, will meet without delay.

Article V

Germany, Italy and Japan affirm that the aforesaid terms do not in any way affect the political status which exists at present as between each of the three Contracting parties and Soviet Russia.

THE UNITED NATIONS DECLARATION [1]

AFTER THE fall of France, Great Britain and the Dominions fought on almost alone. Allied with them were only the governments-in-exile from Nazi-occupied Europe. To these few were subsequently added other victims of Axis attack—the Soviet Union in June, 1941, and the United States in December of the same year. Many Latin-American republics then joined the great wartime coalition.

On January 1, 1942, the coalition was officially named, at President Roosevelt's suggestion, the "United Nations." Each of the twenty-six nations named in the first paragraph of the Declaration accepted the principles of the Atlantic Charter and pledged a common fight and no separate peace. The somewhat odd phraseology of (1), below, was made necessary by the fact that the Soviet Union was not at war at that time with Japan.

It was from the wartime coalition that the present organization of the United Nations grew. It is helpful in studying the organization to remember that it originated in this way and that the Charter of the United Nations (see Document 39) was framed particularly to prevent the Axis nations from again threatening the peace of the world.

A joint declaration by the United States of America, the United Kingdom of Great Britain and Northern Ireland, the Union of Soviet Socialist Republics, China, Australia, Belgium, Canada,

[1] Department of State Publication 1732, *United States Executive Agreement Series,* No. 236, Washington, 1942.

Costa Rica, Cuba, Czechoslovakia, Dominican Republic, El Salvador, Greece, Guatemala, Haiti, Honduras, India, Luxembourg, Netherlands, New Zealand, Nicaragua, Norway, Panama, Poland, South Africa, Yugoslavia.

The Governments signatory hereto,

Having subscribed to a common program of purposes and principles embodied in the Joint Declaration of the President of the United States of America and the Prime Minister of the United Kingdom of Great Britain and Northern Ireland dated August 14, 1941, known as the Atlantic Charter,

Being convinced that complete victory over their enemies is essential to defend life, liberty, independence and religious freedom, and to preserve human rights and justice in their own lands as well as in other lands, and that they are now engaged in a common struggle against savage and brutal forces seeking to subjugate the world, declare:

(1) Each Government pledges itself to employ its full resources, military or economic, against those members of the Tripartite Pact and its adherents with which such government is at war.

(2) Each Government pledges itself to cooperate with the Governments signatory hereto and not to make a separate armistice or peace with the enemies.

The foregoing declaration may be adhered to by other nations which are, or which may be, rendering material assistance and contributions in the struggle for victory over Hitlerism.

LEND-LEASE AGREEMENT OF THE UNITED STATES AND GREAT BRITAIN [1]

THE LEND-LEASE Act of March 11, 1941, made it possible to transform the United States, in President Roosevelt's phrase, into "the arsenal of democracy" even before our official entry into the war. By this means the productive capacity of America was harnessed to provide the sinews of war to what ultimately became the United Nations (see Document 29).

Aid unparalleled in the history of coalition warfare was thus made available to our allies. Some fifty billions of dollars were ultimately appropriated by Congress for this purpose, with over eleven billions' worth of material shipped abroad, mainly to Great Britain and the Soviet Union.

The Lend-Lease Agreement of February 23, 1942, between the United States and Great Britain (below) is typical of those later concluded as well with the other United Nations under the authority of the Lend-Lease Act.

Article I

The Government of the United States of America will continue to supply the Government of the United Kingdom with such defense articles, defense services, and defense information as the President shall authorize to be transferred or provided.

Article II

The Government of the United Kingdom will continue to contribute to the defense of the United States of America and

[1] Department of State Publication 1790, *United States Executive Agreement Series,* No. 241, Washington, 1942.

the strengthening thereof and will provide such articles, services, facilities or information as it may be in a position to supply.

Article III

The Government of the United Kingdom will not without the consent of the President of the United States of America transfer title to, or possession of, any defense article or defense information transferred to it under the Act or permit the use thereof by anyone not an officer, employee, or agent of the Government of the United Kingdom.

Article IV

If, as a result of the transfer to the Government of the United Kingdom of any defense article or defense information, it becomes necessary for that Government to take any action or make any payment in order fully to protect any of the rights of a citizen of the United States of America who has patent rights in and to any such defense article or information, the Government of the United Kingdom will take such action or make such payment when requested to do so by the President of the United States of America.

Article V

The Government of the United Kingdom will return to the United States of America at the end of the present emergency, as determined by the President, such defense articles transferred under this Agreement as shall not have been destroyed, lost or consumed and as shall be determined by the President to be useful in the defense of the United States of America or of the Western Hemisphere or to be otherwise of use to the United States of America.

Article VI

In the final determination of the benefits to be provided to the United States of America by the Government of the United Kingdom full cognizance shall be taken of all property, services, information, facilities, or other benefits or considerations provided by the Government of the United Kingdom subsequent to March 11, 1941, and accepted or acknowledged by the President on behalf of the United States of America.

Article VII

In the final determination of the benefits to be provided to the United States of America by the Government of the United Kingdom in return for aid furnished under the Act of Congress of March 11, 1941, the terms and conditions thereof shall be such as not to burden commerce between the two countries, but to promote mutually advantageous economic relations between them and the betterment of world-wide economic relations. To that end, they shall include provision for agreed action by the United States of America and the United Kingdom, open to participation by all other countries of like mind, directed to the expansion, by appropriate international and domestic measures, of production, employment, and the exchange and consumption of goods, which are the material foundations of the liberty and welfare of all peoples; to the elimination of all forms of discriminatory treatment in international commerce, and to the reduction of tariffs and other trade barriers; and, in general, to the attainment of all the economic objectives set forth in the Joint Declaration made on August 14, 1941, by the President of the United States of America and the Prime Minister of the United Kingdom.

At an early convenient date, conversations shall be begun between the two Governments with a view to determining, in the light of governing economic conditions, the best means of attaining the above-stated objectives by their own agreed action and of seeking the agreed action of other like-minded Governments.

Article VIII

This Agreement shall take effect as from this day's date. It shall continue in force until a date to be agreed upon by the two Governments.

THE ANGLO-SOVIET TREATY OF ALLIANCE [1]

THE ANGLO-SOVIET Treaty of Alliance, signed on May 26, 1942, came into force following the exchange of ratifications at Moscow on July 4, 1942. It is divided into two parts: Part I is to be in effect until Great Britain and the Soviet Union have concluded peace with Germany. Treaties of peace have already been agreed to by these powers for the other Axis allies in Europe mentioned in the treaty.

Article 7 provides that each party will refrain from concluding any alliance directed against the other party. The Soviet Union claimed (see note preceding Document 50) that Great Britain violated the treaty by ratifying the North Atlantic Pact. The Russians consider the Atlantic Pact as directed against themselves. In the face of East-West tension and while Germany remains disarmed and therefore not an active threat, it is likely that this treaty will remain a reflection of past events rather than an indication of future alignments. Nevertheless, the treaty is still in effect.

PART I

Article 1

In virtue of the alliance established between the United Kingdom and the Union of Soviet Socialist Republics, the high contracting parties mutually undertake to afford one another military and other assistance and support of all kinds in war against

[1] *Great Britain, Treaty Series,* No. 2 (1942), *Command Paper* No. 6376.

Germany and all those States which are associated with her in acts of aggression in Europe.

Article 2

The high contracting parties undertake not to enter into any negotiations with the Hitlerite Government or any other government in Germany that does not clearly renounce all aggressive intentions, and not to negotiate or conclude, except by mutual consent, any armistice or peace treaty with Germany or any other State associated with her in acts of aggression in Europe.

PART II

Article 3

1. The high contracting parties declare their desire to unite with other like-minded States in adopting proposals for common action to preserve peace and resist aggression in the post-war period.

2. Pending adoption of such proposals, they will after the termination of hostilities take all the measures in their power to render impossible a repetition of aggression and violation of the peace by Germany or any of the States associated with her in acts of aggression in Europe.

Article 4

Should one of the high contracting parties during the post-war period become involved in hostilities with Germany or any of the States mentioned in Article 3, Section 2, in consequence of the attack by that State against that party, the other high contracting party will at once give to the contracting party so involved in hostilities all military and other support and assistance in his power.

This article shall remain in force until the high contracting parties, by mutual agreement, shall recognize that it is superseded by adoption of the proposals contemplated in Article 3, (1). In default of the adoption of such proposals, it shall remain

in force for a period of twenty years and thereafter until terminated by either high contracting party as provided in Article 8.

Article 5

The high contracting parties, having regard to the interests of
the security of each of them, agree to work together in close and
friendly collaboration after re-establishment of peace for the organization of security and economic prosperity in Europe.

They will take into account the interests of the United Nations in these objects and they will act in accordance with the
two principles of not seeking territorial aggrandizement for
themselves and of non-interference in the internal affairs of other
States.

Article 6

The high contracting parties agree to render one another all
possible economic assistance after the war.

Article 7

Each high contracting party undertakes not to conclude any
alliance and not to take part in any coalition directed against
the other high contracting party.

Article 8

The present Treaty is subject to ratification in the shortest possible time and instruments of ratification shall be exchanged in
Moscow as soon as possible. . . .

Part I of the present Treaty shall remain in force until the re-
establishment of peace between the high contracting parties and
Germany and the powers associated with her in acts of aggression in Europe.

Part II of the present Treaty shall remain in force for a period
of twenty years. Thereafter, unless twelve months' notice has
been given by either party to terminate the Treaty at the end of
the said period of twenty years, it shall continue in force until
twelve months after either high contracting party shall have
given notice to the other in writing of his intention to terminate it. . . .

DISSOLUTION OF THE COMINTERN [1]

THE RESOLUTION of the Presidium of the Communist International, issued in Moscow on May 22, 1943, dissolving the Comintern (the Communist International), marked the high-water mark of friendly feelings among the Big Three. Its existence had been an active cause of dissension, and its termination gave rise to hopes in the Western world that the Soviet Union had abandoned her plans for world revolution. These hopes were short-lived. Even before the definitive defeat of the Axis, disturbing signs of increasing friction began to appear. These were the first symptoms of what broadened into the cold war.

In September of 1947, a conference of Communist party representatives from Yugoslavia, Poland, Bulgaria, Rumania, Hungary, Russia, Czechoslovakia, Italy, and France met in Poland and drafted a declaration which said in part:

Fundamental changes have taken place in the international situation as a result of the Second World War and in the post-war period. . . . The Soviet Union and the other democratic countries regarded as their basic war aims the restoration and consolidation of democratic order in Europe, the eradication of fascism and the prevention of the possibility of new aggression on the part of Germany, and the establishment of a lasting all-round cooperation among the nations of Europe. The United States of America, and Britain in agreement with them, set themselves another aim in the war: to rid themselves of competitors on the markets (Germany and Japan) and to establish their dominant position. This difference in the definition of war aims

[1] *New York Times,* May 23, 1943.

and the tasks of the post-war settlement grew more profound after the war. . . .

Under these circumstances it is necessary that the antiimperialist, democratic camp should close its ranks, draw up an agreed program of actions and work out its own tactics against the main forces of the imperialist camp, against American imperialism and its British and French allies, against the right-wing Socialists, primarily in Britain and France.[2]

Accordingly, a resolution was adopted which said in part:

The Conference states that the absence of contacts among the Communist Parties participating at this Conference is a serious shortcoming in the present situation. Experience has shown that such lack of contacts among the Communist Parties is wrong and harmful. . . .[3]

To remedy the situation, a Communist Information Bureau was to be created at Belgrade to organize "interchange of experience, and if need be, coordination of the activities of the Communist Parties on the basis of mutual agreement" (Article 2 of the resolution). On October 5, 1947, it was announced from Moscow that the newly formed Communist Information Bureau, or Cominform, would, as its first activity, oppose the "Truman-Marshall Plan." Thus, after four years, the Comintern was succeeded by a very similar Cominform.

The historic role of the Communist International, which was founded in 1919 as a result of a political union of the great majority of the old prewar working-class parties, consisted in upholding the principles of the working-class movement, in helping to promote consolidation in a number of countries of the vanguard of the foremost workers in the real working-class parties,

[2] *North Atlantic Treaty*, Senate Document No. 48, 81st Congress, 1st Session, pp. 116*ff*.

[3] *Ibid.*

and in helping them mobilize workers for the defense of their economic and political interests, and for the struggle against Fascism and the war which the latter was preparing, and for the support of the Soviet Union as the chief bulwark against Fascism.

The Communist International from the first exposed the real meaning of the Anti-Comintern Pact as a weapon for the preparation of war by the Hitlerites. Long before the war it ceaselessly and tirelessly exposed the vicious, subversive work of the Hitlerites, who masked it by their screams about so-called interference of the Communist International in the internal affairs of these states.

But long before the war it became more and more clear that, with increasing complications in internal and international relations of various countries, any sort of international center would encounter insuperable obstacles in solving the problems facing the movement in each separate country.

Deep differences of the historic paths of development of various countries, differences in their character and even contradictions in their social orders, differences in the level and the tempo of their economic and political development, differences finally in the degree of consciousness and organization of workers, conditioned different problems affecting the working class of the various countries.

The whole development of events in the last quarter of a century and the experience accumulated by the Communist International convincingly showed that the organizational form of uniting workers, chosen by the First Congress of the Communist International, answered conditions of the first stages of the working-class movement, but it has been outgrown by the growth of this movement and by the complications of its problems in separate countries and has even become a drag on the further strengthening of the national working-class parties.

The World War that the Hitlerites have let loose has still further sharpened the differences in the situation of the separate countries and has placed a deep dividing line between those countries that fell under the Hitlerite tyranny and those freedom-loving peoples who have united in a powerful anti-Hitlerite coalition.

In countries of the Hitlerite bloc the fundamental task of the working class, toilers and all honest people consists in giving all help for the defeat of this bloc by sabotage of the Hitlerite military machine from within and by helping to overthrow the governments guilty of war.

In countries of the anti-Hitlerite coalition the sacred duty of the widest masses of the people, and in the first place of foremost workers, consists in aiding by every means the military efforts of the governments of these countries aimed at the speediest defeat of the Hitlerite bloc and the assurance of the friendship of nations based on their equality.

At the same time the fact must not be lost sight of that the separate countries that are members of the anti-Hitlerite coalition have their own particular problems. For example, in countries occupied by the Hitlerites that have lost their state of independence the basic task of the foremost workers and of the wide masses of people consists in promoting the armed struggle developing into a national war of liberation against Hitlerite Germany.

At the same time the war of liberation of freedom-loving peoples against the Hitlerite tyranny, which has brought into movement the masses of people, uniting them without difference of party or religion in the ranks of the powerful anti-Hitlerite coalition, has demonstrated with still greater clearness that the general national uprising and mobilization of people for the speediest victory over the enemy can be best of all and most fruitfully carried out by the vanguard of the working-class movement of each separate country, working within the framework of its own country.

Already the Seventh Congress of the Communist International meeting in 1935, taking into account the change that had taken place both in the international situation and in working-class movements that demanded great flexibility and independence of its sections in deciding the problems confronting them, emphasized the necessity for the Executive Committee of the Communist International, in deciding all questions of the working-class movement arising from concrete conditions and peculiarities of each country, to make a rule of avoiding interference in the internal organizational affairs of the Communist parties.

These same considerations guided the Communist International in considering the resolution of the Communist party of the United States of America of November 1940, on its withdrawal from the ranks of the Communist International.

Guided by the judgment of the founders of Marxism and Leninism, Communists have never been supporters of the conservation of organizational forms that have outlived themselves. They have always subordinated forms of organization of the working-class movement, and methods of working of such organization, to the fundamental political interest of the working-class movement as a whole, to peculiarities of the concrete historical situation and to problems immediately resulting from this situation.

They remember the example of the great Marx, who united foremost workers in the ranks of the Working Men's International Association, and when the First International had fulfilled its historical task of laying the foundations for the development of working-class parties in the countries of Europe and America, and, as a result of the matured situation creating mass national working-class parties, dissolved first the International, inasmuch as this form of organization already no longer corresponded to the demands confronting it.

In consideration of the above and taking into account the growth and the political maturity of Communist parties and their leading cadres in separate countries, and also having in view the fact that during the present war some sections have raised the question of the dissolution of the Communist International as the directing center of the international working-class movement, the Presidium of the Executive Committee of the Communist International, in the circumstances of the World War, not being able to convene a Congress of the Communist International, puts forward the following proposal for ratification by the sections of the Communist International:

The Communist International, as the directing center of the international working-class movement, is to be dissolved, thus freeing the sections of the Communist International from their obligations arising from the statutes and resolutions of the Congresses of the Communist International.

The Presidium of the Executive Committee of the Communist International calls on all supporters of the Communist International to concentrate their energies on the whole-hearted support of and active participation in the war of liberation of the peoples and the states of the anti-Hitlerite coalition for the speediest defeat of the deadly enemy of the working class and toilers—German Fascism and its associates and vassals.

THE MOSCOW DECLARATIONS[1]

THE FIRST wartime conference to achieve a significant degree of coordination among the United States, Great Britain, and the Soviet Union was held in Moscow, October 19 to October 30, 1943. It was attended by the foreign ministers of the Big Three. The communiqué which follows was released on November 1, 1943, and was signed by the United States, Great Britain, and the Soviet Union. The Declaration on Security was signed in addition by the Chinese Ambassador to Moscow on behalf of China. China was not, however, a party to the other declarations which related to European affairs.

In the Declaration on Security, the Soviet Union, together with the other three powers, agreed to the formation of what ultimately became the United Nations organization.

Declaration on General Security:

The Governments of the United States of America, the United Kingdom, the Soviet Union and China: united in their determination, in accordance with the Declaration by the United Nations of January 1, 1942, and subsequent declarations, to continue hostilities against those Axis powers with which they respectively are at war until such powers have laid down their arms on the basis of unconditional surrender; conscious of their responsibility to secure the liberation of themselves and the peoples allied with them from the menace of aggression; recognizing the necessity of ensuring a rapid and orderly transition from war to peace and of establishing and maintaining international peace

[1] *Department of State Bulletin,* Vol. IX, pp. 307*ff.*

and security with the least diversion of the world's human and economic resources for armaments; jointly declare:

1. That their united action, pledged for the prosecution of the war against their respective enemies, will be continued for the organization and maintenance of peace and security.

2. That those of them at war with a common enemy will act together in all matters relating to the surrender and disarmament of that enemy.

3. That they will take all measures deemed by them to be necessary to provide against any violation of the terms imposed upon the enemy.

4. That they recognize the necessity of establishing at the earliest practicable date a general international organization, based on the principle of the sovereign equality of all peace-loving states, and open to membership by all such states, large and small, for the maintenance of international peace and security.

5. That for the purpose of maintaining international peace and security pending the reestablishment of law and order and the inauguration of a system of general security, they will consult with one another and as occasion requires with other members of the United Nations with a view to joint action on behalf of the community of nations.

6. That after the termination of hostilities they will not employ their military forces within the territories of other states except for the purposes envisaged in this declaration and after joint consultation.

7. That they will confer and co-operate with one another and with other members of the United Nations to bring about a practicable general agreement with respect to the regulation of armaments in the post-war period.

Declaration on Italy:

The Foreign Secretaries of the United States of America, the United Kingdom and the Soviet Union have established that their three Governments are in complete agreement that Allied policy towards Italy must be based upon the fundamental principle that Fascism and all its evil influences and emanations shall be utterly destroyed and that the Italian people shall be given every opportunity to establish governmental and other institutions based upon democratic principles.

The Foreign Secretaries of the United States of America and the United Kingdom declare that the action of their Governments from the inception of the invasion of Italian territory, in so far as paramount military requirements have permitted, has been based upon this policy.

In the furtherance of this policy in the future the Foreign Secretaries of the three Governments are agreed that the following measures are important and should be put into effect:

1. It is essential that the Italian Government should be made more democratic by the introduction of representatives of those sections of the Italian people who have always opposed Fascism.

2. Freedom of speech, of religious worship, of political belief, of the press and of public meeting shall be restored in full measure to the Italian people, who shall also be entitled to form anti-Fascist political groups.

3. All institutions and organizations created by the Fascist regime shall be suppressed.

4. All Fascist or pro-Fascist elements shall be removed from the administration and from the institutions and organizations of a public character.

5. All political prisoners of the Fascist regime shall be released and accorded a full amnesty.

6. Democratic organs of local government shall be created.

7. Fascist chiefs and other persons known or suspected to be war criminals shall be arrested and handed over to justice.

In making this declaration the three Foreign Secretaries recognize that so long as active military operations continue in Italy the time at which it is possible to give full effect to the principles set out above will be determined by the Commander-in-Chief on the basis of instructions received through the Combined Chiefs of Staff. The three Governments parties to this declaration will at the request of any one of them consult on this matter.

It is further understood that nothing in this resolution is to operate against the right of the Italian people ultimately to choose their own form of government.

Declaration on Austria:

The Governments of the United Kingdom, the Soviet Union and the United States of America are agreed that Austria, the first free country to fall a victim to Hitlerite aggression, shall be liberated from German domination.

They regard the annexation imposed upon Austria by Germany on March 15, 1938, as null and void. They consider themselves as in no way bound by any changes effected in Austria since that date. They declare that they wish to see reestablished a free and independent Austria, and thereby to open the way for the Austrian people themselves, as well as those neighboring states which will be faced with similar problems, to find that political and economic security which is the only basis for lasting peace.

Austria is reminded, however, that she has a responsibility which she cannot evade for participation in the war on the side of Hitlerite Germany, and that in the final settlement account will inevitably be taken of her own contribution to her liberation.

Declaration on German Atrocities:

The United Kingdom, the United States and the Soviet Union have received from many quarters evidence of atrocities, massacres and cold-blooded mass executions which are being perpetrated by the Hitlerite forces in the many countries they have overrun and from which they are now being steadily expelled. The brutalities of Hitlerite domination are no new thing and all the peoples or territories in their grip have suffered from the worst form of government by terror. What is new is that many of these territories are now being redeemed by the advancing armies of the liberating Powers and that in their desperation, the recoiling Hitlerite Huns are redoubling their ruthless cruelties. This is now evidenced with particular clearness by monstrous crimes of the Hitlerites on the territory of the Soviet Union which is being liberated from the Hitlerites, and on French and Italian territory.

Accordingly, the aforesaid three allied Powers, speaking in the interests of the thirty-three United Nations, hereby solemnly declare and give full warning of their declaration as follows:

At the time of the granting of any armistice to any government which may be set up in Germany, those German officers and men and members of the Nazi party who have been responsible for, or have taken a consenting part in the above atrocities, massacres and executions, will be sent back to the countries in which their abominable deeds were done in order that they may be judged and punished according to the laws of these liberated countries and of the free governments which will be created therein. Lists will be compiled in all possible detail from all these countries having regard especially to the invaded parts of the Soviet Union, to Poland and Czechoslovakia, to Yugoslavia and Greece, including Crete and other islands, to Norway, Denmark, the Netherlands, Belgium, Luxemburg, France and Italy.

Thus, the Germans who take part in wholesale shootings of Italian officers or in the execution of French, Dutch, Belgian or Norwegian hostages or of Cretan peasants, or who have shared in the slaughters inflicted on the people of Poland or in territories of the Soviet Union which are now being swept clear of the enemy, will know that they will be brought back to the scene of their crimes and judged on the spot by the peoples whom they have outraged. Let those who have hitherto not imbrued their hands with innocent blood beware lest they join the ranks of the guilty, for most assuredly the three allied Powers will pursue them to the uttermost ends of the earth and will deliver them to their accusers in order that justice may be done.

The above declaration is without prejudice to the case of the major criminals, whose offenses have no particular geographical localization and who will be punished by the joint decision of the Governments of the Allies.

THE CAIRO CONFERENCE [1]

PRESIDENT ROOSEVELT and Prime Minister Churchill conferred with Generalissimo Chiang Kai-shek at Cairo from November 22 to November 25, 1943. China was promised the return of all territories taken from her by Japan since 1914. Korea, it was agreed, would become "free and independent." The Soviet Union, since it was not at war with Japan, was not represented at the conference and was not a party to the agreement given in the official communiqué below which was signed by the United States, Great Britain, and China. As a result, the agreement of Russia had to be obtained subsequently—especially regarding Korea.

The several military missions have agreed upon future military operations against Japan. The Three Great Allies expressed their resolve to bring unrelenting pressure against their brutal enemies by sea, land, and air. This pressure is already rising.

The Three Great Allies are fighting this war to restrain and punish the aggression of Japan. They covet no gain for themselves and have no thought of territorial expansion. It is their purpose that Japan shall be stripped of all the islands in the Pacific which she has seized or occupied since the beginning of the first World War in 1914, and that all the territories Japan has stolen from the Chinese, such as Manchuria, Formosa, and the Pescadores, shall be restored to the Republic of China. Japan will also be expelled from all other territories which she has taken by violence and greed. The aforesaid three great powers,

[1] *Department of State Bulletin,* Vol. IX, p. 393.

mindful of the enslavement of the people of Korea, are determined that in due course Korea shall become free and independent.

With these objects in view the three Allies, in harmony with those of the United Nations at war with Japan, will continue to persevere in the serious and prolonged operations necessary to procure the unconditional surrender of Japan.

THE TEHERAN CONFERENCE [1]

THE TEHERAN Conference communiqué of December 1, 1943, signed by the United States, Great Britain, and the Soviet Union, consisted of three parts: a Declaration of the Three Powers, a Declaration Regarding Iran, and a Secret Protocol. The first part is reproduced below. The Declaration Regarding Iran expressed the "desire" of the Big Three "for the maintenance of the independence, sovereignty and territorial integrity of Iran." The postwar status of Iran was thus one of the first of the many similar problems which were disposed of in subsequent conferences. The Secret Protocol, not released until March 24, 1947, provided for an offensive to be launched by the Russians to coincide with the approaching landings in Normandy. It was further agreed that Turkey would be urged to enter the war and that the Yugoslav partisans, under the leadership of Marshal Tito, would be supported by the three powers "to the greatest possible extent," since they were actively harassing the German forces in Yugoslavia.

The Teheran Conference brought President Roosevelt face to face with Marshal Stalin for the first time. It was the first of the conferences to be attended by all three heads of state. That the meeting was successful in establishing a working personal relationship among them is evident from the communiqué which reflects the good feeling which animated the conference.

---

[1] *Department of State Bulletin*, Vol. IX, pp. 409*ff*.

We—The President of the United States, the Prime Minister of Great Britain, and the Premier of the Soviet Union, have met these four days past, in this, the Capital of our Ally, Iran, and have shaped and confirmed our common policy.

We express our determination that our nations shall work together in war and in the peace that will follow.

As to war—our military staffs have joined in our round table discussions, and we have concerted our plans for the destruction of the German forces. We have reached complete agreement as to the scope and timing of the operations to be undertaken from the east, west and south.

The common understanding which we have here reached guarantees that victory will be ours.

And as to peace—we are sure that our concord will win an enduring Peace. We recognize fully the supreme responsibility resting upon us and all the United Nations to make a peace which will command the goodwill of the overwhelming mass of the peoples of the world and banish the scourge and terror of war for many generations.

With our Diplomatic advisors we have surveyed the problems of the future. We shall seek the cooperation and active participation of all nations, large and small, whose peoples in heart and mind are dedicated, as are our own peoples, to the elimination of tyranny and slavery, oppression and intolerance. We will welcome them, as they may choose to come, into a world family of Democratic Nations.

No power on earth can prevent our destroying the German armies by land, their U Boats by sea, and their war plants from the air.

Our attack will be relentless and increasing.

Emerging from these cordial conferences we look with confidence to the day when all peoples of the world may live free lives, untouched by tyranny, and according to their varying desires and their own consciences.

We came here with hope and determination. We leave here, friends in fact, in spirit and in purpose.

ROOSEVELT, CHURCHILL AND STALIN

THE FRANCO-SOVIET TREATY
OF ALLIANCE OF 1944 [1]

LIKE THE Anglo-Soviet Treaty of Alliance, the Franco-Soviet treaty contains a stipulation (Article V) that neither party will "conclude alliances" or "participate in any coalition directed against one of them." Since the Soviet Union construed the North Atlantic Pact (to which France is a party) as an alliance directed against her (see Document 50), in her view France has violated the treaty.

Under conditions of tension between the East and West, the treaty remains a reflection of past rather than present conditions. The French, however, remain concerned with the possibility of German rearmament; to the extent that this occurs in the next few years the alliance may take on new life.

The treaty was signed on December 10, 1944.

Article I

Each of the high contracting parties shall continue the struggle on the side of the other party and on the side of the United Nations until final victory over Germany. Each of the high contracting parties undertakes to render the other party aid and assistance in this struggle with all the means at its disposal.

Article II

The high contracting parties shall not agree to enter into separate negotiations with Germany or to conclude, without mutual consent, any armistice or peace treaty either with the

[1] *Department of State Bulletin*, Vol. XII, pp. 39*ff.*

Hitler Government or with any other government or authority set up in Germany for the purpose of the continuation or support of the policy of German aggression.

Article III

The high contracting parties undertake also after the termination of the present war with Germany, to take jointly all necessary measures for the elimination of any new threat coming from Germany and to obstruct such actions as would make possible any new attempt at aggression on her part.

Article IV

In the event either of the high contracting parties finds itself involved in military operations against Germany, whether as a result of aggression committed by the latter or as a result of the operation of the above Article III, the other party shall at once render it every aid and assistance within its power.

Article V

The high contracting parties undertake not to conclude any alliance and not to take part in any coalition directed against either of the high contracting parties.

Article VI

The high contracting parties agree to render each other every possible economic assistance after the war with a view to facilitating and accelerating reconstruction of both countries and in order to contribute to the cause of world prosperity.

Article VII

The present treaty does not in any way affect obligations undertaken previously by the high contracting parties in regard to third states in virtue of published treaties.

Article VIII

The present treaty, whose Russian and French texts are equally valid, shall be ratified and ratification instruments shall be exchanged in Paris as early as possible. It comes into force from the moment of the exchange of ratification instruments and shall be valid for twenty years. If the treaty is not denounced by either of the high contracting parties at least one year before the expiration of this term, it shall remain valid for an unlimited time; each of the high contracting parties will be able to terminate its operation by giving notice to that effect one year in advance.

THE CRIMEA (YALTA) CONFERENCE [1]

THE YALTA Conference met in the Crimea from February 4 to February 11, 1945. It was attended by the Big Three heads of state. The Protocol of the Crimea Conference (below), signed by the United States, Great Britain, and the Soviet Union, was issued in its entirety on March 24, 1947. Previously, the agreements contained therein had been released from time to time as follows: on February 11, 1945, sections II, VI to VIII, and XIII; on March 5, 1945, the invitation to the San Francisco Conference (in section I); on February 11, 1946, the supplemental Yalta agreement on the Far East; on March 19, 1947, section V; on March 24, 1947, sections III, IV, IX to XII, and XIV. The remaining portion of section I, relating to the admission of two Soviet Republics, was made known at the San Francisco Conference.

The invitations to the United Nations Conference on International Organization were extended in the name of the Big Three plus China. France, which had not taken part in the Dumbarton Oaks conversations which gave rise to the preliminary plans for the organization of the United Nations, declined the invitation to be a sponsoring government, although she became an original member of the United Nations.

The "Yalta voting formula" (see section I) subsequently became Article 27 of the UN Charter. The only changes which were made in it were changes of references—Chapter VIII, Section A, and Chapter VIII, Section C, paragraph 1

[1] *Department of State Press Release,* No. 239, Mar. 24, 1947.

of the Dumbarton Oaks Agreement becoming respectively Chapter VI and Article 52, paragraph 3 of the Charter (see also Documents 38 and 39).

The most controversial of the Yalta agreements was that pertaining to the Far East in which Russia was assured the Kurile Islands, as well as other gains—in effect restoring to the Russians their position prior to the Russo-Japanese War. This was kept secret until after the war in both Europe and Asia was over. The grounds for keeping it secret until Russia was able to declare war on Japan are obvious. The wisdom of keeping it secret beyond that time is debatable. The further criticism has been made that decisions affecting China's future were made without the participation of China in the Conference. Nationalist China subsequently concurred in these decisions although it might plausibly be argued that her freedom of action was seriously curtailed. In any case, the provisions reinforced in the American people a suspicion of secret arrangements which has attached to the name "Yalta" a connotation not necessarily justified by the actual content of the agreements made there.

I. World Organization

It was decided:

1. That a United Nations Conference on the proposed world organization should be summoned for Wednesday, 25 April, 1945, and should be held in the United States of America.

2. The nations to be invited to this Conference should be:

(a) The United Nations as they existed on 8 February, 1945; and

(b) Such of the Associated Nations as have declared war on the common enemy by 1 March, 1945. (For this purpose, by the term "Associated Nations" was meant the eight Associated Nations and Turkey.) When the Conference on World Organization is held, the delegates of the United Kingdom and United States of America will support a proposal to admit to original membership two Soviet Socialist Republics, *i.e.,* the Ukraine and White Russia.

3. That the United States Government, on behalf of the three Powers, should consult the Government of China and the French Provisional Government in regard to decisions taken at the present Conference concerning the proposed World Organization.

4. That the text of the invitation to be issued to all the nations which would take part in the United Nations Conference should be as follows:

Invitation

"The Government of the United States of America on behalf of itself and the Governments of the United Kingdom, the Union of Soviet Socialist Republics, and the Republic of China and of the Provisional Government of the French Republic, invite the Government of —— to send representatives to a Conference of the United Nations to be held on the 25th of April, 1945, or soon thereafter, at San Francisco, in the United States of America to prepare for a General International Organization for the maintenance of international peace and security.

"The above named Governments suggest that the Conference consider as affording a basis for such a Charter the Proposals for the Establishment of a General International Organization which were made public last October as a result of the Dumbarton Oaks Conference, and which have now been supplemented by the following provisions for Section C of Chapter VI:

C. Voting

" '1. Each member of the Security Council should have one vote.

" '2. Decisions of the Security Council on procedural matters should be made by an affirmative vote of seven members.

" '3. Decisions of the Security Council on all other matters should be made by an affirmative vote of seven members including the concurring votes of the permanent members; provided that, in decisions under Chapter VIII, Section A and under the second sentence of paragraph 1 of Chapter VIII, Section C, a party to a dispute should abstain from voting.'

"Further information as to arrangements will be transmitted subsequently. . . ."

Territorial trusteeship:

It was agreed that the five nations which will have permanent seats on the Security Council should consult each other prior to the United Nations Conference on the question of territorial trusteeship.

The acceptance of this recommendation is subject to its being made clear that territorial trusteeship will only apply to (a) existing mandates of the League of Nations; (b) territories detached from the enemy as a result of the present war; (c) any other territory which might voluntarily be placed under trusteeship; and (d) no discussion of actual territories is contemplated at the forthcoming United Nations Conference or in the preliminary consultations, and it will be a matter for subsequent agreement which territories within the above categories will be placed under trusteeship.

II. Declaration on Liberated Europe

The following declaration has been approved:

"The Premier of the Union of Soviet Socialist Republics, the Prime Minister of the United Kingdom and the President of the United States of America have consulted with each other in the common interests of the peoples of their countries and those of liberated Europe. They jointly declare their mutual agreement to concert during the temporary period of instability in liberated Europe the policies of their three Governments in assisting the peoples liberated from the domination of Nazi Germany and the peoples of the former Axis satellite States of Europe to solve by democratic means their pressing political and economic problems.

"The establishment of order in Europe and the rebuilding of national economic life must be achieved by processes which will enable the liberated peoples to destroy the last vestiges of Nazism and Fascism and to create democratic institutions of their own choice. This is a principle of the Atlantic Charter—the right of all peoples to choose the form of government under which they will live—the restoration of sovereign rights and self-government to those peoples who have been forcibly deprived of them by the aggressor nations.

"To foster the conditions in which the liberated peoples may exercise these rights, the three Governments will jointly assist the people in any European liberated State or former Axis satellite State in Europe where in their judgment conditions require (a) to establish conditions of internal peace; (b) to carry out emergency measures for the relief of distressed peoples; (c) to form interim governmental authorities broadly representative of all democratic elements in the population and pledged to the earliest possible establishment through free elections of Governments responsive to the will of the people; and (d) to facilitate where necessary the holding of such elections.

"The three Governments will consult the other United Nations and provisional authorities or other Governments in Europe when matters of direct interest to them are under consideration.

"When, in the opinion of the three Governments, conditions in any European liberated State or any former Axis satellite State in Europe make such action necessary, they will immediately consult together on the measures necessary to discharge the joint responsibilities set forth in this declaration.

"By this declaration we reaffirm our faith in the principles of the Atlantic Charter, our pledge in the Declaration by the United Nations, and our determination to build in cooperation with other peace-loving nations world order under law, dedicated to peace, security, freedom and general well-being of all mankind.

"In issuing this declaration, the three Powers express the hope that the Provisional Government of the French Republic may be associated with them in the procedure suggested."

III. Dismemberment of Germany

It was agreed that Article 12 (a) of the Surrender Terms for Germany should be amended to read as follows:

"The United Kingdom, the United States of America and the Union of Soviet Socialist Republics shall possess supreme authority with respect to Germany. In the case of such authority they will take such steps, including the complete disarmament, demilitarization and dismemberment of Germany as they deem requisite for future peace and security."

The study of the procedure of the dismemberment of Germany was referred to a Committee. . . .

IV. Zone of Occupation for the French and Control Council for Germany

It was agreed that a zone in Germany, to be occupied by the French forces, should be allocated to France. This zone would be formed out of the British and American zones and its extent would be settled by the British and Americans in consultation with the French Provisional Government.

It was also agreed that the French Provisional Government should be invited to become a member of the Allied Control Council for Germany.

V. Reparation

The following protocol has been approved:

Protocol on the Talks Between the Heads of Three Governments At the Crimean Conference on the German Reparations in Kind

1. Germany must pay in kind for the losses caused by her to the Allied nations in the course of the war. Reparations are to be received in the first instance by those countries which have borne the main burden of the war, have suffered the heaviest losses and have organized victory over the enemy.

2. Reparation in kind is to be exacted from Germany in three following forms:

(a) Removals within two years from the surrender of Germany or the cessation of organized resistance from the national wealth of Germany located on the territory of Germany herself as well as outside her territory (equipment, machine-tools, ships, rolling stock, German investments abroad, shares of industrial, transport and other enterprises in Germany, etc.), these removals to be carried out chiefly for purpose of destroying the war potential of Germany.

(b) Annual deliveries of goods from current production for a period to be fixed.

(c) Use of German labor.

3. For the working out on the above principles of a detailed plan for exaction of reparation from Germany an Allied Reparation Commission will be set up in Moscow. It will consist of three representatives—one from the Union of Soviet Socialist Republics, one from the United Kingdom and one from the United States of America.

4. With regard to the fixing of the total sum of the reparation as well as the distribution of it among the countries which suffered from the German aggression, the Soviet and American delegations agreed as follows:

"The Moscow Reparation Commission should take in its initial studies as a basis for discussion the suggestion of the Soviet Government that the total sum of the reparation in accordance with the points (a) and (b) of the Paragraph 2 should be 20 billion dollars and that 50 per cent of it should go to the Union of Soviet Socialist Republics."

The British delegation was of the opinion that pending consideration of the reparation question by the Moscow Reparation Commission no figures of reparation should be mentioned.

The above Soviet-American proposal has been passed to the Moscow Reparation Commission as one of the proposals to be considered by the Commission.

. . . .

VII. Poland

The following declaration on Poland was agreed by the Conference:

"A new situation has been created in Poland as a result of her complete liberation by the Red Army. This calls for the establishment of a Polish Provisional Government which can be more broadly based than was possible before the recent liberation of the western part of Poland. The Provisional Government which is now functioning in Poland should therefore be reorganized on a broader democratic basis with the inclusion of democratic leaders from Poland itself and from Poles abroad. This new Government should then be called the Polish Provisional Government of National Unity.

"M. Molotov, Mr. Harriman, and Sir A. Clark Kerr are authorized as a commission to consult in the first instance in Moscow with members of the present Provisional Government and with other Polish democratic leaders from within Poland and from abroad, with a view to the reorganization of the present Government along the above lines. This Polish Provisional Government of National Unity shall be pledged to the holding of free and unfettered elections as soon as possible on the basis of universal suffrage and secret ballot. In these elections all democratic and anti-Nazi Parties shall have the right to take part and to put forward candidates.

"When a Polish Provisional Government of National Unity has been properly formed in conformity with the above, the Government of the U.S.S.R., which now maintains diplomatic relations with the present Provisional Government of Poland, and the Government of the United Kingdom and the Government of the United States of America will establish diplomatic relations with the new Polish Provisional Government of National Unity, and will exchange ambassadors by whose reports the respective Governments will be kept informed about the situation in Poland.

"The three heads of Government consider that the eastern frontier of Poland should follow the Curzon Line with digressions from it in some regions of five to eight kilometers in favor of Poland. They recognize that Poland must receive substantial accessions of territory in the north and west. They feel that the opinion of the new Polish Provisional Government of National

Unity should be sought in due course of the extent of these accessions and that the final delimitation of the western frontier of Poland should thereafter await the Peace Conference."

. . . .

XIII. Meetings of the Three Foreign Secretaries

The Conference agreed that permanent machinery should be set up for consultation between the three Foreign Secretaries; they should meet as often as necessary, probably about every three or four months.

These meetings will be held in rotation in the three capitals, the first meeting being held in London.

XIV. The Montreux Convention and the Straits

It was agreed that at the next meeting of the three Foreign Secretaries to be held in London, they should consider proposals which it was understood the Soviet Government would put forward in relation to the Montreux Convention, and report to their Governments. The Turkish Government should be informed at the appropriate moment.

The foregoing protocol was approved and signed by the three Foreign Secretaries at the Crimean Conference, February 11, 1945.

. . . .

Agreement Regarding Japan

The leaders of the three Great Powers—the Soviet Union, the United States of America and Great Britain—have agreed that in two or three months after Germany has surrendered and the war in Europe has terminated the Soviet Union shall enter into the war against Japan on the side of the Allies on condition that:

1. The status quo in Outer-Mongolia (the Mongolian People's Republic) shall be preserved;

2. The former rights of Russia violated by the treacherous attack of Japan in 1904 shall be restored, viz.:

(a) The southern part of Sakhalin as well as the islands adjacent to it shall be returned to the Soviet Union;

(b) The commercial port of Dairen shall be internationalized, the pre-eminent interests of the Soviet Union in this port being safeguarded, and the lease of Port Arthur as a naval base of the U.S.S.R. restored;

(c) The Chinese-Eastern Railroad and the South Manchurian Railroad, which provides an outlet to Dairen, shall be jointly operated by the establishment of a joint Soviet-Chinese company, it being understood that the pre-eminent interests of the Soviet Union shall be safeguarded and that China shall retain full sovereignty in Manchuria;

3. The Kurile Islands shall be handed over to the Soviet Union.

It is understood that the agreement concerning Outer-Mongolia and the ports and railroads referred to above will require concurrence of Generalissimo Chiang Kai-shek. The President will take measures in order to obtain this concurrence on advice from Marshal Stalin.

The Heads of the three Great Powers have agreed that these claims of the Soviet Union shall be unquestionably fulfilled after Japan has been defeated.

For its part the Soviet Union expresses its readiness to conclude with the National Government of China a pact of friendship and alliance between the U.S.S.R. and China in order to render assistance to China with its armed forces for the purpose of liberating China from the Japanese yoke.

Joseph V. Stalin

Franklin D. Roosevelt

Winston S. Churchill

STATEMENT BY THE SPONSORING GOVERNMENTS ON SECURITY COUNCIL VOTING [1]

THE "YALTA voting formula" (see note preceding Document 37) was the subject of much controversy at the San Francisco Conference. There was a widespread feeling among the middle and small powers against the veto power which was proposed for the sponsoring governments (the United States, the Soviet Union, Great Britain, and China) and France. There were many doubts as to the wisdom of incorporating it into the Charter. Accordingly, the sponsoring governments, on June 7, 1945, issued a statement designed to clarify the issue. In the statement it was made perfectly clear by the great powers that they would agree to nothing less than the proposed veto, although assurances were extended that it would not be lightly used. France declared her complete agreement with the statement.[2]

The chapters and sections referred to in the statement are from the Dumbarton Oaks Proposals (since the Charter was still being drafted at this time); the equivalent parts of the United Nations Charter in its final form are indicated in brackets immediately following.

The veto under the Charter can be applied by any permanent member of the Security Council, under any chapter of the Charter, except (1) where that member is a party to a

[1] *United Nations Conference on International Organization: Documents*, Vol. XI, pp. 710ff.

[2] The Chairman of Committee III/1 declared that "the Delegation of France associates itself completely with this statement." *Ibid.*, p. 710.

dispute under Chapter VI or Article 52, paragraph 3, or (2) where it is a question of procedure. All matters which are not procedural are by definition substantive and subject to the veto. In case of a difference of opinion as to whether a matter is procedural or substantive, the sponsoring governments claimed (Part II, paragraph 2) the right to decide that preliminary question by a substantive vote.

The statement of the sponsoring governments was neither officially accepted nor officially rejected at the Conference; the small powers made it clear that they preferred not to be bound by its provisions. In practice, the sponsoring governments have acted thus far as though the statement were binding.

Specific questions covering the voting procedure in the Security Council have been submitted by a Sub-Committee of the Conference Committee on Structure and Procedures of the Security Council to the Delegations of the four Governments sponsoring the Conference—The United States of America, the United Kingdom of Great Britain and Northern Ireland, the Union of Soviet Socialist Republics, and the Republic of China. In dealing with these questions, the four Delegations desire to make the following statement of their general attitude towards the whole question of unanimity of permanent members in the decisions of the Security Council.

Part I

1. The Yalta voting formula recognizes that the Security Council, in discharging its responsibilities for the maintenance of international peace and security, will have two broad groups of functions. Under Chapter VIII [Chs. VI & VII], the Council will have to make decisions which involve its taking direct measures in connection with settlement of disputes, adjustment of situations likely to lead to disputes, determination of threats to the peace, removal of threats to the peace, and suppression of breaches of the peace. It will also have to make decisions which do not involve the taking of such measures. The Yalta formula provides that the second of these two groups of decisions will be governed by a procedural vote—that is, the vote of any seven members. The first group of decisions will be governed by a qualified vote—that is, the vote of seven members, including the concurring votes of the five permanent members, subject to the proviso that in decisions under Section A [Ch. VI] and a part of Section C of Chapter VIII [Art. 52, para. 3] parties to a dispute shall abstain from voting.

2. For example, under the Yalta formula a procedural vote will govern the decisions made under the entire Section D of Chapter VI [Arts. 28–32]. This means that the Council will, by a vote of any seven of its members, adopt or alter its rules of procedure; determine the method of selecting its President; organize itself in such a way as to be able to function continuously; select the times and places of its regular and special meetings; establish such bodies or agencies as it may deem necessary for the performance of its functions; invite a Member of the Organization not represented on the Council to participate in its discussions when that Member's interests are specially affected; and invite any state when it is a party to a dispute being considered by the Council to participate in the discussion relating to that dispute.

3. Further, no individual member of the Council can alone prevent consideration and discussion by the Council of a dispute or situation brought to its attention under paragraph 2, Section A, Chapter VIII [Ch. VI]. Nor can parties to such dispute be prevented by these means from being heard by the Council. Likewise, the requirement for unanimity of the permanent members cannot prevent any member of the Council from reminding the Members of the Organization of their general obligations assumed under the Charter as regards peaceful settlement of international disputes.

4. Beyond this point, decisions and actions by the Security Council may well have major political consequences and may

even initiate a chain of events which might, in the end, require the Council under its responsibilities to invoke measures of enforcement under Section B, Chapter VIII [Ch. VII]. This chain of events begins when the Council decides to make an investigation, or determines that the time has come to call upon states to settle their differences, or makes recommendations to the parties. It is to such decisions and actions that unanimity of the permanent members applies, with the important proviso, referred to above, for abstention from voting by parties to a dispute.

5. To illustrate: in ordering an investigation, the Council has to consider whether the investigation—which may involve calling for reports, hearing witnesses, dispatching a commission of inquiry, or other means—might not further aggravate the situation. After investigation, the Council must determine whether the continuance of the situation or dispute would be likely to endanger international peace and security. If it so determines, the Council would be under obligation to take further steps. Similarly, the decision to make recommendations, even when all parties request it to do so, or to call upon parties to a dispute to fulfill their obligations under the Charter, might be the first step on a course of action from which the Security Council could withdraw only at the risk of failing to discharge its responsibilities.

6. In appraising the significance of the vote required to take such decisions or actions, it is useful to make comparison with the requirements of the League Covenant with reference to decisions of the League Council. Substantive decisions of the League of Nations Council could be taken only by the unanimous vote of all its members, whether permanent or not, with the exception of parties to a dispute under Article XV of the League Covenant. Under Article XI, under which most of the disputes brought before the League were dealt with and decisions to make investigations taken, the unanimity rule was invariably interpreted to include even the votes of the parties to a dispute.

7. The Yalta voting formula substitutes for the rule of complete unanimity of the League Council a system of qualified majority voting in the Security Council. Under this system non-permanent members of the Security Council individually would have no "veto." As regards the permanent members, there is no question under the Yalta formula of investing them with a new right, namely, the right to veto, a right which the permanent members of the League Council always had. The formula proposed for the taking of action in the Security Council by a majority of seven would make the operation of the Council less subject to obstruction than was the case under the League of Nations rule of complete unanimity.

8. It should also be remembered that under the Yalta formula the five major powers could not act by themselves, since even under the unanimity requirement any decisions of the Council would have to include the concurring votes of at least two of the non-permanent members. In other words, it would be possible for five non-permanent members as a group to exercise a "veto." It is not to be assumed, however, that the permanent members, any more than the non-permanent members, would use their "veto" power wilfully to obstruct the operation of the Council.

9. In view of the primary responsibilities of the permanent members, they could not be expected, in the present condition of the world, to assume the obligation to act in so serious a matter as the maintenance of international peace and security in consequence of a decision in which they had not concurred. Therefore, if a majority voting in the Security Council is to be made possible, the only practicable method is to provide, in respect of non-procedural decisions, for unanimity of the permanent members plus the concurring votes of at least two of the non-permanent members.

10. For all these reasons, the four Sponsoring Governments agreed on the Yalta formula and have presented it to this Conference as essential if an international organization is to be created through which all peace-loving nations can effectively discharge their common responsibilities for the maintenance of international peace and security.

Part II

In the light of the considerations set forth in Part I of this statement, it is clear what the answers to the questions submitted by the Subcommittee should be, with the exception of Question 19. The answer to that question is as follows:

1. In the opinion of the Delegations of the Sponsoring Governments, the Draft Charter itself contains an indication of the application of the voting procedures to the various functions of the Council.

2. In this case, it will be unlikely that there will arise in the future any matters of great importance on which a decision will have to be made as to whether a procedural vote would apply. Should, however, such a matter arise, the decision regarding the preliminary question as to whether or not such a matter is procedural must be taken by a vote of seven members of the Security Council, including the concurring votes of the permanent members.

DOCUMENT 39

CHARTER OF THE UNITED NATIONS [1]

THE CHARTER of the United Nations, signed on June 26, 1945, came into force on October 24, 1945. The original members of the United Nations, those who took part in the San Francisco Conference or who had previously signed the United Nations Declaration of January 1, 1942, and signed and ratified the Charter are

Argentine Republic	Dominican Republic	Liberia
Australia	Ecuador	Luxembourg
Belgium	Egypt	Mexico
Bolivia	El Salvador	Netherlands
Brazil	Ethiopia	New Zealand
Byelorussian S.S.R.	France	Nicaragua
Canada	Greece	Norway
Chile	Guatemala	Panama
China	Haiti	Paraguay
Colombia	Honduras	Peru
Costa Rica	India	Philippine Republic
Cuba	Iran	Poland[2]
Czechoslovakia	Iraq	Saudi Arabia
Denmark	Lebanon	Syria

[1] *United Nations Conference on International Organization: Documents,* Vol. XV, pp. 273*ff.*

[2] Poland had not attended the San Francisco Conference owing to disagreement among the Big Three as to the Polish Provisional Government but was admitted, Oct. 24, 1945.

Turkey   Union of Soviet   United States
Ukrainian S.S.R.   Socialist Repub-   Uruguay
Union of South   lics   Venezuela
   Africa   United Kingdom   Yugoslavia

All these states ratified the Charter and deposited their ratifications as provided under Article 111. Their original membership commenced upon deposit of ratification, and in
every case this was 1945. In addition the following new
members have been admitted:

Afghanistan (Nov. 19, 1946)   Sweden (Nov. 19, 1946)
Iceland (Nov. 19, 1946)   Union of Burma (Apr. 19,
Israel (May 11, 1949)   1948)
Pakistan (Sept. 30, 1947)   Yemen (Sept. 30, 1947)
Siam (Dec. 16, 1946)

No member has yet been suspended or expelled.

We the peoples of the United Nations, determined to save
succeeding generations from the scourge of war, which twice in
our lifetime has brought untold sorrow to mankind, and

to reaffirm faith in fundamental human rights, in the dignity
and worth of the human person, in the equal rights of men and
women and of nations large and small, and

to establish conditions under which justice and respect for the
obligations arising from treaties and other sources of international law can be maintained, and

to promote social progress and better standards of life in larger
freedom,

and for these ends to practice tolerance and live together in
peace with one another as good neighbors, and

to unite our strength to maintain international peace and
security, and

to ensure, by the acceptance of principles and the institution of methods, that armed force shall not be used, save in the common interest, and

to employ international machinery for the promotion of the economic and social advancement of all peoples,

have resolved to combine our efforts to accomplish these aims.

Accordingly, our respective Governments, through representatives assembled in the City of San Francisco, who have exhibited their full powers found to be in good and due form, have agreed to the present Charter of the United Nations and do hereby establish an international organization to be known as the United Nations.

CHAPTER I: PURPOSES AND PRINCIPLES

Article 1

The purposes of the United Nations are:

1. To maintain international peace and security, and to that end: to take effective collective measures for the prevention and removal of threats to the peace, and for the suppression of acts of aggression or other breaches of the peace, and to bring about by peaceful means, and in conformity with the principles of justice and international law, adjustment or settlement of international disputes or situations which might lead to a breach of the peace;

2. To develop friendly relations among nations based on respect for the principle of equal rights and self-determination of peoples, and to take other appropriate measures to strengthen universal peace;

3. To achieve international cooperation in solving international problems of an economic, social, cultural, or humanitarian character, and in promoting and encouraging respect for human rights and for fundamental freedoms for all without distinction as to race, sex, language, or religion; and

4. To be a center for harmonizing the actions of nations in the attainment of these common ends.

Article 2

The Organization and its Members, in pursuit of the Purposes stated in Article 1, shall act in accordance with the following Principles.

1. The Organization is based on the principle of the sovereign equality of all its Members.

2. All Members, in order to ensure to all of them the rights and benefits resulting from membership, shall fulfill in good faith the obligations assumed by them in accordance with the present Charter.

3. All Members shall settle their international disputes by peaceful means in such a manner that international peace and security, and justice, are not endangered.

4. All Members shall refrain in their international relations from the threat or use of force against the territorial integrity or political independence of any state, or in any other manner inconsistent with the Purposes of the United Nations.

5. All Members shall give the United Nations every assistance in any action it takes in accordance with the present Charter, and shall refrain from giving assistance to any state against which the United Nations is taking preventive or enforcement action.

6. The Organization shall ensure that states which are not Members of the United Nations act in accordance with these Principles so far as may be necessary for the maintenance of international peace and security.

7. Nothing contained in the present Charter shall authorize the United Nations to intervene in matters which are essentially within the domestic jurisdiction of any state or shall require the Members to submit such matters to settlement under the present Charter; but this principle shall not prejudice the application of enforcement measures under Chapter VII.

CHAPTER II: MEMBERSHIP

Article 3

The original Members of the United Nations shall be the states which, having participated in the United Nations Conference on International Organization at San Francisco, or having previously signed the Declaration by United Nations of January 1, 1942, sign the present Charter and ratify it in accordance with Article 110.

Article 4

1. Membership in the United Nations is open to all other peace-loving states which accept the obligations contained in the present Charter, and, in the judgment of the Organization, are able and willing to carry out these obligations.

2. The admission of any such state to membership in the United Nations will be effected by a decision of the General Assembly upon the recommendation of the Security Council.

Article 5

A member of the United Nations against which preventive or enforcement action has been taken by the Security Council may be suspended from the exercise of the rights and privileges of membership by the General Assembly upon the recommendation of the Security Council. The exercise of these rights and privileges may be restored by the Security Council.

Article 6

A Member of the United Nations which has persistently violated the Principles contained in the present Charter may be expelled from the Organization by the General Assembly upon the recommendation of the Security Council.

CHAPTER III: ORGANS

Article 7

1. There are established as the principal organs of the United Nations: a General Assembly, a Security Council, an Economic and Social Council, a Trusteeship Council, an International Court of Justice, and a Secretariat.

2. Such subsidiary organs as may be found necessary may be established in accordance with the present Charter.

Article 8

The United Nations shall place no restrictions on the eligibility of men and women to participate in any capacity and under conditions of equality in its principal and subsidiary organs.

CHAPTER IV: THE GENERAL ASSEMBLY

COMPOSITION

Article 9

1. The General Assembly shall consist of all the Members of the United Nations.

2. Each member shall have not more than five representatives in the General Assembly.

FUNCTIONS AND POWERS

Article 10

The General Assembly may discuss any questions or any matters within the scope of the present Charter or relating to the powers and functions of any organs provided for in the present Charter, and, except as provided in Article 12, may make recommendations to the Members of the United Nations or to the Security Council or to both on any such questions or matters.

Article 11

1. The General Assembly may consider the general principles of cooperation in the maintenance of international peace and security, including the principles governing disarmament and the regulation of armaments, and may make recommendations with regard to such principles to the Members or to the Security Council or to both.

2. The General Assembly may discuss any questions relating to the maintenance of international peace and security brought before it by any Member of the United Nations, or by the Security Council, or by a state which is not a Member of the United Nations in accordance with Article 35, paragraph 2, and,

except as provided in Article 12, may make recommendations with regard to any such questions to the state or states concerned or to the Security Council or to both. Any such question on which action is necessary shall be referred to the Security Council by the General Assembly either before or after discussion.

3. The General Assembly may call the attention of the Security Council to situations which are likely to endanger international peace and security.

4. The powers of the General Assembly set forth in this Article shall not limit the general scope of Article 10.

Article 12

1. While the Security Council is exercising in respect of any dispute or situation the functions assigned to it in the present Charter, the General Assembly shall not make any recommendations with regard to that dispute or situation unless the Security Council so requests.

2. The Secretary-General, with the consent of the Security Council, shall notify the General Assembly at each session of any matters relative to the maintenance of international peace and security which are being dealt with by the Security Council and shall similarly notify the General Assembly, or the Members of the United Nations if the General Assembly is not in session, immediately the Security Council ceases to deal with such matters.

Article 13

1. The General Assembly shall initiate studies and make recommendations for the purpose of:

a. promoting international cooperation in the political field and encouraging the progressive development of international law and its codification.

b. promoting international cooperation in the economic, social, cultural, educational, and health fields, and assisting in the realization of human rights and fundamental freedoms for all without distinction as to race, sex, language, or religion.

2. The further responsibilities, functions, and powers of the

General Assembly with respect to matters mentioned in paragraph 1 (b) above are set forth in Chapters IX and X.

Article 14

Subject to the provisions of Article 12, the General Assembly may recommend measures for the peaceful adjustment of any situation, regardless of origin, which it deems likely to impair the general welfare or friendly relations among nations, including situations resulting from a violation of the provisions of the present Charter setting forth the Purposes and Principles of the United Nations.

Article 15

1. The General Assembly shall receive and consider annual and special reports from the Security Council; these reports shall include an account of the measures that the Security Council has decided upon or taken to maintain international peace and security.

2. The General Assembly shall receive and consider reports from the other organs of the United Nations.

Article 16

The General Assembly shall perform such functions with respect to the international trusteeship system as are assigned to it under Chapters XII and XIII, including the approval of the trusteeship agreements for areas not designated as strategic.

Article 17

1. The General Assembly shall consider and approve the budget of the Organization.

2. The expenses of the Organization shall be borne by the Members as apportioned by the General Assembly.

3. The General Assembly shall consider and approve any financial and budgetary arrangements with specialized agencies referred to in Article 57 and shall examine the administrative budgets of such specialized agencies with a view to making recommendations to the agencies concerned.

VOTING

Article 18

1. Each member of the General Assembly shall have one vote.

2. Decisions of the General Assembly on important questions shall be made by a two-thirds majority of the members present and voting. These questions shall include: recommendations with respect to the maintenance of international peace and security, the election of the non-permanent members of the Security Council, the election of the members of the Economic and Social Council, the election of members of the Trusteeship Council in accordance with paragraph 1 (c) of Article 86, the admission of new Members to the United Nations, the suspension of the rights and privileges of membership, the expulsion of Members, questions relating to the operation of the trusteeship system, and budgetary questions.

3. Decisions on other questions, including the determination of additional categories of questions to be decided by a two-thirds majority, shall be made by a majority of the members present and voting.

Article 19

A Member of the United Nations which is in arrears in the payment of its financial contributions to the Organization shall have no vote in the General Assembly if the amount of its arrears equals or exceeds the amount of the contributions due from it for the preceding two full years. The General Assembly may, nevertheless, permit such a Member to vote if it is satisfied that the failure to pay is due to conditions beyond the control of the Member.

PROCEDURE

Article 20

The General Assembly shall meet in regular annual sessions and in such special sessions as occasion may require. Special sessions shall be convoked by the Secretary-General at the request of the Security Council or of a majority of the Members of the United Nations.

Article 21

The General Assembly shall adopt its own rules of procedure. It shall elect its President for each session.

Article 22

The General Assembly may establish such subsidiary organs as it deems necessary for the performance of its functions.

CHAPTER V: THE SECURITY COUNCIL

COMPOSITION

Article 23

1. The Security Council shall consist of eleven Members of the United Nations. The Republic of China, France, the Union of Soviet Socialist Republics, the United Kingdom of Great Britain and Northern Ireland, and the United States of America shall be permanent members of the Security Council. The General Assembly shall elect six other Members of the United Nations to be non-permanent members of the Security Council, due regard being specially paid, in the first instance to the contribution of Members of the United Nations to the maintenance of international peace and security and to the other purposes of the Organization and also to equitable geographical distribution.

2. The non-permanent members of the Security Council shall be elected for a term of two years. In the first election of the non-permanent members, however, three shall be chosen for a term of one year. A retiring member shall not be eligible for immediate re-election.

3. Each member of the Security Council shall have one representative.

FUNCTIONS AND POWERS

Article 24

1. In order to ensure prompt and effective action by the United Nations, its Members confer on the Security Council primary responsibility for the maintenance of international peace

and security, and agree that in carrying out its duties under this responsibility the Security Council acts on their behalf.

2. In discharging these duties the Security Council shall act in accordance with the Purposes and Principles of the United Nations. The specific powers granted to the Security Council for the discharge of these duties are laid down in Chapters VI, VII, VIII, and XII.

3. The Security Council shall submit annual and, when necessary, special reports to the General Assembly for its consideration.

Article 25

The Members of the United Nations agree to accept and carry out the decisions of the Security Council in accordance with the present Charter.

Article 26

In order to promote the establishment and maintenance of international peace and security with the least diversion for armaments of the world's human and economic resources, the Security Council shall be responsible for formulating, with the assistance of the Military Staff Committee referred to in Article 47, plans to be submitted to the Members of the United Nations for the establishment of a system for the regulations of armaments.

VOTING

Article 27

1. Each member of the Security Council shall have one vote.

2. Decisions of the Security Council on procedural matters shall be made by an affirmative vote of seven members.

3. Decisions of the Security Council on all other matters shall be made by an affirmative vote of seven members including the concurring votes of the permanent members; provided that, in decisions under Chapter VI, and under paragraph 3 of Article 52, a party to a dispute shall abstain from voting.

PROCEDURE

Article 28

1. The Security Council shall be so organized as to be able to function continuously. Each member of the Security Council shall for this purpose be represented at all times at the seat of the Organization.

2. The Security Council shall hold periodic meetings at which each of its members may, if it so desires, be represented by a member of the government or by some other specially designated representative.

3. The Security Council may hold meetings at such places other than the seat of the Organization as in its judgment will best facilitate its work.

Article 29

The Security Council may establish such subsidiary organs as it deems necessary for the performance of its functions.

Article 30

The Security Council shall adopt its own rules of procedure, including the method of selecting its President.

Article 31

Any Member of the United Nations which is not a member of the Security Council may participate, without vote, in the discussion of any question brought before the Security Council whenever the latter considers that the interests of that Member are specially affected.

Article 32

Any Member of the United Nations which is not a member of the Security Council or any state which is not a Member of the United Nations, if it is a party to a dispute under consideration by the Security Council, shall be invited to participate, without vote, in the discussion relating to the dispute. The Security Council shall lay down such conditions as it deems just for the participation of a state which is not a Member of the United Nations.

CHAPTER VI: PACIFIC SETTLEMENT OF DISPUTES

Article 33

1. The parties to any dispute, the continuance of which is likely to endanger the maintenance of international peace and security, shall, first of all, seek a solution by negotiation, enquiry, mediation, conciliation, arbitration, judicial settlement, resort to regional agencies or arrangements, or other peaceful means of their own choice.

2. The Security Council shall, when it deems necessary, call upon the parties to settle their dispute by such means.

Article 34

The Security Council may investigate any dispute, or any situation which might lead to international friction or give rise to a dispute, in order to determine whether the continuance of the dispute or situation is likely to endanger the maintenance of international peace and security.

Article 35

1. Any Member of the United Nations may bring any dispute, or any situation of the nature referred to in Article 34, to the attention of the Security Council or of the General Assembly.

2. A state which is not a Member of the United Nations may bring to the attention of the Security Council or of the General Assembly any dispute to which it is a party if it accepts in advance, for the purposes of the dispute, the obligations of pacific settlement provided in the present Charter.

3. The proceedings of the General Assembly in respect of matters brought to its attention under this Article will be subject to the provisions of Articles 11 and 12.

Article 36

1. The Security Council may, at any stage of a dispute of the nature referred to in Article 33 or of a situation of like nature,

recommend appropriate procedures or methods of adjustment.

2. The Security Council should take into consideration any procedures for the settlement of the dispute which have already been adopted by the parties.

3. In making recommendations under this Article the Security Council should also take into consideration that legal disputes should as a general rule be referred by the parties to the International Court of Justice in accordance with the provisions of the Statute of the Court.

Article 37

1. Should the parties to a dispute of the nature referred to in Article 33 fail to settle it by the means indicated in that Article, they shall refer it to the Security Council.

2. If the Security Council deems that the continuance of the dispute is in fact likely to endanger the maintenance of international peace and security, it shall decide whether to take action under Article 36 or to recommend such terms of settlement as it may consider appropriate.

Article 38

Without prejudice to the provisions of Articles 33 to 37, the Security Council may, if all the parties to any dispute so request, make recommendations to the parties with a view to a pacific settlement of the dispute.

CHAPTER VII: ACTION WITH RESPECT TO THREATS TO THE PEACE, BREACHES OF THE PEACE, AND ACTS OF AGGRESSION

Article 39

The Security Council shall determine the existence of any threat to the peace, breach of the peace, or act of aggression and shall make recommendations, or decide what measures shall be taken in accordance with Articles 41 and 42, to maintain or restore international peace and security.

Article 40

In order to prevent an aggravation of the situation, the Security Council may, before making the recommendations or deciding upon the measures provided for in Article 39, call upon the parties concerned to comply with such provisional measures as it deems necessary or desirable. Such provisional measures shall be without prejudice to the rights, claims, or position of the parties concerned. The Security Council shall duly take account of failure to comply with such provisional measures.

Article 41

The Security Council may decide what measures not involving the use of armed force are to be employed to give effect to its decisions, and it may call upon the Members of the United Nations to apply such measures. These may include complete or partial interruption of economic relations and of rail, sea, air, postal, telegraphic, radio, and other means of communication, and the severance of diplomatic relations.

Article 42

Should the Security Council consider that measures provided for in Article 41 would be inadequate or have proved to be inadequate, it may take such action by air, sea, or land forces as may be necessary to maintain or restore international peace and security. Such action may include demonstrations, blockade, and other operations by air, sea, or land forces of Members of the United Nations.

Article 43

1. All Members of the United Nations, in order to contribute to the maintenance of international peace and security, undertake to make available to the Security Council, on its call and in accordance with a special agreement or agreements, armed forces, assistance, and facilities, including rights of passage, necessary for the purpose of maintaining international peace and security.

2. Such agreement or agreements shall be negotiated as soon

as possible on the initiative of the Security Council. They shall
be concluded between the Security Council and Members or
between the Security Council and groups of Members and shall
be subject to ratification by the signatory states in accordance
with their respective constitutional processes.

Article 44

When the Security Council has decided to use force it shall,
before calling upon a Member not represented on it to provide
armed forces in fulfillment of the obligations assumed under
Article 43, invite that Member, if the Member so desires, to
participate in the decisions of the Security Council concerning
the employment of contingents of that Member's armed forces.

Article 45

In order to enable the United Nations to take urgent military
measures, Members shall hold immediately available national
air-force contingents for combined international enforcement
action. The strength and degree of readiness of these contingents
and plans for their combined action shall be determined, within
the limits laid down in the special agreement or agreements referred to in Article 43, by the Security Council with the assistance of the Military Staff Committee.

Article 46

Plans for the application of armed force shall be made by the
Security Council with the assistance of the Military Staff Committee.

Article 47

1. There shall be established a Military Staff Committee to advise and assist the Security Council on all questions relating to
the Security Council's military requirements for the maintenance
of international peace and security, the employment and command of forces placed at its disposal, the regulation of armaments,
and possible disarmament.

2. The Military Staff Committee shall consist of the Chiefs of
Staff of the permanent members of the Security Council or their

representatives. Any Member of the United Nations not permanently represented on the Committee shall be invited by the Committee to be associated with it when the efficient discharge of the Committee's responsibilities requires the participation of that Member in its work.

3. The Military Staff Committee shall be responsible under the Security Council for the strategic direction of any armed forces placed at the disposal of the Security Council. Questions relating to the command of such forces shall be worked out subsequently.

4. The Military Staff Committee, with the authorization of the Security Council and after consultation with appropriate regional agencies, may establish regional subcommittees.

Article 48

1. The action required to carry out the decisions of the Security Council for the maintenance of international peace and security shall be taken by all the Members of the United Nations or by some of them, as the Security Council may determine.

2. Such decisions shall be carried out by the Members of the United Nations directly and through their action in the appropriate international agencies of which they are members.

Article 49

The Members of the United Nations shall join in affording mutual assistance in carrying out the measures decided upon by the Security Council.

Article 50

If preventive or enforcement measures against any state are taken by the Security Council, any other state, whether a Member of the United Nations or not, which finds itself confronted with special economic problems arising from the carrying out of those measures shall have the right to consult the Security Council with regard to a solution of those problems.

Article 51

Nothing in the present Charter shall impair the inherent right of individual or collective self-defense if an armed attack occurs against a Member of the United Nations, until the Security Council has taken the measures necessary to maintain international peace and security. Measures taken by Members in the exercise of this right of self-defense shall be immediately reported to the Security Council and shall not in any way affect the authority and responsibility of the Security Council under the present Charter to take at any time such action as it deems necessary in order to maintain or restore international peace and security.

CHAPTER VIII: REGIONAL ARRANGEMENTS

Article 52

1. Nothing in the present Charter precludes the existence of regional arrangements or agencies for dealing with such matters relating to the maintenance of international peace and security as are appropriate for regional action, provided that such arrangements or agencies and their activities are consistent with the Purposes and Principles of the United Nations.

2. The Members of the United Nations entering into such arrangements or constituting such agencies shall make every effort to achieve pacific settlement of local disputes through such regional arrangements or by such regional agencies before referring them to the Security Council.

3. The Security Council shall encourage the development of pacific settlement of local disputes through such regional arrangements or by such regional agencies either on the initiative of the states concerned or by reference from the Security Council.

4. This Article in no way impairs the application of Articles 34 and 35.

Article 53

1. The Security Council shall, where appropriate, utilize such regional arrangements or agencies for enforcement action under its authority. But no enforcement action shall be taken under regional arrangements or by regional agencies without the authorization of the Security Council, with the exception of meas-

ures against any enemy state, as defined in paragraph 2 of this Article, provided for pursuant to Article 107 or in regional arrangements directed against renewal of aggressive policy on the part of any such state, until such times as the Organization may, on request of the Governments concerned, be charged with the responsibility for preventing further aggression by such a state.

2. The term enemy state as used in paragraph 1 of this Article applies to any state which during the Second World War has been an enemy of any signatory of the present Charter.

Article 54

The Security Council shall at all times be kept fully informed of activities undertaken or in contemplation under regional arrangements or by regional agencies for the maintenance of international peace and security.

CHAPTER IX: INTERNATIONAL ECONOMIC AND SOCIAL COOPERATION

Article 55

With a view to the creation of conditions of stability and well-being which are necessary for peaceful and friendly relations among nations based on respect for the principle of equal rights and self-determination of peoples, the United Nations shall promote:

a. higher standards of living, full employment, and conditions of economic and social progress and development;

b. solutions of international economic, social, health, and related problems; and international cultural and educational cooperation; and

c. universal respect for, and observance of, human rights and fundamental freedoms for all without distinction as to race, sex, language, or religion.

Article 56

All Members pledge themselves to take joint and separate action in cooperation with the Organization for the achievement of the purposes set forth in Article 55.

Article 57

1. The various specialized agencies, established by intergovernmental agreement and having wide international responsibilities, as defined in their basic instruments, in economic, social, cultural, educational, health, and related fields, shall be brought into relationship with the United Nations in accordance with the provisions of Article 63.

2. Such agencies thus brought into relationship with the United Nations are hereinafter referred to as specialized agencies.

Article 58

The Organization shall make recommendations for the coordination of the policies and activities of the specialized agencies.

Article 59

The Organization shall, where appropriate, initiate negotiations among the states concerned for the creation of any new specialized agencies required for the accomplishment of the purposes set forth in Article 55.

Article 60

Responsibility for the discharge of the functions of the Organization set forth in this Chapter shall be vested in the General Assembly and, under the authority of the General Assembly, in the Economic and Social Council, which shall have for this purpose the powers set forth in Chapter X.

CHAPTER X: THE ECONOMIC AND SOCIAL COUNCIL

COMPOSITION

Article 61

1. The Economic and Social Council shall consist of eighteen Members of the United Nations elected by the General Assembly.

2. Subject to the provisions of paragraph 3, six members of the Economic and Social Council shall be elected each year

for a term of three years. A retiring member shall be eligible for immediate re-election.

3. At the first election, eighteen members of the Economic and Social Council shall be chosen. The term of office of six members so chosen shall expire at the end of one year, and of six other members at the end of two years, in accordance with arrangements made by the General Assembly.

4. Each member of the Economic and Social Council shall have one representative.

FUNCTIONS AND POWERS

Article 62

1. The Economic and Social Council may make or initiate studies and reports with respect to international economic, social, cultural, educational, health, and related matters and may make recommendations with respect to any such matters to the General Assembly, to the Members of the United Nations, and to the specialized agencies concerned.

2. It may make recommendations for the purpose of promoting respect for, and observance of, human rights and fundamental freedoms for all.

3. It may prepare draft conventions for submission to the General Assembly, with respect to matters falling within its competence.

4. It may call, in accordance with the rules prescribed by the United Nations, international conferences on matters falling within its competence.

Article 63

1. The Economic and Social Council may enter into agreements with any of the Agencies referred to in Article 57, defining the terms on which the agency concerned shall be brought into relationship with the United Nations. Such agreements shall be subject to approval by the General Assembly.

2. It may coordinate the activities of the specialized agencies through consultation with and recommendations to such agencies

and through recommendations to the General Assembly and to the Members of the United Nations.

Article 64

1. The Economic and Social Council may take appropriate steps to obtain regular reports from the specialized agencies. It may make arrangements with the Members of the United Nations and with the specialized agencies to obtain reports on the steps taken to give effect to its own recommendations and to recommendations on matters falling within its competence made by the General Assembly.

2. It may communicate its observations on these reports to the General Assembly.

Article 65

The Economic and Social Council may furnish information to the Security Council and shall assist the Security Council upon its request.

Article 66

1. The Economic and Social Council shall perform such functions as fall within its competence in connection with the carrying out of the recommendations of the General Assembly.

2. It may, with the approval of the General Assembly, perform services at the request of Members of the United Nations and at the request of specialized agencies.

3. It shall perform such other functions as are specified elsewhere in the present Charter or as may be assigned to it by the General Assembly.

VOTING

Article 67

1. Each member of the Economic and Social Council shall have one vote.

2. Decisions of the Economic and Social Council shall be made by a majority of the members present and voting.

PROCEDURE

Article 68

The Economic and Social Council shall set up commissions in economic and social fields and for the promotion of human rights, and such other commissions as may be required for the performance of its functions.

Article 69

The Economic and Social Council shall invite any Member of the United Nations to participate, without vote, in its deliberations on any matter of particular concern to that Member.

Article 70

The Economic and Social Council may make arrangements for representatives of the specialized agencies to participate, without vote, in its deliberations and in those of the commissions established by it, and for its representatives to participate in the deliberations of the specialized agencies.

Article 71

The Economic and Social Council may make suitable arrangements for consultation with non-governmental organizations which are concerned with matters within its competence. Such arrangements may be made with international organizations and, where appropriate, with national organizations after consultation with the Member of the United Nations concerned.

Article 72

1. The Economic and Social Council shall adopt its own rules of procedure, including the method of selecting its President.

2. The Economic and Social Council shall meet as required in accordance with its rules, which shall include provisions for the convening of meetings on the request of a majority of its members.

CHAPTER XI: DECLARATION REGARDING NON-SELF-GOVERNING TERRITORIES

Article 73

Members of the United Nations which have or assume responsibilities for the administration of territories whose peoples have not yet attained a full measure of self-government recognize the principle that the interests of the inhabitants of these territories are paramount, and accept as a sacred trust the obligation to promote to the utmost, within the system of international peace and security established by the present Charter, the well-being of the inhabitants of these territories, and, to this end:

a. to ensure, with due respect for the culture of the peoples concerned, their political, economic, social, and educational advancement, their just treatment, and their protection against abuses;

b. to develop self-government, to take due account of the political aspirations of the peoples, and to assist them in the progressive development of their free political institutions, according to the particular circumstances of each territory and its peoples and their varying stages of advancement;

c. to further international peace and security;

d. to promote constructive measures of development, to encourage research, and to cooperate with one another and, when and where appropriate, with specialized international bodies with a view to the practical achievement of the social, economic, and scientific purposes set forth in this Article; and

e. to transmit regularly to the Secretary-General for information purposes, subject to such limitation as security and constitutional considerations may require, statistical and other information of a technical nature relating to economic, social, and educational conditions in the territories for which they are respectively responsible other than those territories to which Chapters XII and XIII apply.

Article 74

Members of the United Nations also agree that their policy in respect of the territories to which this Chapter applies, no less than in respect of their metropolitan areas, must be based on the general principle of good-neighborliness, due account being taken of the interests and well-being of the rest of the world, in social, economic, and commercial matters.

CHAPTER XII: INTERNATIONAL TRUSTEESHIP SYSTEM

Article 75

The United Nations shall establish under its authority an international trusteeship system for the administration and supervision of such territories as may be placed thereunder by subsequent individual agreements. These territories are hereinafter referred to as trust territories.

Article 76

The basic objectives of the trusteeship system, in accordance with the Purposes of the United Nations laid down in Article 1 of the present Charter, shall be:

a. to further international peace and security;

b. to promote the political, economic, social, and educational advancement of the inhabitants of the trust territories, and their progressive development towards self-government or independence as may be appropriate to the particular circumstances of each territory and its peoples and the freely expressed wishes of the peoples concerned, and as may be provided by the terms of each trusteeship agreement;

c. to encourage respect for human rights and for fundamental freedoms for all without distinction as to race, sex, language, or religion, and to encourage recognition of the interdependence of the peoples of the world; and

d. to ensure equal treatment in social, economic, and commercial matters for all Members of the United Nations and their nationals, and also equal treatment for the latter in the administration of justice, without prejudice to the attainment of the foregoing objectives and subject to the provisions of Article 80.

Article 77

1. The trusteeship system shall apply to such territories in the following categories as may be placed thereunder by means of trusteeship agreements:

a. territories now held under mandate;

b. territories which may be detached from enemy states as a result of the Second World War; and

c. territories voluntarily placed under the system by states responsible for their administration.

2. It will be a matter for subsequent agreement as to which territories in the foregoing categories will be brought under the trusteeship system and upon what terms.

Article 78

The trusteeship system shall not apply to territories which have become Members of the United Nations, relationship among which shall be based on respect for the principle of sovereign equality.

Article 79

The terms of trusteeship for each territory to be placed under the trusteeship system, including any alteration or amendment, shall be agreed upon by the states directly concerned, including the mandatory power in the case of territories held under mandate by a Member of the United Nations, and shall be approved as provided for in Articles 83 and 85.

Article 80

1. Except as may be agreed upon in individual trusteeship agreements, made under Articles 77, 79, and 81, placing each territory under the trusteeship system, and until such agreements have been concluded, nothing in this Chapter shall be construed in or of itself to alter in any manner the rights whatsoever of any states or any peoples or the terms of existing international

instruments to which Members of the United Nations may respectively be parties.

2. Paragraph 1 of this Article shall not be interpreted as giving grounds for delay or postponement of the negotiation and conclusion of agreements for placing mandated and other territories under the trusteeship system as provided for in Article 77.

Article 81

The trusteeship agreement shall in each case include the terms under which the trust territory will be administered and designate the authority which will exercise the administration of the trust territory. Such authority, hereinafter called the administering authority, may be one or more states or the Organization itself.

Article 82

There may be designated, in any trusteeship agreement, a strategic area or areas which may include part or all of the trust territory to which the agreement applies, without prejudice to any special agreement or agreements made under Article 43.

Article 83

1. All functions of the United Nations relating to strategic areas, including the approval of the terms of the trusteeship agreements and of their alteration or amendment, shall be exercised by the Security Council.

2. The basic objectives set forth in Article 76 shall be applicable to the people of each strategic area.

3. The Security Council shall, subject to the provisions of the trusteeship agreements and without prejudice to security considerations, avail itself of the assistance of the Trusteeship Council to perform those functions of the United Nations under the trusteeship system relating to political, economic, social, and educational matters in the strategic areas.

Article 84

It shall be the duty of the administering authority to ensure that the trust territory shall play its part in the maintenance of international peace and security. To this end the administering authority may make use of volunteer forces, facilities, and assistance from the trust territory in carrying out the obligations towards the Security Council undertaken in this regard by the administering authority, as well as for local defense and the maintenance of law and order within the trust territory.

Article 85

1. The functions of the United Nations with regard to trusteeship agreements for all areas not designated as strategic, including the approval of the terms of the trusteeship agreements and of their alteration or amendment, shall be exercised by the General Assembly.

2. The Trusteeship Council, operating under the authority of the General Assembly, shall assist the General Assembly in carrying out these functions.

CHAPTER XIII: THE TRUSTEESHIP COUNCIL

COMPOSITION

Article 86

1. The Trusteeship Council shall consist of the following Members of the United Nations:

a. those Members administering trust territories;

b. such of those Members mentioned by name in Article 23 as are not administering trust territories; and

c. as many other Members elected for three-year terms by the General Assembly as may be necessary to ensure that the total number of members of the Trusteeship Council is equally divided between those Members of the United Nations which administer trust territories and those which do not.

2. Each member of the Trusteeship Council shall designate one specially qualified person to represent it therein.

FUNCTIONS AND POWERS

Article 87

The General Assembly and, under its authority, the Trusteeship Council, in carrying out their functions, may:

a. consider reports submitted by the administering authority;

b. accept petitions and examine them in consultation with the administering authority;

c. provide for periodic visits to the respective trust territories at times agreed upon with the administering authority; and

d. take these and other actions in conformity with the terms of the trusteeship agreements.

Article 88

The Trusteeship Council shall formulate a questionnaire on the political, economic, social, and educational advancement of the inhabitants of each trust territory, and the administering authority for each trust territory within the competence of the General Assembly shall make an annual report to the General Assembly upon the basis of such questionnaire.

VOTING

Article 89

1. Each member of the Trusteeship Council shall have one vote.

2. Decisions of the Trusteeship Council shall be made by a majority of the members present and voting.

PROCEDURE

Article 90

1. The Trusteeship Council shall adopt its own rules of procedure, including the method of selecting its President.

2. The Trusteeship Council shall meet as required in accordance with its rules, which shall include provision for the convening of meetings on the request of a majority of its members.

Article 91

The Trusteeship Council shall, when appropriate, avail itself of the assistance of the Economic and Social Council and of the specialized agencies in regard to matters with which they are respectively concerned.

CHAPTER XIV: THE INTERNATIONAL COURT OF JUSTICE

Article 92

The International Court of Justice shall be the principal judicial organ of the United Nations. It shall function in accordance with the annexed Statute, which is based upon the Statute of the Permanent Court of International Justice and forms an integral part of the present Charter.

Article 93

1. All Members of the United Nations are *ipso facto* parties to the Statute of the International Court of Justice.

2. A state which is not a Member of the United Nations may become a party to the Statute of the International Court of Justice on conditions to be determined in each case by the General Assembly upon the recommendation of the Security Council.

Article 94

1. Each Member of the United Nations undertakes to comply with the decision of the International Court of Justice in any case to which it is a party.

2. If any party to a case fails to perform the obligations incumbent upon it under a judgment rendered by the Court, the other party may have recourse to the Security Council, which may, if it deems necessary, make recommendations or decide upon measures to be taken to give effect to the judgment.

Article 95

Nothing in the present Charter shall prevent Members of the United Nations from entrusting the solution of their differences to other tribunals by virtue of agreements already in existence or which may be concluded in the future.

Article 96

1. The General Assembly or the Security Council may request the International Court of Justice to give an advisory opinion on any legal question.

2. Other organs of the United Nations and specialized agencies, which may at any time be so authorized by the General Assembly, may also request advisory opinions of the Court on legal questions arising within the scope of their activities.

CHAPTER XV: THE SECRETARIAT

Article 97

The Secretariat shall comprise a Secretary-General and such staff as the Organization may require. The Secretary-General shall be appointed by the General Assembly upon the recommendation of the Security Council. He shall be the chief administrative officer of the Organization.

Article 98

The Secretary-General shall act in that capacity in all meetings of the General Assembly, of the Security Council, of the Economic and Social Council, and of the Trusteeship Council, and shall perform such other functions as are entrusted to him by these organs. The Secretary-General shall make an annual report to the General Assembly on the work of the Organization.

Article 99

The Secretary-General may bring to the attention of the Security Council any matter which in his opinion may threaten the maintenance of international peace and security.

Article 100

1. In the performance of their duties the Secretary-General and the staffs shall not seek or receive instructions from any

government or from any other authority external to the Organization. They shall refrain from any action which might reflect on their position as international officials responsible only to the Organization.

2. Each Member of the United Nations undertakes to respect the exclusively international character of the responsibilities of the Secretary-General and the staff and not to seek to influence them in the discharge of their responsibilities.

Article 101

1. The staff shall be appointed by the Secretary-General under regulations established by the General Assembly.

2. Appropriate staffs shall be permanently assigned to the Economic and Social Council, the Trusteeship Council, and, as required, to other organs of the United Nations. These staffs shall form a part of the Secretariat.

3. The paramount consideration in the employment of the staff and in the determination of the conditions of service shall be the necessity of securing the highest standards of efficiency, competence, and integrity. Due regard shall be paid to the importance of recruiting the staff on as wide a geographical basis as possible.

CHAPTER XVI: MISCELLANEOUS PROVISIONS

Article 102

1. Every treaty and every international agreement entered into by any Member of the United Nations after the present Charter comes into force shall as soon as possible be registered with the Secretariat and published by it.

2. No party to any such treaty or international agreement which has not been registered in accordance with the provisions of paragraph 1 of this Article may invoke that treaty or agreement before any organ of the United Nations.

Article 103

In the event of a conflict between the obligations of the Members of the United Nations under the present Charter and their obligations under any other international agreement, their obligations under the present Charter shall prevail.

Article 104

The Organization shall enjoy in the territory of each of its Members such legal capacity as may be necessary for the exercise of its functions and the fulfillment of its purposes.

Article 105

1. The Organization shall enjoy in the territory of each of its Members such privileges and immunities as are necessary for the fulfillment of its purposes.

2. Representatives of the Members of the United Nations and officials of the Organization shall similarly enjoy such privileges and immunities as are necessary for the independent exercise of their functions in connection with the Organization.

3. The General Assembly may make recommendations with a view to determining the details of the application of paragraphs 1 and 2 of this Article or may propose conventions to the Members of the United Nations for this purpose.

CHAPTER XVII: TRANSITIONAL SECURITY ARRANGEMENTS

Article 106

Pending the coming into force of such special agreements referred to in Article 43 as in the opinion of the Security Council enable it to begin the exercise of its responsibilities under Article 42, the parties to the Four-Nation Declaration, signed at Moscow, October 30, 1943, and France, shall, in accordance with the provisions of paragraph 5 of that Declaration, consult with one another and as occasion requires with other Members of the United Nations with a view to such joint action on behalf of the

Organization as may be necessary for the purpose of maintaining international peace and security.

Article 107

Nothing in the present Charter shall invalidate or preclude action, in relation to any state which during the Second World War has been an enemy of any signatory to the present Charter, taken or authorized as a result of that war by the Governments having responsibility for such action.

CHAPTER XVIII: AMENDMENTS

Article 108

Amendments to the present Charter shall come into force for all Members of the United Nations when they have been adopted by a vote of two-thirds of the members of the General Assembly and ratified in accordance with their respective constitutional processes by two-thirds of the Members of the United Nations, including all the permanent members of the Security Council.

Article 109

1. A General Conference of the Members of the United Nations for the purpose of reviewing the present Charter may be held at a date and place to be fixed by a two-thirds vote of the members of the General Assembly and by a vote of any seven members of the Security Council. Each Member of the United Nations shall have one vote in the conference.

2. Any alteration of the present Charter recommended by a two-thirds vote of the conference shall take effect when ratified in accordance with their respective constitutional processes by two-thirds of the Members of the United Nations including all the permanent members of the Security Council.

3. If such a conference has not been held before the tenth annual session of the General Assembly following the coming into force of the present Charter, the proposal to call such a conference shall be placed on the agenda of that session of the General Assembly, and the conference shall be held if so decided by

a majority vote of the members of the General Assembly and by a vote of any seven members of the Security Council.

CHAPTER XIX: RATIFICATION AND SIGNATURE

Article 110

1. The present Charter shall be ratified by the signatory states in accordance with their respective constitutional processes.

2. The ratifications shall be deposited with the Government of the United States of America, which shall notify all the signatory states of each deposit as well as the Secretary-General of the Organization when he has been appointed.

3. The present Charter shall come into force upon the deposit of ratifications by the Republic of China, France, the Union of Soviet Socialist Republics, the United Kingdom of Great Britain and Northern Ireland, and the United States of America, and by a majority of the other signatory states. A protocol of the ratifications deposited shall thereupon be drawn up by the Government of the United States of America which shall communicate copies thereof to all the signatory states.

4. The states signatory to the present Charter which ratify it after it has come into force will become original Members of the United Nations on the date of the deposit of their respective ratifications.

Article 111

The present Charter, of which the Chinese, French, Russian, English, and Spanish texts are equally authentic, shall remain deposited in the archives of the Government of the United States of America. Duly certified copies thereof shall be transmitted by that Government to the Governments of the other signatory states.

DOCUMENT 40

STATUTE OF THE INTERNATIONAL COURT OF JUSTICE [1]

OF THE two methods of legal settlement of international disputes, adjudication (judicial settlement) has been used far more often since 1922 than has arbitration (see Document 8). The Permanent Court of International Justice, which formed part of the League of Nations system, was replaced, following World War II, by the International Court of Justice which forms part of the United Nations system. The Statute of the International Court of Justice, signed on June 26, 1945, as an integral part of the United Nations Charter to which it was annexed, came into force on October 24, 1945.

Both the League Court and the present court are courts of adjudication. The decisions of the judges are binding upon the parties to a dispute. However, no nation is required to submit a dispute to the court unless it so desires.[1a] A nation may elect to submit certain classes of legal disputes automatically to the court, provided that the other party to the dispute has assumed a similar obligation. This is done by adhering to Article 36, the so-called "optional clause." A great power adhering frequently enumerates certain types of disputes to be excluded, however, from the compulsory jurisdiction of the court. The United States accepted the

[1] *United Nations Conference on International Organization: Documents,* Vol. XV, pp. 293ff.

[1a] An exception to this is in a case where a nation has agreed (usually in a peace treaty following its defeat) that the court will automatically have jurisdiction in certain disputes.

"optional clause" in the following proclamation, August 14, 1946:

. . . The United States of America recognizes as compulsory *ipso facto* and without special agreement, in relation to any other state accepting the same obligation, the jurisdiction of the International Court of Justice in all legal disputes hereafter arising concerning

a. the interpretation of a treaty;

b. any question of international law;

c. the existence of any fact which, if established, would constitute a breach of an international obligation;

d. the nature or extent of the reparation to be made for the breach of an international obligation;

Provided, that this declaration shall not apply to

a. disputes the solution of which the parties shall entrust to other tribunals by virtue of agreements already in existence or which may be concluded in the future; or

b. disputes with regard to matters which are essentially within the domestic jurisdiction of the United States of America as determined by the United States of America; or

c. disputes arising under a multilateral treaty, unless (1) all parties to the treaty affected by the decision are also parties to the case before the Court, or (2) the United States of America specially agrees to jurisdiction; and

Provided further, that this declaration shall remain in force for a period of five years and thereafter until the expiration of six months after notice may be given to terminate this declaration. . . .[2]

Thirty nations have accepted the optional clause with varying reservations.

The Statute of the International Court of Justice is substantially the same as that of the Permanent Court of International Justice. A primary reason for creating a new court

[2] *Department of State Bulletin,* Vol. XV, pp. 452*ff.*

was that neither the United States nor the Soviet Union had been members of the League Court. All members of the United Nations are automatically members as well of the present court.[3] It is possible for a nation to become a member of the court without becoming a member, however, of the United Nations. On July 28, 1948, Switzerland became the first nonmember of the United Nations to do so.[4]

In addition to its function of deciding upon disputes submitted directly to it, the League Court was empowered, upon request of the Assembly or Council, to render an advisory opinion upon the legal aspects of a dispute before the League. The present court is similarly empowered to issue advisory opinions. While these carry great weight because of the prestige of the court, they are not binding decisions but are more in the nature of legal advice which can be accepted or rejected by the Assembly or Council.

Article 1

The International Court of Justice established by the Charter of the United Nations as the principal judicial organ of the United Nations shall be constituted and shall function in accordance with the provisions of the present Statute.

CHAPTER I: ORGANIZATION OF THE COURT

Article 2

The Court shall be composed of a body of independent judges, elected regardless of their nationality from among persons of

---

[3] See note preceding Document 39 for the membership of the United Nations.

[4] The General Assembly defined the terms of Switzerland's admission in a resolution of Dec. 11, 1946. The principal reason Switzerland has not become a member of the UN is because of her traditional neutrality which is incompatible with participation in the sanctions provided for in Chapter VII of the Charter.

high moral character, who possess the qualifications required in their respective countries for appointment to the highest judicial offices, or are jurisconsults of recognized competence in international law.

Article 3

1. The Court shall consist of fifteen members, no two of whom may be nationals of the same state.

2. A person who for the purposes of membership in the Court could be regarded as a national of more than one state shall be deemed to be a national of the one in which he ordinarily exercises civil and political rights.

Article 4

1. The members of the Court shall be elected by the General Assembly and by the Security Council from a list of persons nominated by the national groups in the Permanent Court of Arbitration, in accordance with the following provisions.

2. In the case of Members of the United Nations not represented in the Permanent Court of Arbitration, candidates shall be nominated by national groups appointed for this purpose by their governments under the same conditions as those prescribed for members of the Permanent Court of Arbitration by Article 44 of the Convention of The Hague of 1907 for the pacific settlement of international disputes.

3. The conditions under which a state which is a party to the present Statute but is not a Member of the United Nations may participate in electing the members of the Court shall, in the absence of a special agreement, be laid down by the General Assembly upon recommendation of the Security Council.

Article 5

1. At least three months before the date of the election, the Secretary-General of the United Nations shall address a written request to the members of the Permanent Court of Arbitration belonging to the states which are parties to the present Statute, and to the members of the national groups appointed under

Article 4, paragraph 2, inviting them to undertake, within a given time, by national groups, the nomination of persons in a position to accept the duties of a member of the Court.

2. No group may nominate more than four persons, not more than two of whom shall be of their own nationality. In no case may the number of candidates nominated by a group be more than double the number of seats to be filled.

Article 6

Before making these nominations, each national group is recommended to consult its highest court of justice, its legal faculties and schools of law, and its national academies and national sections of international academies devoted to the study of law.

Article 7

1. The Secretary-General shall prepare a list in alphabetical order of all the persons thus nominated. Save as provided in Article 12, paragraph 2, these shall be the only persons eligible.

2. The Secretary-General shall submit this list to the General Assembly and to the Security Council.

Article 8

The General Assembly and the Security Council shall proceed independently of one another to elect the members of the Court.

Article 9

At every election, the electors shall bear in mind not only that the persons to be elected should individually possess the qualifications required, but also that in the body as a whole the representation of the main forms of civilization and of the principal legal systems of the world should be assured.

Article 10

1. Those candidates who obtain an absolute majority of votes in the General Assembly and in the Security Council shall be considered as elected.

2. Any vote of the Security Council, whether for the election of judges or for the appointment of members of the conference envisaged in Article 12, shall be taken without any distinction between permanent and non-permanent members of the Security Council.

3. In the event of more than one national of the same state obtaining an absolute majority of the votes both of the General Assembly and of the Security Council, the eldest of these only shall be considered as elected.

Article 11

If, after the first meeting held for the purpose of the election, one or more seats remain to be filled, a second and, if necessary, a third meeting shall take place.

Article 12

1. If, after the third meeting, one or more seats still remain unfilled, a joint conference consisting of six members, three appointed by the General Assembly and three by the Security Council, may be formed at any time at the request of either the General Assembly or the Security Council, for the purpose of choosing by the vote of an absolute majority one name for each seat still vacant, to submit to the General Assembly and the Security Council for their respective acceptance.

2. If the joint conference is unanimously agreed upon any person who fulfills the required conditions, he may be included in its list, even though he was not included in the list of nominations referred to in Article 7.

3. If the joint conference is satisfied that it will not be successful in procuring an election, those members of the Court who have already been elected shall, within a period to be fixed by the Security Council, proceed to fill the vacant seats by selection from among those candidates who have obtained votes either in the General Assembly or in the Security Council.

4. In the event of an equality of votes among the judges, the eldest judge shall have a casting vote.

Article 13

1. The members of the Court shall be elected for nine years and may be re-elected; provided, however, that of the judges elected at the first election, the terms of five judges shall expire at the end of three years and the terms of five more judges shall expire at the end of six years.

2. The judges whose terms are to expire at the end of the above-mentioned initial periods of three and six years shall be chosen by lot to be drawn by the Secretary-General immediately after the first election has been completed.

3. The members of the Court shall continue to discharge their duties until their places have been filled. Though replaced, they shall finish any cases which they may have begun.

4. In the case of the resignation of a member of the Court, the resignation shall be addressed to the President of the Court for transmission to the Secretary-General. This last notification makes the place vacant.

Article 14

Vacancies shall be filled by the same method as that laid down for the first election, subject to the following provision: the Secretary-General shall, within one month of the occurrence of the vacancy, proceed to issue the invitations provided for in Article 5, and the date of the election shall be fixed by the Security Council.

Article 15

A member of the Court elected to replace a member whose term of office has not expired shall hold office for the remainder of his predecessor's term.

Article 16

1. No member of the Court may exercise any political or administrative function, or engage in any other occupation of a professional nature.

2. Any doubt on this point shall be settled by the decision of the Court.

Article 17

1. No member of the Court may act as agent, counsel, or advocate in any case.

2. No member may participate in the decision of any case in which he has previously taken part as agent, counsel, or advocate for one of the parties, or as a member of a national or international court, or of a commission of enquiry, or in any other capacity.

3. Any doubt on this point shall be settled by the decision of the Court.

Article 18

1. No member of the Court can be dismissed unless, in the unanimous opinion of the other members, he has ceased to fulfill the required conditions.

2. Formal notification thereof shall be made to the Secretary-General by the Registrar.

3. This notification makes the place vacant.

Article 19

The members of the Court, when engaged on the business of the Court, shall enjoy diplomatic privileges and immunities.

Article 20

Every member of the Court shall, before taking up his duties, make a solemn declaration in open court that he will exercise his powers impartially and conscientiously.

Article 21

1. The Court shall elect its President and Vice-President for three years; they may be re-elected.

2. The Court shall appoint its Registrar and may provide for the appointment of such other officers as may be necessary.

Article 22

1. The seat of the Court shall be established at The Hague. This, however, shall not prevent the Court from sitting and ex-

ercising its functions elsewhere whenever the Court considers it desirable.

2. The President and the Registrar shall reside at the seat of the Court.

Article 23

1. The Court shall remain permanently in session, except during the judicial vacations, the dates and duration of which shall be fixed by the Court.

2. Members of the Court are entitled to periodic leave, the dates and duration of which shall be fixed by the Court, having in mind the distance between The Hague and the home of each judge.

3. Members of the Court shall be bound, unless they are on leave or prevented from attending by illness or other serious reasons duly explained to the President, to hold themselves permanently at the disposal of the Court.

Article 24

1. If, for some special reason, a member of the Court considers that he should not take part in the decision of a particular case, he shall so inform the President.

2. If the President considers that for some special reason one of the members of the Court should not sit in a particular case, he shall give him notice accordingly.

3. If in any such case the member of the Court and the President disagree, the matter shall be settled by the decision of the Court.

Article 25

1. The full Court shall sit except when it is expressly provided otherwise in the present Statute.

2. Subject to the condition that the number of judges available to constitute the Court is not thereby reduced below eleven, the Rules of the Court may provide for allowing one or more judges, according to circumstances and in rotation, to be dispensed from sitting.

3. A quorum of nine judges shall suffice to constitute the Court.

Article 26

1. The Court may from time to time form one or more chambers, composed of three or more judges as the Court may determine, for dealing with particular categories of cases; for example, labor cases and cases relating to transit and communications.

2. The Court may at any time form a chamber for dealing with a particular case. The number of judges to constitute such a chamber shall be determined by the Court with the approval of the parties.

3. Cases shall be heard and determined by the chamber provided for in this Article if the parties so request.

Article 27

A judgment given by any of the chambers provided for in Articles 26 and 29 shall be considered as rendered by the Court.

Article 28

The chambers provided for in Articles 26 and 29 may, with the consent of the parties, sit and exercise their functions elsewhere than at The Hague.

Article 29

With a view to the speedy despatch of business, the Court shall form annually a chamber composed of five judges which, at the request of the parties, may hear and determine cases by summary procedure. In addition, two judges shall be selected for the purpose of replacing judges who find it impossible to sit.

Article 30

1. The Court shall frame rules for carrying out its functions. In particular, it shall lay down rules of procedure.

2. The Rules of the Court may provide for assessors to sit with the Court or with any of its chambers, without the right to vote.

Article 31

1. Judges of the nationality of each of the parties shall retain their right to sit in the case before the Court.

2. If the Court includes upon the Bench a judge of the nationality of one of the parties, any other party may choose a person to sit as judge. Such person shall be chosen preferably from among those persons who have been nominated as candidates as provided in Articles 4 and 5.

3. If the Court includes upon the Bench no judge of the nationality of the parties, each of these parties may proceed to choose a judge as provided in paragraph 2 of this Article.

4. The provisions of this Article shall apply to the case of Articles 26 and 29. In such cases, the President shall request one or, if necessary, two of the members of the Court forming the chamber to give place to the members of the Court of the nationality of the parties concerned, and, failing such, or if they are unable to be present, to the judges specially chosen by the parties.

5. Should there be several parties in the same interest, they shall, for the purpose of the preceding provisions, be reckoned as one party only. Any doubt upon this point shall be settled by the decision of the Court.

6. Judges chosen as laid down in paragraphs 2, 3, and 4 of this Article shall fulfill the conditions required by Articles 2, 17 (paragraph 2), 20, and 24 of the present Statute. They shall take part in the decision on terms of complete equality with their colleagues.

Article 32

1. Each member of the Court shall receive an annual salary.

2. The President shall receive a special annual allowance.

3. The Vice-President shall receive a special allowance for every day on which he acts as President.

4. The judges chosen under Article 31, other than members of the Court, shall receive compensation for each day on which they exercise their functions.

5. These salaries, allowances, and compensation shall be fixed

by the General Assembly. They may not be decreased during the term of office.

6. The salary of the Registrar shall be fixed by the General Assembly on the proposal of the Court.

7. Regulations made by the General Assembly shall fix the conditions under which retirement pensions may be given to members of the Court and to the Registrar, and the conditions under which members of the Court and the Registrar shall have their traveling expenses refunded.

8. The above salaries, allowances, and compensation shall be free of all taxation.

Article 33

The expenses of the Court shall be borne by the United Nations in such a manner as shall be decided by the General Assembly.

CHAPTER II: COMPETENCE OF THE COURT

Article 34

1. Only states may be parties in cases before the Court.

2. The Court, subject to and in conformity with its Rules, may request of public international organizations information relevant to cases before it, and shall receive such information presented by such organizations on their own initiative.

3. Whenever the construction of the constituent instrument of a public international organization or of an international convention adopted thereunder is in question in a case before the Court, the Registrar shall so notify the public international organization concerned and shall communicate to it copies of all the written proceedings.

Article 35

1. The Court shall be open to the states parties to the present Statute.

2. The conditions under which the Court shall be open to other states shall, subject to the special provisions contained in treaties in force, be laid down by the Security Council, but in no

case shall such conditions place the parties in a position of inequality before the Court.

3. When a state which is not a Member of the United Nations is a party to a case, the Court shall fix the amount which that party is to contribute towards the expenses of the Court. This provision shall not apply if such state is bearing a share of the expenses of the Court.

Article 36

1. The jurisdiction of the Court comprises all cases which the parties refer to it and all matters specially provided for in the Charter of the United Nations or in treaties and conventions in force.

2. The states parties to the present Statute may at any time declare that they recognize as compulsory *ipso facto* and without special agreement in relation to any other state accepting the same obligation, the jurisdiction of the Court in all legal disputes concerning:

a. the interpretation of a treaty;

b. any question of international law;

c. the existence of any fact which, if established, would constitute a breach of an international obligation;

d. the nature or extent of the reparation to be made for the breach of an international obligation.

3. The declarations referred to above may be made unconditionally or on condition of reciprocity on the part of several or certain states, or for a certain time.

4. Such declarations shall be deposited with the Secretary-General of the United Nations, who shall transmit copies thereof to the parties to the Statute and to the Registrar of the Court.

5. Declarations made under Article 36 of the Statute of the Permanent Court of International Justice and which are still in force shall be deemed, as between the parties to the present Statute, to be acceptances of the compulsory jurisdiction of the International Court of Justice for the period which they still have to run and in accordance with their terms.

6. In the event of a dispute as to whether the Court has jurisdiction, the matter shall be settled by the decision of the Court.

Article 37

Whenever a treaty or convention in force provides for reference of a matter to a tribunal to have been instituted by the League of Nations, or to the Permanent Court of International Justice, the matter shall, as between the parties to the present Statute, be referred to the International Court of Justice.

Article 38

1. The Court, whose function is to decide in accordance with international law such disputes as are submitted to it, shall apply:

a. international conventions, whether general or particular, establishing rules expressly recognized by the contesting states;

b. international custom, as evidence of a general practice accepted as law;

c. the general principles of law recognized by civilized nations;

d. subject to the provisions of Article 59, judicial decisions and the teachings of the most highly qualified publicists of the various nations, as subsidiary means for the determination of rules of law.

2. This provision shall not prejudice the power of the Court to decide a case *ex aequo et bono,* if the parties agree thereto.

CHAPTER III: PROCEDURE

Article 39

1. The official languages of the Court shall be French and English. If the parties agree that the case shall be conducted in French, the judgment shall be delivered in French. If the parties agree that the case shall be conducted in English, the judgment shall be delivered in English.

2. In the absence of an agreement as to which language shall be employed, each party may, in the pleadings, use the language which it prefers; the decision of the Court shall be given in

French and English. In this case the Court shall at the same time determine which of the two texts shall be considered as authoritative.

3. The Court shall, at the request of any party, authorize a language other than French or English to be used by that party.

Article 40

1. Cases are brought before the Court, as the case may be, either by the notification of the special agreement or by a written application addressed to the Registrar. In either case the subject of the dispute and the parties shall be indicated.

2. The Registrar shall forthwith communicate the application to all concerned.

3. He shall also notify the Members of the United Nations through the Secretary-General, and also any other states entitled to appear before the Court.

Article 41

1. The Court shall have the power to indicate, if it considers that circumstances so require, any provisional measures which ought to be taken to preserve the respective rights of either party.

2. Pending the final decision, notice of the measures suggested shall forthwith be given to the parties and to the Security Council.

Article 42

1. The parties shall be represented by agents.

2. They may have the assistance of counsel or advocates before the Court.

3. The agents, counsel, and advocates of parties before the Court shall enjoy the privileges and immunities necessary to the independent exercise of their duties.

Article 43

1. The procedure shall consist of two parts: written and oral.

2. The written proceedings shall consist of the communication to the Court and to the parties of memorials, counter-

memorials and, if necessary, replies; also all papers and documents in support.

3. These communications shall be made through the Registrar, in the order and within the time fixed by the Court.

4. A certified copy of every document produced by one party shall be communicated to the other party.

5. The oral proceedings shall consist of the hearing by the Court of witnesses, experts, agents, counsel, and advocates.

Article 44

1. For the service of all notices upon persons other than the agents, counsel, and advocates, the Court shall apply direct to the government of the state upon whose territory the notice has to be served.

2. The same provision shall apply whenever steps are to be taken to procure evidence on the spot.

Article 45

The hearing shall be under the control of the President or, if he is unable to preside, of the Vice-President; if neither is able to preside, the senior judge present shall preside.

Article 46

The hearing in Court shall be public, unless the Court shall decide otherwise, or unless the parties demand that the public be not admitted.

Article 47

1. Minutes shall be made at each hearing and signed by the Registrar and the President.

2. These minutes alone shall be authentic.

Article 48

The Court shall make orders for the conduct of the case, shall decide the form and time in which each party must conclude its arguments, and make all arrangements connected with the taking of evidence.

Article 49

The Court may, even before the hearing begins, call upon the agents to produce any document or to supply any explanations. Formal note shall be taken of any refusal.

Article 50

The Court may, at any time, entrust any individual, body, bureau, commission, or other organization that it may select, with the task of carrying out an enquiry or giving an expert opinion.

Article 51

During the hearing any relevant questions are to be put to the witnesses and experts under the conditions laid down by the Court in the rules of procedure referred to in Article 30.

Article 52

After the Court has received the proofs and evidence within the time specified for the purpose, it may refuse to accept any further oral or written evidence that one party may desire to present unless the other side consents.

Article 53

1. Whenever one of the parties does not appear before the Court, or fails to defend its case, the other party may call upon the Court to decide in favor of its claim.

2. The Court must, before doing so, satisfy itself, not only that it has jurisdiction in accordance with Articles 36 and 37, but also that the claim is well founded in fact and law.

Article 54

1. When, subject to the control of the Court, the agents, counsel, and advocates have completed their presentation of the case, the President shall declare the hearing closed.

2. The Court shall withdraw to consider the judgment.

3. The deliberations of the Court shall take place in private and remain secret.

Article 55

1. All questions shall be decided by a majority of the judges present.

2. In the event of an equality of votes, the President or the judge who acts in his place shall have a casting vote.

Article 56

1. The judgment shall state the reasons on which it is based.

2. It shall contain the names of the judges who have taken part in the decision.

Article 57

If the judgment does not represent in whole or in part the unanimous opinion of the judges, any judge shall be entitled to deliver a separate opinion.

Article 58

The judgment shall be signed by the President and by the Registrar. It shall be read in open court, due notice having been given to the agents.

Article 59

The decision of the Court has no binding force except between the parties and in respect of that particular case.

Article 60

The judgment is final and without appeal. In the event of dispute as to the meaning or scope of the judgment, the Court shall construe it upon the request of any party.

Article 61

1. An application for revision of a judgment may be made only when it is based upon the discovery of some fact of such a nature as to be a decisive factor, which fact was, when the judgment was given, unknown to the Court and also to the party claiming revision, always provided that such ignorance was not due to negligence.

2. The proceedings for revision shall be opened by a judgment of the Court expressly recording the existence of the new fact, recognizing that it has such a character as to lay the case open to revision, and declaring the application admissible on this ground.

3. The Court may require previous compliance with the terms of the judgment before it admits proceedings in revision.

4. The application for revision must be made at latest within six months of the discovery of the new fact.

5. No application for revision may be made after the lapse of ten years from the date of the judgment.

Article 62

1. Should a state consider that it has an interest of a legal nature which may be affected by the decision in the case, it may submit a request to the Court to be permitted to intervene.

2. It shall be for the Court to decide upon this request.

Article 63

1. Whenever the construction of a convention to which states other than those concerned in the case are parties is in question, the Registrar shall notify all such states forthwith.

2. Every state so notified has the right to intervene in the proceedings; but if it uses this right, the construction given by the judgment will be equally binding upon it.

Article 64

Unless otherwise decided by the Court, each party shall bear its own costs.

CHAPTER IV: ADVISORY OPINIONS

Article 65

1. The Court may give an advisory opinion on any legal question at the request of whatever body may be authorized by or in accordance with the Charter of the United Nations to make such a request.

2. Questions upon which the advisory opinion of the Court is asked shall be laid before the Court by means of a written request containing an exact statement of the question upon which an opinion is required, and accompanied by all documents likely to throw light upon the question.

Article 66

1. The Registrar shall forthwith give notice of the request for an advisory opinion to all states entitled to appear before the Court.

2. The Registrar shall also, by means of a special and direct communication, notify any state entitled to appear before the Court or international organization considered by the Court, or, should it not be sitting, by the President, as likely to be able to furnish information on the question, that the Court will be prepared to receive, within a time limit to be fixed by the President, written statements, or to hear, at a public sitting to be held for the purpose, oral statements relating to the question.

3. Should any such state entitled to appear before the Court have failed to receive the special communication referred to in paragraph 2 of this Article, such state may express a desire to submit a written statement or to be heard; and the Court will decide.

4. States and organizations having presented written or oral statements or both shall be permitted to comment on the statements made by other states or organizations in the form, to the extent, and within the time limits which the Court, or, should it not be sitting, the President, shall decide in each particular case. Accordingly, the Registrar shall in due time communicate any such written statements to states and organizations having submitted similar statements.

Article 67

The Court shall deliver its advisory opinions in open Court, notice having been given to the Secretary-General and to the representatives of Members of the United Nations, or other states and of international organizations immediately concerned.

Article 68

In the exercise of its advisory functions the Court shall further be guided by the provisions of the present Statute which apply in contentious cases to the extent to which it recognizes them to be applicable.

CHAPTER V: AMENDMENT

Article 69

Amendments to the present Statute shall be effected by the same procedure as is provided by the Charter of the United Nations for amendments to that Charter, subject however to any provisions which the General Assembly upon recommendation of the Security Council may adopt concerning the participation of states which are parties to the present Statute but are not Members of the United Nations.

Article 70

The Court shall have power to propose such amendments to the present Statute as it may deem necessary, through written communications to the Secretary-General, for consideration in conformity with the provisions of Article 69.

THE BERLIN (POTSDAM) CONFERENCE [1]

THE BERLIN (Potsdam) Conference, held from July 17 to August 2, 1945, has been the only Big Three meeting to be held following the end of the war in Europe. President Truman here met Marshal Stalin for the first time. Owing to the Conservative party's defeat in the British general elections which occurred during the Conference, and for which the Conference was interrupted (July 26 to July 27), Prime Minister Churchill was replaced by Clement Attlee in the conversations. The major part of the protocol of proceedings, signed by the United States, Great Britain, and the Soviet Union, was released at the close of the Conference, the full text being released on March 24, 1947. [2]

The results of the Conference were twofold. A comprehensive agreement was made for the occupation and administration of Germany pending the peace settlement, and arrangements were made for preparatory work looking toward the conclusion of treaties of peace with the minor Axis nations in Europe. Secondly, a warning was given to Japan (July 26, 1945) that she would face "inevitable and complete destruction" unless she agreed to the "unconditional surrender of all Japanese armed forces." [3] Although the warn-

---

[1] *Department of State Bulletin,* Vol. XIII, pp. 153*ff.*

[2] The most important agreement not made public immediately related to the Black Sea Straits (section XVI). The three governments agreed "that the Convention concluded at Montreux should be revised as failing to meet present-day conditions." *New York Times,* March 25, 1947. This has not been done.

[3] *Department of State Bulletin,* Vol. XII, pp. 137*ff.*

ing was not signed by Russia, its issuance from the Conference suggested the possibility of forthcoming Soviet action in the Far East.

II. ESTABLISHMENT OF A COUNCIL OF FOREIGN MINISTERS

The Conference reached an agreement for the establishment of a Council of Foreign Ministers . . . to continue the necessary preparatory work for the peace settlements. . . .

1

There shall be established a Council composed of the Foreign Ministers of the United Kingdom, the U.S.S.R., China, France and the U.S.

2

(i) The Council shall normally meet in London, which shall be the permanent seat of the joint secretariat which the Council will form. Each of the Foreign Ministers will be accompanied by a high-ranking deputy, duly authorized to carry on the work of the Council in the absence of his Foreign Minister, and by a small staff of technical advisers.

(ii) The first meeting of the Council shall be held in London not later than September 1, 1945. Meetings may be held by common agreement in other capitals as may be agreed from time to time.

3

(i) As its immediate important task the Council shall be authorized to draw up, with a view to their submission to the United Nations, treaties of peace with Italy, Rumania, Bulgaria, Hungary and Finland, and to propose settlements of territorial questions outstanding on the termination of the war in Europe. The Council shall be utilized for the preparation of a peace settlement for Germany to be accepted by the Government of Germany when a Government adequate for the purpose is established.

(ii) For the discharge of each of these tasks the Council will be composed of the members representing those States which were signatory to the terms of surrender imposed upon the enemy State concerned. For the purpose of the peace settlement for Italy, France shall be regarded as a signatory to the terms of surrender for Italy. Other members will be invited to participate when matters directly concerning them are under discussion.

(iii) Other matters may from time to time be referred to the Council by agreement between the member Governments.

4

(i) Whenever the Council is considering a question of direct interest to a State not represented thereon, such State should be invited to send representatives to participate in the discussion and study of that question.

(ii) The Council may adapt its procedure to the particular problems under consideration. In some cases it may hold its own preliminary discussions prior to the participation of other interested States. In other cases, the Council may convoke a formal conference of the State chiefly interested in seeking a solution of the particular problem.

In accordance with the decision of the conference the three Governments have each addressed an identical invitation to the Governments of China and France to adopt this text and to join in establishing the Council. . . .

III. THE POLITICAL AND ECONOMIC PRINCIPLES TO GOVERN THE TREATMENT OF GERMANY IN THE INITIAL CONTROL PERIOD

A. POLITICAL PRINCIPLES

1

In accordance with the agreement on control machinery in Germany, supreme authority in Germany is exercised, on instructions from their respective Governments, by the Commanders in Chief of the armed forces of the U.S.A., the United Kingdom, the U.S.S.R. and the French Republic, each in his own zone of occupation, and also jointly, in matters affecting Germany as a whole, in their capacity as members of the Control Council. . . .

. . . .

3

The purposes of the occupation of Germany by which the Control Council shall be guided are:

(i) The complete disarmament and demilitarization of Germany and the elimination or control of all German industry that could be used for military production. To these ends:

(a) All German land, naval and air forces, the SS, SA, SD and Gestapo . . . shall be completely and finally abolished. . . .

(b) All arms, ammunition and implements of war and all specialized facilities for their production shall be held at the disposal of the Allies or destroyed. . . .

(ii) To convince the German people that they have suffered a total military defeat and that they cannot escape responsibility for what they have brought upon themselves. . . .

(iii) To destroy the National Socialist Party. . . .

(iv) To prepare for the eventual reconstruction of German political life on a democratic basis and for eventual peaceful cooperation in international life by Germany.

4

All Nazi laws which provide the basis of the Hitler regime or established discrimination on grounds of race, creed or political opinion shall be abolished. . . .

5

War criminals and those who have participated in planning or carrying out Nazi enterprises involving or resulting in atrocities or war crimes shall be arrested and brought to judgment. . . .

7

German education shall be so controlled as completely to eliminate Nazi and militarist doctrines. . . .

8

The judicial system will be reorganized. . . .

9

The administration in Germany should be directed toward the decentralization of the political structure and the development of local responsibility. To this end:

(i) Local self-government shall be restored throughout Germany. . . .

(ii) All democratic political parties with rights of assembly and of public discussion shall be allowed and encouraged throughout Germany. . . .

(iv) For the time being, no central German Government shall be established. Notwithstanding this, however, certain essential central German administrative departments headed by state secretaries shall be established, particularly in the fields of finance, transport, communications, foreign trade and industry. . . .

10

Subject to the necessity for maintaining military security, freedom of speech, press and religion shall be permitted, and religious institutions shall be respected. Subject likewise to the maintenance of military security, the formation of free trade unions shall be permitted.

B. ECONOMIC PRINCIPLES

11

In order to eliminate Germany's war potential, the production of arms, ammunition and implements of war as well as all types of aircraft and sea-going ships shall be prohibited and prevented. Production of metals, chemicals, machinery and other items that are directly necessary to a war economy shall be rigidly controlled and restricted to Germany's approved post-war peacetime needs to meet the objectives stated in paragraph 15. Productive capacity not needed for permitted production shall be removed in accordance with the reparations plan recommended by the

Allied Commission on Reparations and approved by the Governments concerned, or if not removed, shall be destroyed.

12

At the earliest practicable date, the German economy shall be decentralized for the purpose of eliminating the present excessive concentration of economic power as exemplified in particular by cartels, syndicates, trusts and other monopolistic arrangements.

13

In organizing the German economy, primary emphasis shall be given to the development of agriculture and peaceful domestic industries.

14

During the period of occupation Germany shall be treated as a single economic unit. . . .

15

Allied controls shall be imposed upon the German economy, but only to the extent necessary:

(a) To carry out programs of industrial disarmament, demilitarization, of reparations and of approved exports and imports.

(b) To assure the production and maintenance of goods and services required to meet the needs of the occupying forces and displaced persons in Germany and essential to maintain in Germany average living standards not exceeding the average of the standards of living of European countries. (European countries means all European countries, excluding the United Kingdom and the U.S.S.R.). . . .

16

In the imposition and maintenance of economic controls established by the Control Council, German administrative machinery shall be created and the German authorities shall be required to the fullest extent practicable to proclaim and assume administration of such controls. Thus it should be brought home to the

German people that the responsibility for the administration of such controls and any breakdown in these controls will rest with themselves. . . .

.   .   .   .

19

Payment of reparations should leave enough resources to enable the German people to subsist without external assistance. In working out the economic balance of Germany, the necessary means must be provided to pay for imports approved by the Control Council in Germany. The proceeds of exports from current production and stocks shall be available in the first place for payment for such imports.

The above clause will not apply to the equipment and products referred to in paragraphs 4(A) and 4(B) of the reparations agreement.

IV. REPARATIONS FROM GERMANY

1

Reparation claims of the U.S.S.R. shall be met by removals from the zone of Germany occupied by the U.S.S.R. and from appropriate German external assets.

2

The U.S.S.R. undertakes to settle the reparation claims of Poland from its own share of reparations.

3

The reparation claims of the United States, the United Kingdom and other countries entitled to reparations shall be met from the western zones and from appropriate German external assets.

4

In addition to the reparations to be taken by the U.S.S.R. from its own zone of occupation, the U.S.S.R. shall receive additionally from the western zones:

(A) 15 per cent of such usable and complete industrial capital equipment, in the first place from the metallurgical, chemical and machine manufacturing industries as is unnecessary for the German peace economy and should be removed from the western zones of Germany, in exchange for an equivalent value of food, coal, potash, zinc, timber, clay products, petroleum products and such other commodities as may be agreed upon.

(B) 10 per cent of such industrial capital equipment as is unnecessary for the German peace economy and should be removed from the western zones, to be transferred to the Soviet Government on reparations account without payment or exchange of any kind in return.

Removals of equipment as provided in (A) and (B) above shall be made simultaneously.

5

The amount of equipment to be removed from the western zones on account of reparations must be determined within six months from now at the latest.

6

Removals of industrial capital equipment shall begin as soon as possible and shall be completed within two years from the determination specified in paragraph 5. The delivery of products covered by 4(A) above shall begin as soon as possible and shall be made by the U.S.S.R. in agreed installments within five years of the date hereof. The determination of the amount and character of the industrial capital equipment unnecessary for the German peace economy and therefore available for reparation shall be made by the Control Council under policies fixed by the Allied Commission on Reparations, with the participation of France, subject to the final approval of the zone commander in the zone from which the equipment is to be removed. . . .

V. DISPOSAL OF THE GERMAN NAVY AND MERCHANT MARINE

The conference agreed in principle upon arrangements for the use and disposal of the surrendered German fleet and merchant ships. . . . A further joint statement will be published. . . .[4]

VI. CITY OF KOENIGSBERG AND THE ADJACENT AREA

The conference examined a proposal by the Soviet Government that pending the final determination of territorial questions at the peace settlement the section of the western frontier of the Union of Soviet Socialist Republics which is adjacent to the Baltic Sea should pass from a point on the eastern shore of the Bay of Danzig to the east, north of Braunsberg-Doldap, to the meeting point of the frontiers of Lithuania, the Polish Republic and East Prussia.

The conference has agreed in principle to the proposal of the Soviet Government concerning the ultimate transfer to the Soviet Union of the City of Koenigsberg and the area adjacent to it as described above subject to expert examination of the actual frontier.

The President of the United States and the British Prime Minister have declared that they will support the proposal of the conference at the forthcoming peace settlement.

.   .   .   ., ...

IX. POLAND

A.

We have taken note with pleasure of the agreement reached among representative Poles from Poland and abroad which has made possible the formation, in accordance with the decisions reached at the Crimea Conference, of a Polish Provisional Government of National Unity recognized by the three Powers. The establishment by the British and United States Governments of diplomatic relations with the Polish Provisional Government has

[4] The further statement said: ". . . operable surface units which could be made operable within a specified time together with 30 U-boats should be divided equally between the Three Powers and . . . the remainder of the German fleet should be destroyed." *Department of State Bulletin*, Vol. XIV, p. 173.

resulted in the withdrawal of their recognition from the former Polish Government in London, which no longer exists.

The British and United States Governments have taken measures to protect the interest of the Polish Provisional Government as the recognized Government of the Polish State in the property belonging to the Polish State located in their territories and under their control, whatever the form of this property may be. They have further taken measures to prevent alienation to third parties of such property. All proper facilities will be given to the Polish Provisional Government for the exercise of the ordinary legal remedies for the recovery of any property belonging to the Polish State which may have been wrongfully alienated.

The three Powers are anxious to assist the Polish Provisional Government in facilitating the return to Poland as soon as practicable of all Poles abroad who wish to go, including members of the Polish armed forces and the Merchant Marine. They ex- pect that those Poles who return home shall be accorded personal and property rights on the same basis as all Polish citizens.

The three Powers note that the Polish Provisional Government, in accordance with the decisions of the Crimea Conference has agreed to the holding of free and unfettered elections as soon as possible on the basis of universal suffrage and secret ballot in which all democratic and anti-Nazi parties shall have the right to take part and to put forward candidates, and that representatives of the Allied press shall enjoy full freedom to report to the world upon developments in Poland before and during the elections.

B.

. . . In conformity with the agreement on Poland reached at the Crimea Conference, the three heads of Government have sought the opinion of the Polish Provisional Government of National Unity in regard to the accession of territory in the north and west which Poland should receive. The President of the National Council of Poland and members of the Polish Provisional Government of National Unity have been received at the Conference and have fully presented their views. The three heads of Government reaffirm their opinion that the final delimitation of the western frontier of Poland should await the peace settlement.

The three heads of Government agree that, pending the final determination of Poland's western frontier, the former German territories east of a line running from the Baltic Sea immediately west of Swinemunde, and thence along the Oder River to the confluence of the Western Neisse River and along the Western Neisse to the Czechoslovak frontier, including that portion of East Prussia not placed under the administration of the Union of Soviet Socialist Republics in accordance with the understanding reached at this Conference and including the area of the former free city of Danzig, shall be under the administration of the Polish State and for such purposes should not be considered as part of the Soviet zone of occupation in Germany.

X. CONCLUSION OF PEACE TREATIES AND ADMISSION TO THE UNITED NATIONS ORGANIZATION

The three Governments consider it desirable that the present anomalous position of Italy, Bulgaria, Finland, Hungary and Rumania should be terminated by the conclusion of peace treaties. . . . The conclusion of peace treaties with recognized democratic governments in these States will also enable the three Governments to support applications from them for membership of the United Nations. . . . The three Governments feel bound, however, to make it clear that they, for their part, would not favor any application for membership put forward by the present Spanish Government. . . .

DOCUMENT 42

THE NUREMBERG INDICTMENT [1]

THE NUREMBERG Indictment was signed on October 6, 1945, in Berlin by the United States, France, Great Britain, and the Soviet Union. Copies were given the defendants named in the indictment, and after a suitable period of preparation the trial began (November 20, 1945). In Appendix C to the indictment [2] a long list of treaties alleged to have been violated under Count Two of the indictment was given. Among these were the Hague Conventions for Peaceful Settlement, the Versailles treaty, the Locarno Treaty of Mutual Guarantee, the Kellogg-Briand Pact, and many others. On October 1, 1946, the verdicts were announced, and sentences were passed several days later. The sentences were: Göring, von Ribbentrop, Keitel, Kaltenbrunner, Rosenberg, Frank, Frick, Streicher, Sauckel, Jodl, Seyss-Inquart, Bormann (tried *in absentia*), to be hanged; Hess, Funk, and Raeder, life imprisonment; von Schirach and Speer, twenty years' imprisonment; von Neurath, fifteen years' imprisonment; Doenitz, ten years' imprisonment; Schacht, von Papen, and Fritzsche, acquitted. Göring took poison and died before he could be executed.

The Nuremberg Trials aroused considerable controversy. Many complex questions were involved. Did the trials, for example, involve ex post facto law? In the final analysis, however, it should be remembered that international law continually evolves. Since nations in addition to being the

[1] *Trial of the Major War Criminals before the International Military Tribunal, Official Documents,* Vol. I, pp. 27*ff.*
[2] *Ibid.,* pp. 84*ff.*

main subjects of the law, are themselves the formulators of the law, international law, when debatable, must be what the nations themselves agree it is. It is significant that the decisions of the Nuremberg Tribunal were approved by fifty-five states during the General Assembly of the United Nations in 1946.[3]

THE UNITED STATES OF AMERICA, THE FRENCH REPUBLIC, THE UNITED KINGDOM OF GREAT BRITAIN AND NORTHERN IRELAND, AND THE UNION OF SOVIET SOCIALIST REPUBLICS

—against—

HERMANN WILHELM GOERING, RUDOLF HESS, JOACHIM VON RIBBENTROP, ROBERT LEY, WILHELM KEITEL, ERNST KALTENBRUNNER, ALFRED ROSENBERG, HANS FRANK, WILHELM FRICK, JULIUS STREICHER, WALTER FUNK, HJALMAR SCHACHT, GUSTAV KRUPP VON BOHLEN UND HALBACH, KARL DOENITZ, ERICH RAEDER, BALDUR VON SCHIRACH, FRITZ SAUCKEL, ALFRED JODL, MARTIN BORMANN, FRANZ VON PAPEN, ARTHUR SEYSS-INQUART, ALBERT SPEER, CONSTANTIN VON NEURATH, and HANS FRITZCHE, Individually and as Members of Any of the Following Groups or Organizations to which They Respectively Belonged, Namely: DIE REICHSREGIERUNG (REICH CABINET); DAS KORPS DER POLITISCHEN LEITER DER NATIONALSOZIALISTISCHEN DEUTSCHEN ARBEITERPARTEI (LEADERSHIP CORPS OF THE NAZI PARTY); DIE SCHUTZSTAFFELN DER NATIONALSOZIALISTISCHEN DEUTSCHEN ARBEITERPARTEI (commonly known as the "SS") and including DER SICHERHEITSDIENST (commonly known as the "SD"); DIE GEHEIME STAATSPOLIZEI (SECRET STATE POLICE, commonly known as the "GESTAPO"); DIE STURMABTEILUNGEN DER NSDAP (commonly known as the "SA"); and the GENERAL STAFF and HIGH COMMAND of the GERMAN ARMED FORCES. . . .

Defendants.

. . . .

[3] *Resolutions of the General Assembly,* No. 95 (I), p. 188.

COUNT ONE—THE COMMON PLAN OR CONSPIRACY

Statement of the Offense

All the defendants, with divers other persons, during a period of years preceding 8 May 1945, participated as leaders, organizers, instigators, or accomplices in the formulation or execution of a common plan or conspiracy to commit, or which involved the commission of, Crimes against Peace, War Crimes, and Crimes against Humanity, as defined in the Charter of this Tribunal, and, in accordance with the provisions of the Charter, are individually responsible for their own acts and for all acts committed by any persons in the execution of such plan or conspiracy. The common plan or conspiracy embraced the commission of Crimes against Peace, in that the defendants planned, prepared, initiated, and waged wars of aggression, which were also wars in violation of international treaties, agreements, or assurances. In the development and course of the common plan or conspiracy it came to embrace the commission of War Crimes, in that it contemplated, and the defendants determined upon and carried out, ruthless wars against countries and populations, in violation of the rules and customs of war, including as typical and systematic means by which the wars were prosecuted, murder, ill-treatment, deportation for slave labor and for other purposes of civilian populations of occupied territories, murder and ill-treatment of prisoners of war and of persons on the high seas, the taking and killing of hostages, the plunder of public and private property, the indiscriminate destruction of cities, towns, and villages, and devastation not justified by military necessity. The common plan or conspiracy contemplated and came to embrace as typical and systematic means, and the defendants determined upon and committed, Crimes against Humanity, both within Germany and within occupied territories, including murder, extermination, enslavement, deportation, and other inhumane acts committed against civilian populations before and during the war, and persecutions on political, racial or religious grounds, in execution of the plan for preparing and prosecuting aggressive or illegal wars, many of such acts and persecutions being violations of the domestic laws of the countries where perpetrated.

.   .   .   .

COUNT TWO—CRIMES AGAINST PEACE

Statement of the Offense

All the defendants with divers other persons, during a period of years preceding 8 May 1945, participated in the planning, preparation, initiation, and waging of wars of aggression, which were also wars in violation of international treaties, agreements, and assurances.

.   .   .   .

COUNT THREE—WAR CRIMES

Statement of the Offense

All the defendants committed War Crimes between 1 September 1939 and 8 May 1945, in Germany and in all those countries and territories occupied by the German Armed Forces since 1 September 1939, and in Austria, Czechoslovakia, and Italy, and on the High Seas.

All the defendants, acting in concert with others, formulated and executed a Common Plan or Conspiracy to commit War Crimes as defined. . . . This plan involved, among other things, the practice of "total" war including methods of combat and of military occupation in direct conflict with the laws and customs of war, and the commission of crimes perpetrated on the field of battle during encounters with enemy armies, and against prisoners of war, and in occupied territories against the civilian population of such territories.

The said War Crimes were committed by the defendants and by other persons for whose acts the defendants are responsible (under Article 6 of the Charter) as such other persons when committing the said War Crimes performed their acts in execution of a common plan and conspiracy to commit the said War

Crimes, in the formulation and execution of which plan and conspiracy all the defendants participated as leaders, organizers, instigators, and accomplices.

These methods and crimes constituted violations of international conventions, of internal penal laws and of the general principles of criminal law as derived from the criminal law of all civilized nations, and were involved in and part of a systematic course of conduct.

. . . .

COUNT FOUR—CRIMES AGAINST HUMANITY

Statement of the Offense

All the defendants committed Crimes against Humanity during a period of years preceding 8 May 1945 in Germany and in all those countries and territories occupied by the German armed forces since 1 September 1939 and in Austria and Czechoslovakia and in Italy and on the High Seas.

All the defendants, acting in concert with others, formulated and executed a common plan or conspiracy to commit Crimes against Humanity as defined in Article 6(c) of the Charter. This plan involved, among other things, the murder and persecution of all who were or who were suspected of being hostile to the Nazi Party and all who were or who were suspected of being opposed to the common plan alleged in Count One.

The said Crimes against Humanity were committed by the defendants and by other persons for whose acts the defendants are responsible (under Article 6 of the Charter) as such other persons, when committing the said War Crimes, performed their acts in execution of a common plan and conspiracy to commit the said War Crimes, in the formulation and execution of which plan and conspiracy all the defendants participated as leaders, organizers, instigators, and accomplices.

These methods and crimes constituted violations of international conventions, of internal penal laws, of the general principles of criminal law as derived from the criminal law of all civilized nations and were involved in and part of a systematic course of conduct. The said acts were contrary to Article 6 of the Charter.

The Prosecution will rely upon the facts pleaded under Count Three as also constituting Crimes against Humanity.

MOSCOW CONFERENCE OF 1945 [1]

A CONFERENCE of the foreign ministers of the United States, Great Britain, and the Soviet Union was held in Moscow December 16 to December 26, 1945. At the conclusion of the conference a protocol of proceedings was issued as given below. Parts III (Korea), IV (China), V (Rumania), and VI (Bulgaria) have been omitted since they refer, for the most part, to transitional arrangements in those nations which did not come to fruition.

Among the more important decisions made at the Moscow Conference of 1945 were the agreements relating to the interim occupation of Japan (pending the peace treaty), the procedure for making the peace treaties for Europe (other than those for Austria and Germany), and the establishment of an Atomic Energy Commission, to be responsible to the Security Council of the United Nations.

I. PREPARATION OF PEACE TREATIES WITH ITALY, RUMANIA, BULGARIA, HUNGARY, AND FINLAND

As announced on the 24th of December, 1945, the Governments of the Soviet Union, the United Kingdom and the United States have agreed and have requested the adherence of the Governments of France and China to the following procedure with respect to the preparation of peace treaties:

1

In the drawing up by the Council of Foreign Ministers of treaties of peace with Italy, Rumania, Bulgaria, Hungary, Fin-

[1] *Department of State Bulletin,* Vol. XIII, pp. 1027ff.

land, only members of the Council who are, or under the terms of the agreement establishing the Council of Foreign Ministers adopted at the Berlin Conference are deemed to be, signatory of the surrender terms will participate, unless and until the Council takes further action under the agreement to invite other members of the Council to participate on questions directly concerning them. That is to say:

A. The terms of the peace treaty with Italy will be drafted by the Foreign Ministers of the United Kingdom, the United States, the Soviet Union and France;

B. The terms of the peace treaties with Rumania, Bulgaria and Hungary by the Foreign Ministers of the Soviet Union, the United States and the United Kingdom;

C. The terms of the peace treaty with Finland by the Foreign Ministers of the Soviet Union and the United Kingdom.

The deputies of the Foreign Ministers will immediately resume their work in London on the basis of understandings reached on the questions discussed at the first plenary session of the Council of Foreign Ministers in London.

2

When the preparation of all these drafts has been completed, the Council of Foreign Ministers will convoke a conference for the purpose of considering treaties of peace with Italy, Rumania, Bulgaria, Hungary and Finland. The conference will consist of the five members of the Council of Foreign Ministers together with all members of the United Nations which actively waged war with substantial military force against European enemy states, namely: U.S.S.R., U.K., U.S.A., China, France, Australia, Belgium, Byelorussian S.S.R., Brazil, Canada, Czechoslovakia, Ethiopia, Greece, India, the Netherlands, New Zealand, Norway, Poland, Union of South Africa, Yugoslavia, Ukrainian S.S.R. The Conference will be held not later than May 1, 1946.

3

After the conclusion of the deliberations of the conference and upon consideration of its recommendations, the States signatory to the terms of armistice with Italy, Rumania, Bulgaria, Hungary and Finland—France being regarded as such for the purposes of the peace treaty with Italy—will draw up final texts of peace treaties.

4

The final texts of the respective peace treaties as so drawn up will be signed by representatives of the States represented at the conference which are at war with the enemy States in question. The texts of the respective peace treaties will then be submitted to the other United Nations which are at war with the enemy States in question.

5

The peace treaties will come into force immediately after they have been ratified by the Allied States signatory to the respective armistices, France being regarded as such in the case of the peace with Italy. These treaties are subject to ratification by the enemy States in question.

II. FAR EASTERN COMMISSION AND ALLIED COUNCIL FOR JAPAN

A. FAR EASTERN COMMISSION

Agreement was reached, with the concurrence of China, for the establishment of a Far Eastern Commission to take the place of the Far Eastern Advisory Commission. The terms of reference for the Far Eastern Commission are as follows:

(i) Establishment of the Commission

A Far Eastern Commission is hereby established composed of the representatives of the U.S.S.R., U.K., U.S., China, France, the Netherlands, Canada, Australia, New Zealand, India and the Philippine Commonwealth.

(ii) Functions

(A) The functions of the Far Eastern Commission shall be:
1. To formulate the policies, principles and standards in

conformity with which the fulfillment by Japan of its obligations under the terms of surrender may be accomplished.

2. To review, on the request of any member, any directive issued to the Supreme Commander for the Allied Powers or any action taken by the Supreme Commander involving policy decisions within the jurisdiction of the Commission.

3. To consider such other matters as may be assigned to it by agreement among the participating Governments reached in accordance with the voting procedure provided for in Article V-2 hereunder.

(B) The Commission shall not make recommendations with regard to the conduct of military operations nor with regard to territorial adjustments.

(C) The Commission in its activities will proceed from the fact that there has been formed an Allied Council for Japan and will respect existing control machinery in Japan, including the chain of command from the United States Government to the Supreme Commander and the Supreme Commander's command of occupational forces.

(iii) *Functions of the United States Government*

1. The U.S. Government shall prepare directives in accordance with policy decisions of the Commission and shall transmit them to the Supreme Commander through the appropriate U.S. Government agency. The Supreme Commander shall be charged with the implementation of the directives which express the policy decisions of the Commission.

2. If the Commission decides that any directive or action reviewed in accordance with Article (ii)-(A)-2 should be modified, its decision shall be regarded as a policy decision.

3. The U.S. Government may issue interim directives to the Supreme Commander pending action by the Commission whenever urgent matters arise not covered by policies already formulated by the Commission; provided that any directives dealing with fundamental changes in the Japanese constitutional structure or in the regime of control, or dealing with a change in the

Japanese Government as a whole, will be issued only following consultation and following the attainment of agreement in the Far Eastern Commission.

4. All directives issued shall be filed with the Commission. . . .

(v) Composition

1. The Far Eastern Commission shall consist of one representative of each of the States party to this agreement. . . .

2. The Commission may take action by less than unanimous vote provided that action shall have the concurrence of at least a majority of all the representatives including the representatives of the four following Powers: U.S.S.R., U.K., U.S.A., and China.

(vi) Location and Organization

1. The Far Eastern Commission shall have its headquarters in Washington. It may meet at other places as occasion requires, including Tokyo, if and when it deems it desirable to do so. . . .

(vii) Termination

The Far Eastern Commission shall cease to function when a decision to that effect is taken by the concurrence of at least a majority of all the representatives including the representatives of the four following Powers: U.S.S.R., U.K., U.S.A., and China. . . .

B. ALLIED COUNCIL FOR JAPAN

The following agreement was also reached, with the concurrence of China, for the establishment of an Allied Council for Japan:

1. There shall be established an Allied Council with its seat in Tokyo under the chairmanship of the Supreme Commander for the Allied Powers (or his deputy) for the purpose of consulting with and advising the Supreme Commander in regard to the implementation of the terms of surrender, the occupation and control of Japan, and of directives supplementary thereto; and for the purpose of exercising the control authority herein granted.

2. The membership of the Allied Council shall consist of the Supreme Commander (or his deputy), who shall be Chairman and U.S. member; a U.S.S.R. member; a Chinese member, and a member representing jointly the U.K., Australia, New Zealand and India. . . .

5. The Supreme Commander shall issue all orders for the implementation of the terms of surrender, the occupation and control of Japan, and directives supplementary thereto. In all cases action will be carried out under and through the Supreme Commander who is the sole executive authority for the Allied Powers in Japan. He will consult and advise with the Council in advance of the issuance of orders on matters of substance, the exigencies of the situation permitting. His decisions upon these matters shall be controlling.

6. If, regarding the implementation of policy decisions of the Far Eastern Commission on questions concerning a change in the regime of control, fundamental changes in the Japanese constitutional structure, and a change in the Japanese Government as a whole, a member of the Council disagrees with the Supreme Commander (or his deputy), the Supreme Commander will withhold the issuance of orders on these questions pending agreement thereon in the Far Eastern Commission.

7. In cases of necessity the Supreme Commander may make decisions concerning the change of individual Ministers of the Japanese Government, or concerning the filling of vacancies created by the resignation of individual cabinet members, after appropriate preliminary consultation with the representatives of the other Allied Powers on the Allied Council.

.   .   .   .

VII. THE ESTABLISHMENT BY THE UNITED NATIONS OF A COMMISSION FOR THE CONTROL OF ATOMIC ENERGY

Discussion of the subject of atomic energy related to the question of the establishment of a commission by the General Assembly of the United Nations. The Ministers of Foreign Affairs of the U.S.S.R., the U.S.A. and the U.K. . . . have agreed to invite the other permanent members of the Security Council, France and China, together with Canada, to join with them in assuming the initiative in sponsoring the following resolution at the first session of the General Assembly of the United Nations in January, 1946:

Resolved by the General Assembly of the United Nations to establish a Commission, with the composition and competence set out hereunder, to deal with the problems raised by the discovery of atomic energy and other related matters.

(*i*) *Establishment of the Commission*

A Commission is hereby established by the General Assembly with the terms of reference set out under Section V below.

(*ii*) *Relations of the Commission with the Organs of the United Nations*

A. The Commission shall submit its reports and recommendations to the Security Council, and such reports and recommendations shall be made public unless the Security Council, in the interests of peace and security, otherwise directs. In the appropriate cases the Security Council should transmit these reports to the General Assembly and the members of the United Nations, as well as to the Economic and Social Council and other organs within the framework of the United Nations.

B. In view of the Security Council's primary responsibility under the Charter of the United Nations for the maintenance of international peace and security, the Security Council shall issue directions to the Commission in matters affecting security. On these matters the Commission shall be accountable for its work to the Security Council.

(*iii*) *Composition of the Commission*

The Commission shall be composed of one representative from each of those States represented on the Security Council, and Canada, when that State is not a member of the Security

Council. Each representative on the Commission may have such assistants as he may desire.

(iv) Rules of Procedure

The Commission shall have whatever staff it may deem necessary, and shall make recommendations for its rules of procedure to the Security Council, which shall approve them as a procedural matter.

(v) Terms of Reference of the Commission

The Commission shall proceed with the utmost dispatch and inquire into all phases of the problem, and make such recommendations from time to time with respect to them as it finds possible. In particular the Commission shall make specific proposals:

A. For extending between all nations the exchange of basic scientific information for peaceful ends;

B. For control of atomic energy to the extent necessary to insure its use only for peaceful purposes;

C. For the elimination from national armaments of atomic weapons and of all other major weapons adaptable to mass destruction;

D. For effective safeguards by way of inspection and other means to protect complying states against the hazards of violations and evasions.

The work of the Commission should proceed by separate stages, the successful completion of each of which will develop the necessary confidence of the world before the next stage is undertaken.

The Commission shall not infringe upon the responsibilities of any organ of the United Nations, but should present recommendations for the consideration of those organs in the performance of their tasks under the terms of the United Nations Charter.

DOCUMENT 44

FIRST REPORT OF THE ATOMIC ENERGY COMMISSION TO THE SECURITY COUNCIL [1]

THE FOLLOWING extracts from the First Report of the Atomic Energy Commission to the Security Council, December 31, 1946, contain the principal points upon which the United States and the Soviet Union have failed to agree concerning the question of the international control of atomic energy. Apart from the general position of these powers (the U.S. desiring effective controls prior to destruction of the atomic bomb stock pile, and the U.S.S.R. desiring destruction of the stock pile as a prior condition for accepting international control of activities within the Soviet frontiers), the principal differences related to (1) whether the proposed Control Commission should have authority to *own and manage* atomic installations and activities wherever carried on, as proposed by the United States, or only an inspection power, as proposed by the Soviet Union, and (2) whether the Control Commission should be given power to institute sanctions not subject to veto, which the United States proposed and the Soviet Union opposed. The majority of the Atomic Energy Commission (which is composed of all those nations having a seat on the Security Council and Canada when that state is not a member of the Council) were in general agreement with the United States' position; but the Soviet Union and her satellites refused to yield from their original position, while the United States opposed outlawing the use of the

[1] *United Nations Atomic Energy Commission, Official Records, Special Supplement, Report to the Security Council,* Dec. 31, 1946, pp. 15ff.

atomic bomb and would not agree to the destruction of its stock pile until what it regarded as effective international control was established. The Soviet possession of the atomic bomb will no doubt substantially affect subsequent discussions by the Commission. The report below reflects the majority viewpoint.

PART II. FINDINGS

·   ·   ·   ·   ·   ·   ·   ·   ·   ·   ·   ·

C. General Findings

. . . The Commission has made the following additional findings of a general nature:

1. That scientifically, technologically, and practically, it is feasible,

(a) To extend among "all nations the exchange of basic scientific information" [2] on atomic energy "for peaceful ends," [2]

(b) To control "atomic energy to the extent necessary to insure its use only for peaceful purposes,"

(c) To accomplish "the elimination from national armaments of atomic weapons," and

(d) To provide "effective safeguards by way of inspection and other means to protect complying States against the hazards of violations and evasions."

2. That effective control of atomic energy depends upon effective control of the production and use of uranium, thorium, and their fissionable derivatives. Appropriate mechanisms of control to prevent their unauthorized diversion or clandestine production and use and to reduce the dangers of seizure—including one or more of the following types of safeguards: accounting, inspection, supervision, *management*,[3] and licensing—must be ap-

[2] The quotation marks refer to the Commission's terms of reference, Section 5, Resolution of the General Assembly, Jan. 24, 1946.

[3] Italics added.

plied through the various stages of the processes from the time the uranium and thorium ores are severed from the ground to the time they become nuclear fuel and are used. . . . *Owner-ship by the international control agency of mines and of ores still in the ground is not to be regarded as mandatory.*[4]

3. That whether the ultimate nuclear fuel be destined for peaceful or destructive uses, the productive processes are identical and inseparable up to a very advanced state of manufacture. Thus, the control of atomic energy to insure its use for peaceful purposes, the elimination of atomic weapons from national armaments, and the provision of effective safeguards to protect complying States against the hazards of violations and evasions must be accomplished through a single unified international system of control and inspection designed to carry out all of these related purposes. . . .

5. That an effective system for the control of atomic energy must be international, and must be established by an enforce-able multilateral treaty or convention which in turn must be administered and operated by an international organ or agency within the United Nations, possessing adequate powers and properly organized, staffed, and equipped for the purpose. . . .

PART III. RECOMMENDATIONS

Based upon the findings of the Commission set forth in Part II of this report, the Commission makes the following recommen-dations to the Security Council with respect to certain of the matters covered by the terms of reference of the Commission, which recommendations are interdependent and not severable, embodying the fundamental principles and indicating the basic organizational mechanisms necessary to attain the objectives set forth in Part II [C, General Findings, paragraph 1 (a)-(d) above].

1. There should be a strong and comprehensive international system of control and inspection aimed at attaining the ob-jectives set forth in the Commission's terms of reference.

[4] Italics added.

2. Such an international system of control and inspection should be established and its scope and functions defined by a treaty or convention in which all of the nations Members of the United Nations should be entitled to participate on fair and equitable terms. The international system of control and inspection should become operative only when those Members of the United Nations necessary to assure its success by signing and ratifying the treaty or convention have bound themselves to accept and support it. Consideration should be given to the matter of participation by non-Members of the United Nations.

3. The treaty or convention should include, among others, provisions for:

(a) Establishing in the United Nations an international control agency possessing powers and charged with responsibility necessary and appropriate for the prompt and effective discharge of the duties imposed upon it by the terms of the treaty or convention. Its rights, powers, and responsibilities, as well as its relations to the several organs of the United Nations, should be clearly established and defined by the treaty or convention. Such powers should be sufficiently broad and flexible to enable the international control agency to deal with new developments that may hereafter arise in the field of atomic energy. The treaty shall provide that the rule of unanimity of the permanent members, which in certain circumstances exists in the Security Council, shall have no relation to the work of the international control agency. *No government shall possess any right of "veto" over the fulfilment by the international control agency of the obligations imposed upon it by the treaty nor shall any government have the power, through the exercise of any right of "veto" or otherwise, to obstruct the course of control or inspection.*[5]

The international control agency shall promote among all nations the exchange of basic scientific information on atomic energy for peaceful ends, and shall be responsible for preventing the use of atomic energy for destructive purposes, and for the con-

[5] Italics added.

trol of atomic energy to the extent necessary to insure its use only for peaceful purposes.

The international control agency should have positive research and developmental responsibilities in order to remain in the forefront of atomic knowledge so as to render the international control agency more effective in promoting the beneficial uses of atomic energy and in eliminating its destructive ones. The exclusive right to carry on atomic research for destructive purposes should be vested in the international control agency.

Research in nuclear physics having a direct bearing on the use of atomic energy should be subject to appropriate safeguards established by the international control agency in accordance with the treaty or convention. Such safeguards should not interfere with the prosecution of pure scientific research, or the publication of its results, provided no dangerous use or purpose is involved.

Decisions of the international control agency pursuant to the powers conferred upon it by the treaty or convention should govern the operations of national agencies for atomic energy. In carrying out its prescribed functions, however, the international control agency should interfere as little as necessary with the operations of national agencies for atomic energy, or with the economic plans and the private, corporate, and State relationships in the several countries;

(b) Affording the duly accredited representatives of the international control agency unimpeded rights of ingress, egress, and access for the performance of their inspections and other duties into, from and within the territory of every participating nation, unhindered by national or local authorities;

(c) Prohibiting the manufacture, possession, and use of atomic weapons by all nations parties thereto and by all persons under their jurisdiction;

(d) Providing for the disposal of any existing stocks of atomic weapons and for the proper use of nuclear fuel adaptable for use in weapons;

(e) Specifying the means and methods of determining violations of its terms, setting forth such violations as shall constitute international crimes, and establishing the nature of the measures of enforcement and punishment to be imposed upon persons and upon nations guilty of violating the terms of the treaty or convention.

The judicial or other processes for determination of violations of the treaty or convention, and of punishments therefor, should be swift and certain. Serious violations of the treaty shall be reported immediately by the international control agency to the nations parties to the treaty, to the General Assembly and to the Security Council. Once the violations constituting international crimes have been defined and the measures of enforcement and punishment therefor agreed to in the treaty or convention, there shall be no legal right, by "veto" or otherwise, whereby a willful violator of the terms of the treaty or convention shall be protected from the consequences of violation of its terms.

The enforcement and punishment provisions of the treaty or convention would be ineffectual if, in any such situations, they could be rendered nugatory by the "veto" of a State which had voluntarily signed the treaty.

4. In consideration of the problem of violation of the terms of the treaty or convention, it should also be borne in mind that a violation might be of so grave a character as to give rise to the inherent right of self-defense recognized in Article 51 of the Charter of the United Nations.

5. The treaty or convention should embrace the entire program for putting the international system of control and inspection into effect and should provide a schedule for the completion of the transitional process over a period of time, step by step, in an orderly and agreed sequence leading to the full and effective establishment of international control of atomic energy. In order that the transition may be accomplished as rapidly as possible and with safety and equity to all, this Commission should supervise the transitional process, as prescribed in the treaty or convention, and should be empowered to determine when a particular stage or stages have been completed and subsequent ones are to commence.

THE ANGLO-FRENCH TREATY OF ALLIANCE [1]

WORLD WAR II, like most prolonged wars fought by coalitions, saw the conclusion of various treaties among the Allies designed to facilitate their cooperation in war and perpetuate their victory once won. It was for this purpose that the Anglo-Soviet Alliance of 1942 (see Document 31) and the Franco-Soviet Alliance of 1944 (see Document 36) were concluded. To complete the series of pacts among the three European Powers, the Anglo-French Treaty of Alliance was concluded on March 4, 1947, and came into force on September 8, 1947. Like the other two treaties, this was directed specifically against any possible threat of renewed German aggression; unlike the others, and reflecting the more permanent character of Anglo-French common interests, it was concluded for the unusually long period of fifty years. These three treaties differ from later treaties, such as the Brussels Treaty and the Atlantic Pact, which were directed against *any* possible aggressor.

Article I

Without prejudice to any arrangements that may be made under any treaty concluded between all the powers having responsibility for action in relation to Germany under Article 107 of the Charter of the United Nations,[2] for the purpose of pre-

---

[1] *United Nations Treaty Series,* Vol. IX, No. 132 (registered), pp. 187*ff.*

[2] See Document 39.

venting any infringement by Germany of her obligations with regard to disarmament and demilitarization and generally of insuring that Germany shall not again become a menace to peace,

The high contracting parties will, in the event of any threat to the security of either of them arising from the adoption by Germany of a policy of aggression, or from action by Germany designed to facilitate such a policy, take, after consulting with each other and where appropriate with the other Powers having responsibility for actions in relation to Germany, such agreed action (which, so long as the said Article 107 remains operative, shall be action under that article) as is best calculated to put an end to this threat.

Article II

Should either of the high contracting parties become again involved in hostilities with Germany, either in consequence of an armed attack within the meaning of Article 51 of the Charter of the United Nations, by Germany against that party, or as a result of enforcement action taken against Germany by the United Nations Security Council, the other high contracting party will at once give the high contracting party so involved in hostility all the military and other support and assistance in its power.

Article III

In the event of either high contracting party being prejudiced by the failure of Germany to fulfill any obligation of an economic character imposed on her as a result of the instrument of surrender, or arising out of any subsequent settlement, the high contracting parties will consult with each other, and where appropriate with the other powers having responsibilities for action in relation to Germany, with a view to taking agreed actions to deal with the situation.

Article IV

Bearing in mind the interests of the other members of the United Nations, the high contracting parties will, by constant consultation on matters affecting their economic relations with each other, take all possible steps to promote the prosperity and economic security of both countries and thus enable each of them to contribute more effectively to the economic and social objectives of the United Nations.

Article V

(1) Nothing in the present Treaty should be interpreted as derogating in any way from the obligation devolving upon the high contracting parties from the provisions of the Charter of the United Nations or from any special agreement concluded in virtue of Article 43 of the Charter.

(2) Neither of the high contracting parties will conclude any alliance or take part in any coalition directed against the other high contracting party: nor will they enter into any obligation inconsistent with the provisions of the present treaty.

Article VI

(1) The present Treaty is subject to ratification and the instruments of ratification will be exchanged in London as soon as possible.

(2) It will come into force immediately on the exchange of the instruments of ratification and will remain in force for a period of fifty years.

(3) Unless either of the high contracting parties gives to the other notice in writing to terminate it at least one year before the expiration of this period, it will remain in force without any specified time limit, subject to the right of either of the high contracting parties to terminate it by giving to the other in writing a year's notice of his intentions to do so.

THE TRUMAN DOCTRINE [1]

THE FOLLOWING speech, delivered to Congress by President Truman on March 12, 1947, sets forth the principles of American foreign policy which have come to be known as the "Truman Doctrine."

The Truman Doctrine was one of the first major efforts by the United States to implement a policy aimed at the containment of the Soviet Union. It aroused much debate in Congress and among the people generally. Although some questioned the wisdom of involving the United States in the Eastern Mediterranean which was remote from the seat of American power, the greater portion of the criticism reflected concern that the United States was "bypassing" the United Nations. Although the United States ultimately proceeded with its program of unilateral assistance to Greece and Turkey, it also supported fully the attempts of the United Nations Special Balkans Committee to pacify the region. The whole question served to underline the difficulty of adapting the United Nations, founded upon the supposition of cooperation between the United States and the Soviet Union, to conditions of tension between them.

. . . The gravity of the situation which confronts the world today necessitates my appearance before a joint session of the Congress. The foreign policy and the national security of this country are involved.

[1] *Congressional Record,* Vol. 93, 80th Congress, 1st Session, pp. 1980*ff*.

One aspect of the present situation, which I wish to present to you at this time for your consideration and decision, concerns Greece and Turkey.

The United States has received from the Greek Government an urgent appeal for financial and economic assistance. Preliminary reports from the American economic mission now in Greece and reports from the American Ambassador in Greece corroborate the statement of the Greek Government that assistance is imperative if Greece is to survive as a free nation.

I do not believe that the American people and the Congress wish to turn a deaf ear to the appeal of the Greek Government.

Greece is not a rich country. Lack of sufficient natural resources has always forced the Greek people to work hard to make both ends meet. Since 1940, this industrious, peace-loving country has suffered invasion, four years of cruel enemy occupation, and bitter internal strife.

When forces of liberation entered Greece they found that the retreating Germans had destroyed virtually all the railways, roads, port facilities, communications, and merchant marine. More than a thousand villages had been burned. Eighty-five per cent of the children were tubercular. Livestock, poultry, and draft animals had almost disappeared. Inflation had wiped out practically all savings.

As a result of these tragic conditions, a militant minority, exploiting human want and misery, was able to create political chaos which, until now, has made economic recovery impossible.

Greece is today without funds to finance the importation of those goods which are essential to bare subsistence. Under these circumstances the people of Greece cannot make progress in solving their problems of reconstruction. Greece is in desperate need of financial and economic assistance to enable it to resume purchases of food, clothing, fuel and seeds. These are indispensable for the subsistence of its people and are obtainable only from abroad. Greece must have help to import the goods necessary to restore internal order and security so essential for economic and political recovery.

The Greek Government has also asked for the assistance of

experienced American administrators, economists and technicians to insure that the financial and other aid given to Greece shall be used effectively in creating a stable and self-sustaining economy and in improving its public administration.

The very existence of the Greek state is today threatened by the terrorist activities of several thousand armed men, led by Communists, who defy the Government's authority at a number of points, particularly along the northern boundaries. A commission appointed by the United Nations Security Council is at present investigating disturbed conditions in Northern Greece and alleged border violations along the frontiers between Greece on the one hand and Albania, Bulgaria and Yugoslavia on the other.

Meanwhile, the Greek Government is unable to cope with the situation. The Greek Army is small and poorly equipped. It needs supplies and equipment if it is to restore the authority to the Government throughout Greek territory.

Greece must have assistance if it is to become a self-supporting and self-respecting democracy. The United States must supply that assistance. We have already extended to Greece certain types of relief and economic aid but these are inadequate. There is no other country to which democratic Greece can turn. No other nation is willing and able to provide the necessary support for a democratic Greek Government.

The British Government, which has been helping Greece, can give no further financial or economic aid after March 31. Great Britain finds itself under the necessity of reducing or liquidating its commitments in several parts of the world, including Greece.

We have considered how the United Nations might assist in this crisis. But the situation is an urgent one requiring immediate action, and the United Nations and its related organizations are not in a position to extend help of the kind that is required.

It is important to note that the Greek Government has asked for our aid in utilizing effectively the financial and other assistance we may give to Greece, and in improving its public administration. It is of the utmost importance that we supervise the use of any funds made available to Greece, in such a manner that each dollar spent will count toward making Greece self-supporting, and will help to build an economy in which a healthy democracy can flourish.

No government is perfect. One of the chief virtues of a democracy, however, is that its defects are always visible and under democratic processes can be pointed out and corrected. The Government of Greece is not perfect. Nevertheless, it represents 85 per cent of the members of the Greek Parliament who were chosen in an election last year. Foreign observers, including 692 Americans, considered this election to be a fair expression of the views of the Greek people.

The Greek Government has been operating in an atmosphere of chaos and extremism. It has made mistakes. The extension of aid by this country does not mean that the United States condones everything that the Greek Government has done or will do. We have condemned in the past, and we condemn now, extremist measures of the right or the left. We have in the past advised tolerance, and we advise tolerance now.

Greece's neighbor, Turkey, also deserves our attention. The future of Turkey as an independent and economically sound state is clearly no less important to the freedom-loving peoples of the world than the future of Greece. The circumstances in which Turkey finds itself today are considerably different from those of Greece. Turkey has been spared the disasters that have beset Greece. And during the war, the United States and Great Britain furnished Turkey with material aid. Nevertheless, Turkey now needs our support.

Since the war Turkey has sought financial assistance from Great Britain and the United States for the purpose of effecting that modernization necessary for the maintenance of its national integrity. That integrity is essential to the preservation of order in the Middle East.

The British Government has informed us that, owing to its own difficulties, it can no longer extend financial or economic aid to Turkey. As in the case of Greece, if Turkey is to have the assistance it needs, the United States must supply it. We are the only country able to provide that help.

I am fully aware of the broad implications involved if the United States extends assistance to Greece and Turkey, and I shall discuss these implications with you at this time.

One of the primary objectives of the foreign policy of the United States is the creation of conditions in which we and other nations will be able to work out a way of life free from coercion. This was a fundamental issue in the war with Germany and Japan. Our victory was won over countries which sought to impose their will, and their way of life, upon other nations.

To ensure the peaceful development of nations, free from coercion, the United States has taken a leading part in establishing the United Nations. The United Nations is designed to make possible lasting freedom and independence for all its members. We shall not realize our objectives, however, unless we are willing to help free people to maintain their free institutions and their national integrity against aggressive movements that seek to impose upon them totalitarian regimes. This is no more than a frank recognition that totalitarian regimes imposed on free peoples, by direct or indirect aggression, undermine the foundations of international peace and hence the security of the United States.

The peoples of a number of countries of the world have recently had totalitarian regimes forced upon them against their will. The Government of the United States has made frequent protests against coercion and intimidation, in violation of the Yalta Agreement, in Poland, Rumania and Bulgaria. I must also state that in a number of other countries there have been similar developments.

At the present moment in world history nearly every nation must choose between alternative ways of life. The choice is too often not a free one.

One way of life is based upon the will of the majority, and is distinguished by free institutions, representative government, free elections, guarantees of individual liberty, freedom of speech and religion, and freedom from political oppression.

The second way of life is based upon the will of a minority forcibly imposed upon the majority. It relies upon terror and oppression, a controlled press and radio, fixed elections, and the suppression of personal freedoms.

I believe that it must be the policy of the United States to support free peoples who are resisting attempted subjugation by armed minorities or by outside pressures.

I believe that we must assist free peoples to work out their own destinies in their own way.

I believe that our help should be primarily through economic and financial aid which is essential to economic stability and orderly political processes.

The world is not static, and the status quo is not sacred. But we cannot allow changes in the status quo in violation of the Charter of the United Nations by such methods as coercion, or by such subterfuges as political infiltration. In helping free and independent nations to maintain their freedom, the United States will be giving effect to the principles of the Charter of the United Nations.

It is necessary only to glance at a map to realize that the survival and integrity of the Greek nation are of grave importance in a much wider situation. If Greece should fall under the control of an armed minority, the effect upon its neighbor, Turkey, would be immediate and serious. Confusion and disorder might well spread throughout the entire Middle East.

Moreover, the disappearance of Greece as an independent state would have a profound effect upon those countries in Europe whose peoples are struggling against great difficulties to maintain their freedoms and their independence while they repair the damages of war.

It would be an unspeakable tragedy if these countries, which have struggled so long against overwhelming odds, should lose that victory for which they sacrificed so much. Collapse of free institutions and loss of independence would be disastrous not only for them but for the world. Discouragement and possibly failure would quickly be the lot of neighboring peoples striving to maintain their freedom and independence.

Should we fail to aid Greece and Turkey in this fateful hour, the effect will be far reaching to the West as well as to the East. We must take immediate and resolute action.

I therefore ask the Congress to provide authority for assistance to Greece and Turkey in the amount of $400,000,000 for the period ending June 30, 1948. In requesting these funds, I have taken into consideration the maximum amount of relief assistance which would be furnished to Greece out of the $350,000,000 which I recently requested that the Congress authorize for the prevention of starvation and suffering in countries devastated by the war.

In addition to funds, I ask the Congress to authorize the detail of American civilian and military personnel to Greece and Turkey, at the request of those countries, to assist in the tasks of reconstruction, and for the purpose of supervising the use of such financial and material assistance as may be furnished. I recommend that authority also be provided for the instruction and training of selected Greek and Turkish personnel.

Finally, I ask that the Congress provide authority which will permit the speediest and most effective use, in terms of needed commodities, supplies, and equipment, of such funds as may be authorized.

If further funds, or further authority, should be needed for purposes indicated in this message, I shall not hesitate to bring the situation before the Congress. On this subject the Executive and Legislative branches of the Government must work together.

This is a serious course upon which we embark. I would not recommend it except that the alternative is much more serious.

The United States contributed $341,000,000,000 toward winning World War II. This is an investment in world freedom and world peace.

The assistance that I am recommending for Greece and Turkey amounts to little more than 1 tenth of 1 per cent of this investment. It is only common sense that we should safeguard this investment and make sure that it was not in vain.

The seeds of totalitarian regimes are nurtured by misery and want. They spread and grow in the evil soil of poverty and strife. They reach their full growth when the hope of a people for a better life has died. We must keep that hope alive. The free peoples of the world look to us for support in maintaining their freedoms.

If we falter in our leadership, we may endanger the peace of the world—and we shall surely endanger the welfare of our own Nation.

Great responsibilities have been placed upon us by the swift movement of events. I am confident that the Congress will face these responsibilities squarely.

THE MARSHALL PLAN [1]

Much of Europe lay in ruins after World War II. Everywhere a grim struggle for rehabilitation and for the resumption of agricultural and industrial activities was being waged. The progress was slow and uncertain, and the transition to a peacetime world was piecemeal and halting. Under such conditions, it became clear that American assistance in substantial amounts would be needed to hasten recovery and to safeguard against an economic deterioration which might lead to social and political upheaval. Economic and humanitarian motives (and, later, ideological motives as well) combined to suggest the wisdom of putting an end to spasmodic charity and loans and of cooperating with Europe in a full-scale program designed to restore her economic health.

The program which later became known as the Marshall Plan was first stated officially by the then Under-Secretary of State, Dean Acheson. It failed to attract much attention, however, until the principle was restated in a speech by Secretary of State Marshall at Harvard University some weeks later. He made it clear that the main burden of administration and execution of the aid which the United States was prepared to offer must be the responsibility of the nations cooperating in the plan.

The statement by Secretary Marshall was acclaimed with enthusiasm by the nations of Western Europe as they real-

[1] Department of State Publication 2912, *The Development of the Foreign Reconstruction Policy of the United States;* Department of State Publication 2882, *European Initiative Essential to Economic Recovery.*

ized its implications. Immediately after the speech, Great
Britain, France, and the Soviet Union held a joint conference
to consider what might be done. The Russians subsequently
withdrew, and the invitation by the French to a general conference was declined by the Soviet bloc. The conference met
in Paris from July 12 to September 22, 1947, and was attended by Great Britain, Austria, Belgium, Denmark, France,
Greece, Iceland, Ireland, Italy, Luxemburg, Netherlands,
Norway, Portugal, Sweden, Switzerland, and Turkey, who
established a Committee of European Economic Recovery
(CEEC). The CEEC was to come to agreement, through discussion by the nations involved, on the amount of assistance
needed by each nation from the United States after they had
pooled their resources.

In America, stop-gap aid was advanced through the Reconstruction Finance Corporation until the passage, on June
28, 1948, of the Foreign Aid Appropriation Act, which provided $4,000,000,000 for European aid. Further aid was sub-
sequently advanced.

The CEEC established an Organization for European Eco-
nomic Cooperation (OEEC) to work together with the
American administrative agency, the Economic Cooperation
Administration (ECA). The OEEC and the ECA have jointly
administered the program of economic aid under the
Marshall Plan.

Address of Under Secretary of State, Dean Acheson (May 8,
1947):
". . . The facts of international life also mean that the United
States is going to have to undertake further emergency financing
of foreign purchases if foreign countries are to continue to buy in
1948 and 1949 the commodities which they need to sustain life
and at the same time rebuild their economies. . . . No other
country is able to bridge the gap in commodities or dollars . . .

until the various countries of the world get on their feet and become self-supporting there can be no political or economic stability in the world and no lasting peace or prosperity for any of us. Without outside aid, the process of recovery in many countries would take so long as to give rise to hopelessness and despair. In these conditions freedom and democracy and the independence of nations could not long survive, for hopeless and hungry people often resort to desperate measures. The war will not be over until the people of the world can again feed and clothe themselves and face the future with some degree of confidence. . . ."

Address of Secretary of State, George C. Marshall (June 5, 1947):

" . . . Europe's requirements for the next three or four years of foreign food and other essential products—principally from America—are so much greater than her present ability to pay that she must have substantial additional help or face economic, social, and political deterioration of a very grave character.

"The remedy lies in breaking the vicious circle and restoring the confidence of the European people in the economic future of their own countries and of Europe as a whole. The manufacturer and the farmer throughout wide areas must be able and willing to exchange their products for currencies the continuing value of which is not open to question.

" . . . It is logical that the United States should do whatever it is able to do to assist in the return of normal economic health in the world, without which there can be no political stability and no assured peace. Our policy is directed not against any country or doctrine but against hunger, poverty, desperation, and chaos. Its purpose should be the revival of a working economy in the world so as to permit the emergence of political and social conditions in which free institutions can exist. Such assistance, I am convinced, must not be on a piecemeal basis as various crises develop. Any assistance that this Government may render in the future should provide a cure rather than a mere palliative. . . .

"It is already evident that, before the United States Government can proceed much further in its efforts to alleviate the situation and help start the European world on its way to recovery, there must be some agreement among the countries of Europe as to the requirements of the situation and the part those countries themselves will take in order to give proper effect to whatever action might be undertaken by this Government. It would be neither fitting nor efficacious for this Government to undertake to draw up unilaterally a program designed to place Europe on its feet economically. That is the business of the Europeans. The initiative, I think, must come from Europe. The role of this country should consist of friendly aid in the drafting of a European program and of later support of such a program so far as it may be practical for us to do so. The program should be a joint one, agreed to by a number of, if not all, European nations. . . ."

THE RIO PACT [1]

THE RIO Pact, known more formally as the Inter-American Treaty of Reciprocal Assistance, was concluded on September 2, 1947, following a Conference for the Maintenance of Continental Peace and Security at Quitandinha, Brazil, held from August 15 to September 2, 1947. It was signed by the Dominican Republic, Guatemala, Costa Rica, Peru, El Salvador, Panama, Paraguay, Venezuela, Chile, Honduras, Cuba, Bolivia, Colombia, Mexico, Haiti, Ecuador, Uruguay, the United States, Argentina, and Brazil and came into effect on December 3, 1948.[2]

Considered together with the other agreements and treaties comprising the Inter-American System, the Rio Pact is an important step toward the creation of an effective agency for hemispheric cooperation and collective security. By the terms of the Rio Treaty, any threat of aggression may be dealt with by measures up to and including the use of armed force. Votes on such matters require a two-thirds majority of the states ratifying the treaty (Article XVII). They are then binding upon all the parties with the sole exception that no state is required to use armed force without its consent (Article XX).

[1] Department of State Publication 3016, International Organization and Conference Series II, American Republics 1, *Inter-American Conference for the Maintenance of Continental Peace and Security*, pp. 59*ff.*

[2] The United States ratified on Dec. 8, 1947, the second nation to do so. Costa Rica ratified as the fourteenth state, and the treaty came into effect. *Department of State Bulletin*, Vol. XX, p. 707, Vol. XXI, pp. 150*ff.*

Many of the provisions of the Rio Pact, including the obligation to consult in the face of any threat and the stipulation that an armed attack against any of them is considered as an attack against all, are duplicated in the Atlantic Pact (see Document 50). In this respect, the Rio Pact provides an excellent illustration of the way in which multilateral agreements and procedures are evolved out of past experience and adapted to somewhat different subsequent conditions.

Article I

The High Contracting Parties formally condemn war and undertake in their international relations not to resort to the threat or the use of force in any manner inconsistent with the provisions of the Charter of the United Nations or of this Treaty.

Article II

As a consequence of the principle set forth in the preceding Article, the High Contracting Parties undertake to submit every controversy which may arise between them to methods of peaceful settlement and to endeavor to settle any such controversy among themselves by means of the procedures in force in the Inter-American System before referring it to the General Assembly or the Security Council of the United Nations.

Article III

1. The High Contracting Parties agree that an armed attack by any State against an American State shall be considered as an attack against all the American States and, consequently, each one of the said Contracting Parties undertakes to assist in meeting the attack in the exercise of the inherent right of individual or collective self-defense recognized by Article 51 of the Charter of the United Nations.

2. On the request of the State or States directly attacked and until the decision of the Organ of Consultation of the Inter-

American System, each one of the Contracting Parties may determine the immediate measures which it may individually take in fulfillment of the obligation contained in the preceding paragraph and in accordance with the principle of continental solidarity. The Organ of Consultation shall meet without delay for the purpose of examining those measures and agreeing upon the measures of a collective character that should be taken.

3. The provisions of this Article shall be applied in case of any armed attack which takes place within the region described in Article IV or within the territory of an American State. When the attack takes place outside of the said areas, the provisions of Article VI shall be applied.

4. Measures of self-defense provided for under this Article may be taken until the Security Council of the United Nations has taken the measures necessary to maintain international peace and security.

Article IV

The region to which this Treaty refers is bounded as follows: beginning at the North Pole; thence due south to a point 74 degrees north latitude, 10 degrees west longitude; thence by a rhumb line to a point 47 degrees 30 minutes north latitude, 50 degrees west longitude; thence by a rhumb line to a point 35 degrees north latitude, 60 degrees west longitude; thence due south to a point in 20 degrees north latitude; thence by a rhumb line to a point 5 degrees north latitude, 24 degrees west longitude; thence due south to the South Pole; thence due north to a point 30 degrees south latitude, 90 degrees west longitude; thence by a rhumb line to a point on·the Equator at 97 degrees west longitude; thence by a rhumb line to a point 15 degrees north latitude, 120 degrees west longitude; thence by a rhumb line to a point 50 degrees north latitude, 170 degrees east longitude; thence due north to a point in 54 degrees north latitude; thence by a rhumb line to a point 65 degrees 30 minutes north latitude, 168 degrees 58 minutes 5 seconds west longitude; thence due north to the North Pole.

Article V

The High Contracting Parties shall immediately send to the Security Council of the United Nations, in conformity with Articles 51 and 54 of the Charter of the United Nations, complete information concerning the activities undertaken or in contemplation in the exercise of the right of self-defense or for the purpose of maintaining inter-American peace and security.

Article VI

If the inviolability or the integrity of the territory or the sovereignty or political independence of any American State should be affected by an aggression which is not an armed attack or by an extra-continental or intra-continental conflict, or by any other fact or situation that might endanger the peace of America, the Organ of Consultation shall meet immediately in order to agree on the measures which must be taken in case of aggression to assist the victim of the aggression or, in any case, the measures which should be taken for the common defense and for the maintenance of the peace and security of the Continent.

Article VII

In the case of a conflict between two or more American States, without prejudice to the right of self-defense in conformity with Article 51 of the Charter of the United Nations, the High Contracting Parties, meeting in consultation shall call upon the contending States to suspend hostilities and restore matters to the *status quo ante bellum,* and shall take in addition all other necessary measures to reestablish or maintain inter-American peace and security and for the solution of the conflict by peaceful means. The rejection of the pacifying action will be considered in the determination of the aggressor and in the application of the measures which the consultative meeting may agree upon.

Article VIII

For the purposes of this Treaty, the measures on which the Organ of Consultation may agree will comprise one or more of the following: recall of chiefs of diplomatic missions; breaking of diplomatic relations; breaking of consular relations; partial or complete interruption of economic relations or of rail, sea, air, postal, telegraphic, telephonic, and radiotelephonic or radio-telegraphic communications; and use of armed force.

Article IX

In addition to other acts which the Organ of Consultation may characterize as aggression, the following shall be considered as such:

a. Unprovoked armed attack by a State against the territory, the people, or the land, sea or air forces of another State;

b. Invasion, by the armed forces of a State, of the territory of an American State, through the trespassing of boundaries demarcated in accordance with a treaty, judicial decision, or arbitral award, or, in the absence of frontiers thus demarcated, invasion affecting a region which is under the effective jurisdiction of another State.

Article X

None of the provisions of this Treaty shall be construed as impairing the rights and obligations of the High Contracting Parties under the Charter of the United Nations.

Article XI

The consultations to which this Treaty refers shall be carried out by means of the Meetings of Ministers of Foreign Affairs of the American Republics which have ratified the Treaty, or in the manner or by the organ which in the future may be agreed upon.

Article XII

The Governing Board of the Pan American Union may act provisionally as an organ of consultation until the meeting of the Organ of Consultation referred to in the preceding Article takes place.

Article XIII

The consultations shall be initiated at the request addressed to the Governing Board of the Pan American Union by any of the Signatory States which has ratified the Treaty.

Article XIV

In the voting referred to in this Treaty only the representatives of the Signatory States which have ratified the Treaty may take part.

Article XV

The Governing Board of the Pan American Union shall act in all matters concerning this Treaty as an organ of liaison among the Signatory States which have ratified this Treaty and between these States and the United Nations.

Article XVI

The decisions of the Governing Board of the Pan American Union referred to in Articles XIII and XV above shall be taken by an absolute majority of the Members entitled to vote.

Article XVII

The Organ of Consultation shall take its decisions by a vote of two-thirds of the Signatory States which have ratified the Treaty.

Article XVIII

In the case of a situation or dispute between American States, the parties directly interested shall be excluded from the voting referred to in the two preceding Articles.

Article XIX

To constitute a quorum in all the meetings referred to in the previous Articles, it shall be necessary that the number of States represented shall be at least equal to the number of votes necessary for the taking of the decision.

Article XX

Decisions which require the application of the measures specified in Article VIII shall be binding upon all the Signatory States
which have ratified this Treaty, with the sole exception that no
State shall be required to use armed force without its consent.

Article XXI

The measures agreed upon by the Organ of Consultation shall
be executed through the procedures and agencies now existing or
those which may in the future be established.

Article XXII

This treaty shall come into effect between the States which
ratify it as soon as the ratifications of two-thirds of the Signatory
States have been deposited.

Article XXIII

This Treaty is open for signature by the American States at
the city of Rio de Janeiro, and shall be ratified by the Signatory
States as soon as possible in accordance with their respective constitutional processes. The ratifications shall be deposited with the
Pan American Union, which shall notify the Signatory States of
each deposit. Such notification shall be considered as an exchange
of ratifications.

Article XXIV

The present Treaty shall be registered with the Secretariat of
the United Nations through the Pan American Union, when two-
thirds of the Signatory States have deposited their ratification.

Article XXV

This Treaty shall remain in force indefinitely, but may be
denounced by any High Contracting Party by a notification in
writing to the Pan American Union, which shall inform all the
other High Contracting Parties of each notification of denunciation received. After the expiration of two years from the date of
the receipt by the Pan American Union of a notification of de-

nunciation by any High Contracting Party, the present Treaty shall cease to be in force with respect to such State, but shall remain in full force and effect with respect to all the other High Contracting Parties.

Article XXVI

The principles and fundamental provisions of this Treaty shall be incorporated in the Organic Pact of the Inter-American System.

THE BRUSSELS (WESTERN UNION) ALLIANCE [1]

THE BRUSSELS (Western Union) Alliance of March 17, 1948, signed by Belgium, the Netherlands, Luxemburg, Great Britain, and France, came into force on August 25, 1948. It was not merely a military alliance, although it did provide the first step in an unprecedented peacetime coordination among the armed forces of the signatory nations. Viscount Montgomery, with headquarters in France, became the first Supreme Commander. From the military point of view, the conclusion of the treaty underlined the changed condition of Western Europe after World War II. Relative to the military potential of the Soviet Union, the power of any single Western European nation is small. The conclusion of the treaty, therefore, was an essential precondition to the creation of more adequate security conditions for the entire area.

The Brussels Treaty established also a consultative commission designed to assist in the process of coordinating the separate economies, reducing economic friction, and looking toward the eventual elimination of customs barriers which have for centuries impeded the flow of goods and services in a natural economic area.

Article I

Convinced of the close community of their interests and of the necessity of uniting in order to promote the economic recovery

[1] *United Nations Treaty Series,* Vol. XIX, No. 304 (registered), pp. 51 *ff.*

of Europe, the high contracting parties will so organize and coordinate their economic activities as to produce the best possible
results, by the elimination of conflict in their economic policies,
co-ordination of production and development of commercial
exchanges.

The co-operation provided for in the preceding paragraph,
which will be effected through the Consultative Council referred
to in Article VII as well as through other bodies, shall not involve any duplication of or prejudice to the work of other economic organizations in which the high contracting parties are or
may be represented, but shall on the contrary assist the work of
those organizations.

Article II

The high contracting parties will make every effort in common, both by direct consultation and in specialized agencies, to
promote the attainment of a higher standard of living by their
peoples and to develop on corresponding lines the social and
other related services of their countries. The high contracting
parties will consult with the object of achieving the earliest possible application of the recommendations of immediate practical
interest relating to social matters, adopted with their approval
in the specialized agencies. They will endeavor to conclude as
soon as possible conventions with others in the sphere of social
security.

Article III

The high contracting parties will make every effort in common
to lead their peoples towards better understanding of the principles which form the basis of their common civilization, and to
promote cultural exchanges by conventions between themselves
or by other means.

Article IV

If any of the high contracting parties should be the object of
an armed attack in Europe, the other high contracting parties
will, in accordance with the provisions of Article 51 of the
Charter of the United Nations, afford the party so attacked all
military and other aid and assistance in their power.

Article V

All measures taken as a result of the preceding article shall be immediately reported to the Security Council. They shall be terminated as soon as the Security Council has taken the measures necessary to maintain or restore international peace and security.

The present Treaty does not prejudice in any way the obligations of the high contracting parties under the provisions of the Charter of the United Nations. It shall not be interpreted as affecting in any way the authority and responsibility of the Security Council under the Charter to take at any time such action as it deems necessary in order to maintain or restore international peace and security.

Article VI

The high contracting parties declare, each so far as he is concerned, that none of the international engagements now in force between him and any other high contracting party or any third State is in conflict with the provisions of the present treaty. None of the high contracting parties will conclude any alliance or participate in any coalition directed against any other of the high contracting parties.

Article VII

For the purpose of consulting together on all questions dealt with in the present Treaty, the high contracting parties will create a Consultative Council which shall be so organized as to be able to exercise its functions continuously. The Council shall meet at such times as it shall deem fit. At the request of any of the high contracting parties, the Council shall be immediately convened in order to permit the high contracting parties to consult with regard to any situation which may constitute a threat to peace, in whatever area this threat should arise, with regard to the attitude to be adopted and the steps to be taken in the case of a renewal by Germany of an aggressive policy, or with regard to any situation constituting a danger to economic stability.

Article VIII

In pursuance of their determination to settle disputes only by peaceful means, the high contracting parties will apply to disputes between themselves the following provisions:

The high contracting parties will, while the present Treaty remains in force, settle all disputes falling within the scope of Article 36, paragraph 2, of the statute of the International Court of Justice by referring them to the Court, subject only, in the case of each of them, to any reservation already made by that party when accepting this clause for compulsory jurisdiction to the extent that that party may maintain the reservation.

In addition, the high contracting parties will submit to conciliation all disputes outside the scope of Article 36, paragraph 2, of the statute of the International Court of Justice. In the case of a mixed dispute involving both questions for which conciliation is appropriate and other questions for which judicial settlement is appropriate, any party to the dispute shall have the right to insist that the judicial settlement of the legal questions shall precede conciliation.

The preceding provisions of this article in no way affect the application of relevant provisions or agreements prescribing some other method of pacific settlement.

Article IX

The high contracting parties may, by agreement, invite any other State to accede to the present Treaty on conditions to be agreed between them and the State so invited.

Any State so invited may become a party to the Treaty by depositing an instrument of accession with the Belgian Government.

The Belgian Government will inform each of the high contracting parties of the deposit of each instrument of accession.

Article X

The present Treaty shall be ratified and the instruments of ratification shall be deposited as soon as possible with the Belgian Government.

It shall enter into force on the date of deposit of the last instrument of ratification, and shall thereafter remain in force for fifty years.

After the expiry of the period of fifty years, each of the high contracting parties shall have the right to cease to be party thereto, provided that he shall have previously given one year's notice of denunciation to the Belgian Government.

The Belgian Government shall inform the Governments of the other high contracting parties of the deposit of each instrument of ratification and of each notice of denunciation.

THE NORTH ATLANTIC PACT [1]

THE NORTH Atlantic Pact was signed by the United States, Great Britain, France, Italy, Canada, Norway, Belgium, Denmark, the Netherlands, Luxemburg, Portugal, and Iceland on April 4, 1949. It was ratified and came into effect on August 24, 1949. It is the most far-reaching document of its kind ever signed and ratified by the United States. The pact provides that the parties will "consult" together to determine a common course of action as need arises. While it does not commit the United States automatically to war, it does provide that an armed attack against one is an attack against all and that the parties will take "individually and in concert" such action as each of them "deems necessary," up to and including the use of armed force.

The treaty did not arouse as much public interest and discussion as might have been expected. Among the main points which were debated were the following: (1) Did the treaty strengthen or weaken the United Nations? (2) Did it diminish the chances of war? The treaty's relation to the United Nations was perhaps the most ambiguous point. It could be claimed that Article 51 of the United Nations Charter (see Document 39) reserved to each member the right of "individual or collective self-defense." There could be no doubt that the pact was such an arrangement (although from the Soviet viewpoint it was considered as aggressive

[1] Department of State Publication 3464, General Foreign Policy Series 8, *North Atlantic Treaty*.

and as directed against herself [2]). Yet it was also an obvious admission that the United Nations was not sufficient to guarantee the security of its member nations. In the treaty itself it was provided that "all measures taken" would be reported immediately to the Security Council and that the measures would be terminated when the Council had taken steps to "restore and maintain" peace and security. Thus, as a "regional" arrangement, the treaty technically remains within the framework of the United Nations Charter, even though the inclusion of such a vast area in two hemispheres somewhat strains the meaning of the word "region." What has changed is that a new emphasis upon regional collective security has replaced the original emphasis of the United Nations upon world-wide collective security.

Since the Soviet Union has concluded a series of bilateral pacts with the nations in the Communist bloc, two rival regional systems which together stretch most of the way around the world now confront each other. It should be noted in this connection that most of the Soviet pacts so far concluded provide, as in the Soviet-Bulgarian Treaty of March 18, 1948 (Article I), that:

The High Contracting Parties bind themselves to take jointly all measures within their power to set aside all threats of revival of aggression by Germany or any other state whatsoever which

[2] *USSR Information Bulletin,* Apr. 8, 1949, p. 205: ". . . the North Atlantic Treaty . . . creates a closed grouping of states and, what is particularly important, absolutely ignores the possibility of the repetition of German aggression, consequently not having as its aim the prevention of a new German aggression. And inasmuch as, of the Great Powers which comprised the anti-Hitlerite coalition, only the USSR is not a party to this Treaty, the North Atlantic Treaty must be regarded as a treaty directed against one of the chief allies of the United States, Great Britain and France in the late war—against the USSR."

may unite itself with Germany directly or in any other manner whatsoever. . . .[3]

The Soviet-Chinese Treaty of February, 1950, is similar except that the word "Japan" is substituted for "Germany." Unless there exist secret provisions in these pacts which would place them in effect against a power *other than one allied with Germany,* the Soviet Union has not evolved a treaty system as yet strictly comparable to the North Atlantic Pact, which is directed against any aggressor whether allied with Germany or not. Nevertheless, if Russia has not yet done so, it is certainly within her power to do so. The trend, therefore, is toward a system of exclusive regional blocs. How far this differs from a balance-of-power arrangement is questionable. How far these arrangements can be reconciled with the intent of the Charter is even more questionable.

Whether the chances of war are increased or diminished by the North Atlantic Treaty is uncertain. The pact creates a strong alliance, a coalition which, if it must fight, will fight in concert from the very beginning. The obvious advantages of this, compared to the piecemeal formation of coalitions at the very last hour, need no underlining. Had Russia and America fought together with France and Britain beginning in September, 1939, World War II might well have ended long before 1945.

The military coordination already begun in Western Europe under the Brussels Alliance (see Document 49) is being expanded under the North Atlantic Pact. Weapons are to be standardized, with the United States, under the Military Assistance Program, furnishing many of the weapons with which the armed forces of the Atlantic nations will be equipped.

---

[3] *North Atlantic Treaty,* Senate Document No. 48, 81st Congress, 1st Session, p. 111.

The Parties to this Treaty reaffirm their faith in the purposes and principles of the Charter of the United Nations and their desire to live in peace with all peoples and all governments.

They are determined to safeguard the freedom, common heritage and civilization of their peoples, founded on the principles of democracy, individual liberty and the rule of law.

They seek to promote stability and well-being in the North Atlantic area.

They are resolved to unite their efforts for collective defense and for the preservation of peace and security.

They therefore agree to this North Atlantic Treaty:

Article I

The Parties undertake, as set forth in the Charter of the United Nations, to settle any international disputes in which they may be involved by peaceful means in such a manner that international peace and security, and justice, are not endangered, and to refrain in their international relations from the threat or use of force in any manner inconsistent with the purposes of the United Nations.

Article II

The Parties will contribute toward the further development of peaceful and friendly international relations by strengthening their free institutions, by bringing about a better understanding of the principles upon which these institutions are founded, and by promoting conditions of stability and well-being. They will seek to eliminate conflict in their international economic policies and will encourage economic collaboration between any or all of them.

Article III

In order more effectively to achieve the objectives of this Treaty, the Parties, separately and jointly, by means of continuous and effective self-help and mutual aid, will maintain and develop their individual and collective capacity to resist armed attack.

Article IV

The Parties will consult together whenever, in the opinion of any of them, the territorial integrity, political independence or security of any of the Parties is threatened.

Article V

The Parties agree that an armed attack against one or more of them in Europe or North America shall be considered an attack against them all; and consequently they agree that, if such an armed attack occurs, each of them, in exercise of the right of individual or collective self-defense recognized by Article 51 of the Charter of the United Nations, will assist the Party or Parties so attacked by taking forthwith, individually and in concert with the other Parties, such action as it deems necessary, including the use of armed force, to restore and maintain the security of the North Atlantic area.

Any such armed attack and all measures taken as a result thereof shall immediately be reported to the Security Council. Such measures shall be terminated when the Security Council has taken the measures necessary to restore and maintain international peace and security.

Article VI

For the purpose of Article V an armed attack on one or more of the Parties is deemed to include an armed attack on the territory of any of the Parties in Europe or North America, on the Algerian departments of France, on the occupation forces of any Party in Europe, on the islands under the jurisdiction of any Party in the North Atlantic area north of the Tropic of Cancer or on the vessels or aircraft in this area of any of the Parties.

Article VII

This Treaty does not affect, and shall not be interpreted as affecting, in any way the rights and obligations under the Charter of the Parties which are members of the United Nations, or the primary responsibility of the Security Council for the maintenance of international peace and security.

Article VIII

Each Party declares that none of the international engagements now in force between it and any other of the Parties or any third state is in conflict with the provisions of this Treaty, and undertakes not to enter into any international engagement in conflict with this Treaty.

Article IX

The Parties hereby establish a council, on which each of them shall be represented, to consider matters concerning the implementation of this Treaty. The council shall be so organized as to be able to meet promptly at any time. The council shall set up such subsidiary bodies as may be necessary; in particular it shall establish immediately a defense committee which shall recommend measures for the implementation of Articles III and V.

Article X

The Parties may, by unanimous agreement, invite any other European state in a position to further the principles of this Treaty and to contribute to the security of the North Atlantic area to accede to this Treaty. Any state so invited may become a party to the Treaty by depositing its instrument of accession with the Government of the United States of America. The Government of the United States of America will inform each of the Parties of the deposit of each such instrument of accession.

Article XI

This Treaty shall be ratified and its provisions carried out by the Parties in accordance with their respective constitutional processes. The instruments of ratification shall be deposited as soon as possible with the Government of the United States of America, which will notify all the other signatories of each deposit. The Treaty shall enter into force between the states which have ratified it as soon as the ratifications of the majority of the signatories, including the ratifications of Belgium, Canada, France, Luxembourg, the Netherlands, the United Kingdom and the United States, have been deposited and shall come into effect with respect to other states on the date of the deposit of their ratifications.

Article XII

After the Treaty has been in force for ten years, or at any time thereafter, the Parties shall, if any of them so requests, consult together for the purpose of reviewing the Treaty, having regard for the factors then affecting peace and security in the North Atlantic area, including the development of universal as well as regional arrangements under the Charter of the United Nations for the maintenance of international peace and security.

Article XIII

After the Treaty has been in force for twenty years, any Party may cease to be a party one year after its notice of denunciation has been given to the Government of the United States of America, which will inform the Governments of the other Parties of the deposit of each notice of denunciation.

Article XIV

This Treaty, of which the English and French texts are equally authentic, shall be deposited in the archives of the Government of the United States of America. Duly certified copies thereof will be transmitted by that Government to the Governments of the other signatories.

BIBLIOGRAPHICAL NOTE

The purpose of this bibliographical note is to direct the interested student to readily available sources of documentation not already cited in the footnotes in the text. The note is not intended to be a complete listing but is confined to a relatively few selections which, taken together with the footnote sources, contain most of the material likely to be sought.

Many current documents on international relations not otherwise accessible are to be found in *International Organization,* a quarterly publication of the World Peace Foundation. The same is true of *International Conciliation,* which is published monthly (except July and August) by the Carnegie Endowment for International Peace. The Royal Institute of International Affairs has published in Great Britain since 1928 an annual volume of *Documents on International Affairs.* Material specifically relating to international law is to be found in the quarterly, *American Journal of International Law.*

There are many sources of documentary materials on American foreign policy. The Department of State not only publishes the diverse materials cited in the text but publishes also a monthly *Documents and State Papers* series. An unofficial series which is very useful, published by the World Peace Foundation, is *Documents on American Foreign Relations.*

The United Nations publishes a series of *Official Records* for the General Assembly, the Security Council, the Economic and Social Council, and the Trusteeship Council as well as for the Atomic Energy Commission. In the *Yearbook of the United Nations* may be found the texts of the most important resolutions passed during each year by the various organs of the United Nations. For the texts of multipartite international instruments of general interest concluded since World War I, see *International Legislation*, edited by Manley O. Hudson. The eighth volume in this series was published in 1949.

The principal sources of League of Nations documents have been indicated in the footnotes of this book, but it may be useful to distinguish here between the *Official Journal* (which contains the records of the Council and the principal official documents sent or received by the League Secretariat) and the *Records of the Assembly* which were published as *Special Supplements* to the *Official Journal*.

INDEX